Sea.

⟶ • *In recognition* • ⟵

of our over forty years

of association with

Eddie Goodman,

John Labatt is pleased

to provide you

with this

complementary copy

of his memoirs:

LIFE OF THE

LIFE OF THE
PARTY

LIFE OF THE PARTY

THE MEMOIRS OF
EDDIE GOODMAN

KEY PORTER·BOOKS

Canadian Cataloguing in Publication Data

Goodman, Eddie.
  Life of the party

ISBN 1-55013-104-4

1. Goodman, Eddie. 2. Political consultants — Canada — Biography. 3. Canada — Politics and government — 1935 — *I. Title.

FC601.G66A3 1988   971.064'092'4   C88-094280-0
F1034.3.G66A3 1988

The publisher gratefully acknowledges the assistance of the Ontario Arts Council.

Key Porter Books
70 The Esplanade
Toronto, Ontario
Canada M5E 1R2

Printed and bound in Canada

88 89 90 91 92 6 5 4 3 2 1

CONTENTS

These memoirs are dedicated to my family —

To my mother, father and sister Cecily who gave to me the love and affection and sense of values that formed the foundation and direction for my life.

To my dearest daughter, Joanne, who has remained with me every day of my life since her death;

To my much beloved daughter, Diane, upon whom I have unwittingly placed the burden of my mistaken belief that she was me;

And finally, but not least, to my dear Suzie, whose indestructible love has been anchor for the storms of my life.

INTRODUCTION

George Eliot said that to write your memoirs is "the publication of a string of mistakes." That is certainly true about a political organizer. On the other hand, Russell Baker, the author of the delightful memoir *Growing Up* said, "Nobody's life makes any sense. If you are going to make a book out of it, you might as well make it into a story."

Youth, war, the arts and odd snippets of law and politics are fit subjects for memoirs. Unfortunately, most of law and politics are too well chronicled for memories' vagaries and should be autobiographic. I have tried in these pages to be reasonably accurate but they are still memoirs and must be read as such. I am prepared, however, to guarantee the authenticity of the many anecdotes I have related.

When the book was almost completed my wife said to me, "You were crazy to write your memoirs. Once they are published you will have no one to tell your stories to. You won't be a celebrity. You will merely be a bigger bore." I replied, "Now you tell me."

I have not tried to be consistent in my views because I have not been consistent in my life. I have never met a consistent politician, certainly not one who was re-elected. How boring are those whose views have never changed from seven to seventy. My inconsistencies are my private delight. The fifty years that I have spent in law and politics have convinced me that there are no absolutes. Heraclitus was right: "all things are in constant flux."

Throughout the book, I have explained my personal philosophy as a Red Tory. While I am somewhat immoderate in

1

my speech, my guiding principles are moderation and compassion. My personal belief is that if the society we wish to preserve is going to survive, it must be changed, but with care and with joint participation of government and the best minds outside the government. While governments will not survive without a little populism, the world will not survive without a little elitism. Democracy requires leaders who can distinguish between pragmatism and opportunism. I tried hard during all my life in politics to make that distinction. I did not always succeed, but I believe I did on most occasions.

My simple hope before I started writing and now that I am finished is not that my readers will rush out to join the Progressive Conservative Party as they put the book down but that they will say that "the read was worth a few laughs and perhaps I will do something for the community." We are not set on this earth merely for self-gratification but to try to make some small contribution to society.

While I seek the Holy Grail of society's cautious change I confess, however, that for me, personally, not all the change has resulted in a finer person. A modicum of success and a modest degree of affluence do have a deteriorating effect on idealism. As I age I find a tendency to want to keep what I have and stay where I am instead of rolling the dice for one more pass. I constantly fight this type of conservatism.

My pleasure in writing this book has resulted from its having been a private endeavour. However, pre-eminent help came from Anne Holloway, my editor and instructor. Without Anne this book would never have achieved whatever professionalism, excellence, and flow it might possess. It also would have required suitcase wheels to get it home.

To Gerri Savits-Fine, my diligent and careful researcher, I express my sincere appreciation. Ed Stewart and Hugh Segal were of inestimable value in helping me recall factually many of the Davis years as was Michael Daniher. Hugh was particularly generous in assisting in the areas of patriation of the constitution. My partner Michael Levine's advice was also most helpful. To my secretary, Shirley Hodgins, and to Trisha Ellison, and my wife Suzie, my warm thanks for their forbearance.

CHAPTER 1

MANY ARE OUR JOYS

The grey horse and wagon with the diminutive muscular man and his young son sitting up front had just passed through the gates of the Halton County farm. The equipage was immediately surrounded by running children calling out to their mother, "Here comes the Jew, here comes the Jew." This was my father's earliest memory. It was the mid-eighteen nineties and he was a three- or four-year-old child accompanying his dad as he carted his wares of clothing and pots and pans and other bric-a-brac from farm to farm in Halton and Peel counties. A few years later the family moved from Acton, Ontario to Wingham, where my grandfather continued to earn his livelihood in this fashion. While he didn't start a commercial dynasty like Timothy Eaton, he did well enough to move to Toronto, where he bought a house on Centre Avenue, now the site of an addition to the Toronto General Hospital. There he completed his family of four boys and three girls; my father was the second child and eldest son.

Today, as I look back from the perspective of seventy years, the scenes of my memory shift and change; faces and places of my youth flash by, coming in and out of focus like images in a kaleidoscope. I see my family in the foreground, my mother always beautiful at every age, and my younger sister, still lovely today, my father coming home from his law office as my sister and I dashed for the paper to spread on the living-room floor of our house on Palmerston Boulevard. My paternal grandparents sitting in the kitchen of their home on Lennox Street playing gin rummy, my grandmother catching my grandfather cheating.

I see my grandfather as a short, tough, bad-tempered man and my grandmother as a beautiful quiet woman — and the only person alive who could handle my irascible grandfather. Charles Goodman came to Canada in 1881 from the part of Galicia that is now Moravia in Czechoslovakia. He arrived at the age of eleven totally alone and unable to speak English. He was the courageous forerunner of the rest of his family, who were to follow shortly once he had reconnoitred the scene and earned a little money to help them settle here.

Fifty years after my father's family had moved to Toronto from Wingham I had a drink with Jack Hanna, the elderly member of the provincial Legislature for Huron County, which included Wingham. I said to him, "My grandfather lived in Wingham and two of my uncles were born there around the turn of the century."

"Was your grandfather Charles Goodman?" he asked, and I nodded. "Charlie the Jew," he mused, "was the toughest guy that ever came to Wingham. I remember him well. He had to be tough to be the only Jew in Wingham and survive."

Stern and tough though he was, it was not Charles Goodman who made an imprint on his children, it was his wife, Sarah. Every one of the four sons took a second name beginning with B as homage to her maiden name of Brody. Nor did Charles's orthodox religious outlook and his dedication to the synagogue take hold with any of his children. It was their mother's commitment to the cause of a Jewish national homeland through Hadassah-WIZO that shaped their contribution to the Jewish community.

The romance of my parents' marriage always intrigued me. They met at a skating rink, and my dad pursued the auburn beauty from when she was sixteen until he finally captured her at age twenty-one. His chief allies were lilies-of-the-valley and roses and gifts of candy, which he continued to lavish on her until his death, bringing home two pounds of Laura Secord chocolates every Friday night. (I was well into adolescence before I learned that our family's habit of biting into a chocolate and leaving the bitten half for someone else wasn't acceptable social behaviour.)

In September 1917, my parents eloped and were married in Hamilton. They then each returned to their separate homes, telling no one of the wedding. Just why, neither ever explained to me. Unfortunately for their plans of secrecy, a Jewish wedding requires a *minyon*, a quorum of ten men. One of the men they had called in knew my maternal grandfather and telephoned him the next day with the news. My mother then joined her new husband in my grandfather's house on Brunswick Avenue until they were able to buy a house on Indian Road Crescent near High Park in Toronto. I was born there in October 1918 during the great influenza epidemic.

When I shake my memory kaleidoscope it is my mother's image that appears most often. She was a chestnut-haired, blue-eyed, petite beauty whose grandparents came to Canada from Russia via the U.S.A. about the same time as my father's family. She was in charge of my education, both formal and informal, and fortunately for me she was an incurable romantic.

Even in my name my mother's love of romantic history shows. She called me Edwin instead of Elliott, which was closer to my Hebrew name, Elia. Edwin was the name of the king of Northumbria in England in the seventh century about whom my mother had read in one of her much-loved historical novels. Edwin I was the first Northumbrian king to convert to Christianity, an act that so enraged his subjects that they destroyed his heathen temple at Goodmanham. The connection was too much for my mother to resist.

My own first recollection, at the age of three, is of the house on Palmerston Boulevard into which we moved in 1921. Palmerston was a broad boulevard lined with huge trees and elegant gaslight standards whose white globes lent an air of magic to the solid brick houses and the solid burghers who lived there. Garfield Weston and his family lived a few blocks north of our house, and our block boasted the residence of Sam McBride, the future mayor of Toronto. To my mother's consternation, on the very first day, not five minutes into the house, I pedalled my fire engine into a lamp.

We continued to live on Palmerston Boulevard until just after the outbreak of war in 1939. My mother had a quiet confidence that our family was different and that her children should be outfitted to reflect their special status. At three and four I was wearing Eton suits with hard collars and beautiful reefer coats. At six, I was at Clinton Street Public School sporting the only tie in the entire class. Class picture after class picture shows that Goodman alone had a necktie. Goodman alone had to wear shorts and then breeches, never long pants. Not until I was in high school and found myself to be the only person at Harbord Collegiate sporting breeches did I rise in righteous indignation and persuade my mother to buy me long pants.

My enrolment at Harbord was the result of a victory against my mother's well-meaning plans for her only son. She had me entered and accepted at Upper Canada College, but I prevailed on her to let me go with my friends to Harbord, which in those days held the joint records of graduating the most scholarship students in Ontario while expelling more pupils per capita than any other school in the province.

The advantages of my mother's sensitivity, however, far outweighed the momentary embarrassments she caused me. From the age of five I went to the theatre every week. The Ballets Russes de Monte Carlo never came to Toronto without my being privileged to see it. Long before I was old enough to walk alone to the children's public library on St. George Street, my mother would tramp with me through the snow to take out books. To this day my own library sports dozens of old volumes of the Bobbsey Twins series and *Bunnie Brown and His Sister Sue* with the dated inscriptions, "To Edwin from Mother with love — 1925." How fortunate I was to have been born before the age of television and to parents who regularly spent the evenings reading. Our house was always filled with books, and it seems to me that much of what I know today dates back to what I read in my childhood and youth.

In furtherance of my mother's cultural educational program, I used to have to take my sister — then called Cecelé, now Cecily — who was six years my junior, to her ballet lessons at The Boris Volkoff School of ballet. It is my belief that whatever contribution I made to the formation and early survival of the National Ballet of Canada can be traced to those hours I waited around the Volkoff studio wishing fervently that I could have been playing football.

My mother's early disappointment was her failure to make me a concert pianist. A stream of excellent teachers tried pleading, threatening, and in one case even beating my hands to a pulp, to no avail. I would practise my scales desultorily while reading a book. I would push the clock ahead so that I could persuade myself that I wasn't lying about my practice time. My ear for music and for languages has always been of the purest tin.

When I entered public school, my parents were convinced that they had reared a prodigy. Before I started school, they had already taught me to read and write and to recite poetry. My mother was confident that all she had to do was take me to the schoolhouse door and I would be revealed to the world. For the first three years they were right. Thanks largely to their efforts, I was educated far beyond any of my classmates. I received my come-uppance relatively quickly, however. When I was in Senior Second, or Grade 4, a new boy named Walter Edick arrived in the class. Up until that time, I could add faster than anybody, was far better read, and had no problem with my examinations. Imagine my chagrin when I found that Edick could add faster than I could. He went on to trounce me soundly in the examinations, and it was all downhill from there. Apart from achieving a good standing in graduate law school, I was never much of a scholar. Walter taught me one of my most valuable lessons — that there were a lot of people around who were cleverer than I was. I would just have to get along in the world by working harder than the next guy.

I joined the 60th Wolf Cub Pack at the age of seven. It was the beginning of a wonderful association, lasting for more than ten years, with the Boy Scout movement, and today I am proud to be the Honorary President of the Boy Scouts of Canada, Greater Toronto Region. Scouting taught me the importance of such basic values in life as a love of nature, self-reliance, and a sense of community. Much of my pride in being a Canadian and enjoying the great wilderness country comes from the Scout movement.

I was bitten by the political bug just before the onset of puberty, whence I date my other youthful interest — women. But for this accident of chronology, I might never have found politics. In 1930 the country was in the beginning of the Depression, when William Lyon Mackenzie King, the prime minister and leader of the Liberal Party, called an election. My father had articled and spent the first years of his practice as a junior to E.W.J. Owens, a lawyer and Conservative member of the Ontario Legislative Assembly for Toronto Centre West, a part of the city not too far from where we lived. This association had brought many people in public life to our house, including G. Reginald Geary, the former mayor of Toronto, then the federal Member of Parliament for Trinity riding. My dad, though only in his mid-thirties, was Geary's official agent, and as such was responsible for the expenditures made on Geary's campaign.

Joe Eisenberg, then a cigar maker, later a printer, and forever an inveterate cigar smoker (you might say almost an eater), was a friend of my parents and used to drop around to our house. Joe's heavy-jowled and broad-featured face with its cigar protruding would later become well known to thousands of Tories across the whole province. He was one of the party's most ardent workers both federally and provincially. When I ran for the Legislature fifteen years later he was still at my side. For immigrants who had fled Europe, the world "liberal" stood for tolerance, the word "conservative" for oppression. In 1930 Eisenberg was a member of a small group of Jews who were Conservatives. The vast majority were Liberals and remain so today. I was eleven when Joe took me out and gave me my first course in politics. I was to deliver signs up and down College, Clinton, and Manning streets for Colonel Geary. The election focused sharply on the two leaders. King had been Liberal leader since 1919, after he returned to Canada from the United States. The Conservative leader since 1927 was Richard Bedford Bennett, a Calgary lawyer. King was a shrewd, wily bachelor who believed in the spirit world. Bennett was a forceful, abrasive, strong-willed, and stubborn man who believed in reality. Except for a few months in 1926, King had been prime minister since 1921, but the world economic depression made the outcome of the 1930 election so hard to predict that an eleven-year-old had as good a chance of being right as anyone.

I had just come home from one of my signposting forays, during which I had been exposed to the predominantly Liberal sentiments of the Italian and Jewish storekeepers. Fortunately in those days the area still had a strong Anglo-Saxon contingent that was more receptive to my Conservative importuning. Puzzled by the hostility I had encountered, I turned to my father and asked ingenuously, "Why are we Conservatives?"

My dad thought for a moment, then replied, "I guess it's because I have always found them more decent." In retrospect it was not an answer I would have expected from a tolerant, objective man like my father, but I accepted it then without question and it remained in my mind. Since then, I have tried to use decency as the yardstick by which I measure politicians. I also admire people of moderation like my father, and decency and moderation often go hand in hand.

The Tories won the election, and Reginald Geary won in Trinity, going on to become minister of justice. I had backed a winner and in one stroke I was turned into a life-long addict of politics. It would have been hard for Colonel Geary to lose. Toronto in the early thirties had little demographic resemblance to Toronto today, even in its central core. The city was British in population and outlook and, except for a lively Irish community, overwhelmingly Protestant and Orange — and Orange meant Tory. The Orange Order delivered every Toronto seat but one to Bennett in 1930. Sam Factor won a lone victory in Toronto West Centre (later Spadina) riding for the Liberals.

My precocious interest in politics was nurtured by the annual municipal elections. Aspiring candidates sought the benefit of my father's advice, assistance, and prestige. He often helped in getting out the voters on election days and I was soon familiar with many aldermanic committee rooms. There I was attracted by the excitement — and by the corned-beef sandwiches, another of my many enduring weaknesses.

Like most people starting to grow old my memories of my youth appear clear and colourful while I have some difficulty remembering what I had for lunch today. Our family was close, loving, and happy. My early environment was largely Jewish but was influenced more by my parents' Zionist proclivities than by specifically religious concerns. My mother and my father were active in furthering the dream of Theodor Herzl, the intellectual and spiritual founder of the movement for the establishment of a Jewish national homeland in Palestine. At twelve I joined Young Judaea, a youth component of the movement.

I attended Holy Blossom Temple Sunday school from the age of seven. It was a reformed or, if you'll pardon the expression, "liberal" synagogue. It also had the historic honour of being the first synagogue established in Toronto. Originally an orthodox synagogue on Richmond Street where my grandparents on both sides were members, it later moved to Bond Street, and from there to Bathurst Street near Eglinton, where it stands today.

In the early thirties, Holy Blossom did not give young men a bar mitzvah ceremony; they had a later confirmation. I was bar mitzvahed at my grandfather's *shul* (synagogue) on Markham Street, which he and his cronies and grandsons had helped renovate with their own labour. He had gone there when he was ousted as president of the large Galician synagogue on Bay Street, where the Eaton Centre now stands. Despite the months of hard work by my private tutor, I stumbled over the ancient Hebrew words when I read from the scrolls of the Torah. Years later, my two daughters did much better.

My close relationship with my parents made me the recipient of everything that a boy could want — except a bicycle, which my mother felt was too dangerous. I may be the only child ever who received boxing gloves at the age of nine or ten and was encouraged to get knocked out by his older friends, but was denied a bicycle. I got even with mother, however. I now have three bicycles and I ride them everywhere, in traffic whose density was never dreamt of in the 1930s.

At high school, football vied with girls for my interest. Although I weighed only 126 pounds I played end for Harbord's junior team. In my last year, 1935, we defeated North Toronto to win the city championship. With only a few moments to go and North Toronto leading 5-2, we blocked a kick almost on the North Toronto goal line. The ball came falling into my hands and I merely had to step across the line to be a hero forever. I grabbed the ball. My fellow teammate, Noel Zeldin, also grabbed it, only harder, and stepped over the line. The headline in the sports page read "Zeldin leads Harbord to championship." This championship was won only once again by the school in the next fifty years. Immortality had eluded me by inches — perhaps a potent of things to come.

It was fortunate for me that I chose Harbord Collegiate instead of Upper Canada College for my secondary school education. Harbord contained both the most brilliant students in the Ontario secondary school system and a large number who could hold their own today in a high school in the South Bronx. In Second Form, today's Grade 10, I had Johnny Wayne, then called Louis Weingarten, on my left, and Frank Shuster on my right. Their vaudeville career started at Harbord in the Oola Boola Club, and as my seat was directly between them I was their first straight man. Louis Applebaum, the composer, sat behind me. Louis Rasminsky, the future governor of the Bank of Canada, and John Weinzweig, the dean of musical composers, had preceded us by a few years. The principal was Mr. Glassey, a classicist, and I took Latin right through Fifth Form. I also took after-class Greek, but only because my term standings were determined by my total marks. Students who took Greek were allowed to include these marks in their overall total, and my allowance from my parents was determined by my standing. I failed miserably in Greek, but the thirty-eight marks I earned allowed me to stand second in the class, and I was rich for a year.

On the other side of the coin there were those students who were merely putting in occasional time until they began to work or to hustle for a buck. They required serious handling by the staff. The approved method of discipline by the male teachers was physical. My only experience of being on the receiving end of such discipline occurred when Brian McCool, subsequently the director of the Department of Music in Ontario's Ministry of Education, picked up a few deprecating remarks I made about him *sotto voce*. He grabbed me and threw my whole one hundred and twenty-six pounds about ten feet against the metal lockers. It was an effective way of making certain that I didn't express my opinion about teachers for a long time. In today's world a teacher who favoured this style of discipline would probably find himself facing a criminal charge or at least having to appear before the Ontario Human Rights Commission.

My comments about Brian McCool were tame when compared to those of my Grade 11 classmate Solly Clairman. The recipient of a tongue-lashing from an attractive French teacher for having skipped a series of classes, Solly waited until she had completed her tirade and then said simply, "Fuck you, babe," picked up his books, and marched out never to return. He and his brother subsequently made a very good living at the newspaper stand at the corner of Dundas and Yonge streets.

Harbord had one other claim to fame. The best crap games of any school in the city went on in the lane just outside the schoolyard. This game attracted young gamblers from far and wide, and I got into the habit of leaving a good part of my allowance there each week. Fortunately for my finances, a friend of mine on the football team said to me one day, "You just bet when I tell you to and get off when I say stop." I was not doing very well left to my own devices so I followed his instructions and built up a healthy nest-egg of cash.

After a few weeks of good fortune, somebody grabbed for the dice, yelling, "Let me see those." My friend immediately kicked the dice away and smashed the grabber in the face with the cry, "Keep your dirty hands off my dice." In the mêlée that followed I melted away into the schoolyard crowd to get ready for football practice, never to return. I was smart enough not to ask what was so special about those dice. Today on the rare occasions when my wife and I go to a resort with a gaming table she cannot understand why after a half an hour or so I go to bed while she stays rattling the bones. The casinos of the Bahamas and Las Vegas can never be as exciting as the lane behind Harbord Collegiate.

On a late-September morning in 1936 I rose and came down for breakfast. I said to my father, "What a great day to start a new phase of my life. Today I am registering at Varsity." Then in the same breath, "Can I borrow the car? I wish to arrive in appropriate fashion for this occasion. There may be a few girls I'd like to impress." My dad laughed and acquiesced, as he almost invariably walked the three to four miles to the office. Every day for the next four years I cadged the car to drive the mile and a half to school.

That first day at the University of Toronto was too exciting to share with anyone else so I drove alone along College Street to the front campus entrance and parked the car near Simcoe Hall. At the far end of the campus was the neo-Gothic-Romanesque University College building with its wondrous tower that had been the very heart of the university since 1859. Time was to inform me how this great secular, non-sectarian institution had fought to prevent inroads on its endowments and its independence by such religious-based, clergy-dominated institutions as Trinity and Victoria Colleges. While I enjoyed its gargoyles and ornately carved staircases throughout my university stay, I did not then realize that the sectarian attacks on its integrity had been repelled with the assistance of John A. Macdonald, who had advised the college that the endowment inherited from King's College should be put into the building "since not even the opponents of the College can steal bricks and mortar."

After I had registered, under the watchful eye of Professor McAndrew, the registrar, I wandered over to 24 St. George Street, the small house just north of College Street which housed the Department of Law. Law was not yet an independent school or faculty, but was offered as an undergraduate honours arts course. It had been my original intention to enter sociology and philosophy, but Jacob Finkelman, a law professor friend of my father, had convinced me to take law, arguing that it was broad enough to give me a liberal arts education and a great start on my legal career before I entered Osgoode Hall, the graduate law school. He was right. The seven years of academic law that I enjoyed were of inestimable benefit to me in practice. The faculty was headed by Dr. W.P.M. Kennedy, an Irish constitutional historian, one of the great characters of the university, and the most interesting lecturer I ever had. He could dispense information about the importance of Magna Carta, the dangers of sex, and his contribution to the Irish constitution all in the same lecture.

The school's distinguished faculty included many of the most illustrious names in Canadian jurisprudence. There was Norman

MacKenzie, later president of the University of British Columbia, Moffat Hancock, who became an outstanding teacher in the United States, and Jacob Finkelman, who left to chair the Ontario Labour Relations Board. Later future Supreme Court Chief Justice Bora Laskin also joined the staff. Kennedy brought to it his élan and a pride in true scholarship that it has maintained throughout its history. I proudly saw my daughter Diane attend there forty-five years later.

At Varsity, I was more interested in being a jock and a socialite than a scholar. I did, however, take an active role in the University College Parliament and the Macdonald-Cartier Conservative Club. In the latter, I suffered the first of many electoral defeats when I lost the presidency to Charles Dubin, a close friend, now associate chief justice of Ontario, by one vote. I alleged that he, contrary to the dictates of friendship, voted for himself and that I voted for him as well, which he vigorously denied.

In 1938, I was a youth delegate to the Ontario Progressive Party leadership convention that elected George Drew. Little did I realize when I cast my vote for Earl Lawson, the runner-up, that a great forty-two-year provincial Conservative dynasty with which I would be actively involved was to start five years later.

My dad was an ardent college football fan and, from the time I was three until I entered university, he took me to every Varsity home game. I had two youthful ambitions. One was to play football for the University of Toronto and the second was to be a judge. In my first year I played on University College's intramural team and was invited to try out for the University team. It didn't take me long to see that not only was I not going to make the Varsity squad, but that the best I could do would be to sit on the bench of the intermediate team. I consoled myself by joining the *Varsity* newspaper as sports columnist and later assistant sports editor.

When I wasn't in the law library or in the *Varsity* office I would sojourn for many hours in the poolroom at Hart House, which unfortunately has long since disappeared. There, half a dozen of us from our year at law school would hang around talking about cases we had read or lying about the girls we had gone out with.

The hero of this group was George Karry, who became the first lawyer of Greek parentage in Ontario. He was a good, although lazy athlete, and he was an outstanding pool player who became the University snooker champion. Snooker bets financed many an evening for the two of us. If we couldn't find pickings at the school we would go to neighbourhood pool halls to play the local sharks. It all came to an end one day when we bet all we could beg or borrow on a game at Hart House. George spotted his opponent, Freddie Harris, thirteen points. He played carelessly and needed two hooks with only the pink and black balls on the table. He settled down, got the hooks, sank the pink, sank the black with a flourish, and sewered. I was broke for a month.

My social life at university revolved around my fraternity, Pi Lambda Phi. As "rex" of this institution I nearly caused it to be banned on the campus. Using the only key of the graduate room, Dan Stone, Irving Gould, and I took a two-dozen case of Labatt quarts and two quite proper young ladies in for a drink, in flagrant violation of fraternity and university regulations. The result was chaos when we had a bowling game with the empties, but we managed to escape undetected. When the campus authorities got wind of our pranks and came to me for answers, I formally appointed Stone and Gould as a two-man inquiry to find the culprits. They never succeeded.

I fell in love and settled down for the last year and a half of my stay at Varsity. Vernon Singer, the future Ontario MLA, had met a beautiful long-haired, long-legged blonde from Dunnville, Ontario, Barbara Eileen High. She would not go out with him because she had just broken up with Bernie Laski, the leader of the Varsity band who, like Singer, was Jewish. This romance, which had lasted for quite a while, had caused her great anguish. Her aunt, with whom she was staying, was married to the Moderator of the United Church and did not want her niece going out with a Jew. Neither did her fraternity sisters, who passed a formal resolution against bringing Jews to their annual dance. (Thirty-five years later, my daughter Joanne was rushed by and joined that same fraternity at the University of Western

Ontario.) Barbara decided that now that her romance was over, she was not going through that fight again. Singer asked me to argue his case with the young lady. I pleaded the cause of down-trodden Jews so eloquently that Barbara and I fell deeply in love and went "steady" until I went overseas. We had talked of marriage and my parents were very fond of her, but that romance, like many others, became a casualty of the war.

Barbara and I rarely quarrelled. Her only objection was to my manners, which were coarser than hers, my mother's teaching notwithstanding. Her chief complaint centred on my habit of stealing food from her plate to taste. One spring day we were walking past Borden's Dairy on Spadina Avenue north of College Street. I went in to buy two ice cream cones, a strawberry for her and an orange for me. As I was handing her her cone, I took a bite off the top. Incensed, she mashed her cone into my face. In spite of this object lesson, I still taste the food on my wife's plate.

During my third year at university, the war clouds gathered on the horizon and we students began to discuss our obligations in the event of war. My response was clear cut. I was a Tory, a nationalist, and a Jew — on all counts I must participate. British institutions, Canadian independence, and the Jewish people were threatened. In my youth, I was no skeptic; I took the lines from Richard Lovelace's "To Lucasta, going to the Wars" literally: "I could not love thee, Dear, so much,/Loved I not honour more." The theory of the rights of personal conscience of American students during the Vietnam War in the sixties would have been then — and indeed still is — abhorrent to me.

CHAPTER TWO

WAR AGAINST TYRANNY

It was September 1939. The German Panzer divisions had already obliterated the antiquated Polish Army and swallowed up Poland. The university year had just begun, and on every campus students were struggling to face the international reality. One day I walked into the Pi Lambda Phi house on St. George Street to be confronted by my fraternity brother Mel Orenstein dressed as a sapper in the Engineers. Most of us had joined the Canadian Officers Training Corps, but as yet no one from the house had gone on active service. I can still hear him saying, "I did it today, and it's what you fellows should be doing as well."

I had no doubt he was right. The question was: what service and when? With the advantage of an officers' training course right on campus, I decided to stay for most of my last year, do the course, sign up, then come back to graduate law school when it was over. That the Allied victory would be won quickly I had little doubt.

Getting on active service with a commission proved to be more difficult than I imagined. There were still a great number of militia officers with priority over the COTC-trained students, so I looked for other possibilities. A few of my fellow students had joined the navy under a special plan whereby college students came in as ratings and were quickly trained and made officers. I decided that I would lend my many talents to the navy instead of the army. I went down to the HMCS *York* on Lake Ontario to see the naval lieutenant in charge of recruiting volunteers. I was filling out my enlistment application after answering the usual questions, when he said to me, "By the way, are you Jewish?" When I told him that I was, he said, "You look like a decent kid. Forget this program. Most of the applicants will undoubtedly become officers, but I doubt that anyone who is Jewish will be an officer in this man's navy." I stood up, said, "Thank you very much for your advice," tore up my application and was back where I started. The navy was the one branch of the service that had a reputation for bigotry, but that later disappeared with the growing need for recruits.

While in the thirties it was commonplace to run into bigotry and anti-semitism, it had no harmful effect on me either then or throughout my life. When I encountered it, I would be angered, but then I would laugh and feel sorry for the bigots. It has always been my belief that being Jewish gave me a richer life and, in the various non-Jewish worlds I travelled in, drew attention to me, which allowed me to show my mettle. When I ultimately joined the army I saw only one slight incident of anti-semitism directed at a young Jewish trooper. In the services, people were usually accepted on merit.

It was now the fall of 1940 and I had enrolled at Osgoode Hall Law School, articled to my father. The war was going badly and I was growing desperate to right the balance by enlisting. Vernon Singer came over one day and said, "The Royal Canadian Armoured Corps Training School, under the command of Colonel Worthington, have announced they are recruiting officers. They will be interviewing applicants within a week or two." I went immediately to the district headquarters and put my name on the list. A few weeks later I was summoned for my interview.

The panel consisted of three colonels all in command of armoured units at Camp Borden. Most of the applicants were University of Toronto students, principally engineering students, as the Armoured Corps was looking for mechanically oriented officers. Indeed, the Canadian Army was to become the most mechanized army in the world. Of the three commanding officers, two were from former cavalry regiments, then armoured, and the third was the commander of a tank regiment. The senior cavalry officer, after reading my background, asked what my experience with vehicles was. I replied, "Very little, sir."

"What do you know about combustion engines?"

"Nothing, sir."

Looking somewhat bewildered, he asked, "Do you know anything about trucks?"

"Where to put in the gas and how to put the key in the ignition, sir."

"Then do you mind telling me what, in the name of blazes, makes you think you should be an Armoured Corps officer?"

I took a deep breath and told the panel that I had been interested in horses all my life, which was absolutely true, that I had been a riding master at a children's camp for four or five years, which was also true. I then departed somewhat from the truth to enter the realm of diplomacy, saying that I had read a great deal about the history of the British cavalry, and that while the German invasion of Poland had proved there was no future for the horse in war, I was confident that the traditions of gallantry synonymous with the cavalry would be continued in the Armoured Corps. Before they could interrupt me I added breathlessly, "I feel I have some qualities of leadership and am a quick learner. The internal combustion engine holds no fear for me." I was quickly dismissed and left, not too confident of success.

About a month later, I received a letter informing me that I had been one of the few accepted as a second lieutenant in the Armoured Corps and directing me to report to Camp Borden in December. This was my first experience of the well-known Canadian Army maxim that "Bullshit Baffles Brains."

After basic training at the Canadian Armoured Corps School, then under the command of Colonel Frank Worthington, I was posted to the great Manitoba regiment, the Fort Garry Horse. On arrival I found that there were other Eddies so I was nicknamed Benny after the band leader, Benny Goodman.

I have regretted many times since then my mechanical ineptness and ignorance. When the war was over, I did not know a great deal more about the internal combustion engine than I had at the beginning, no matter how hard I tried, although I was to command both the Armoured Corps Tactical School and the Gunnery School. Fortunately, I had the good sense, both as a troop commander and as a squadron commander, to have a talented mechanic close by to deal with the vicissitudes of keeping my vehicles well maintained and running. I'll never forget the occasion when General E.L.M. Burns turned to me and said, "Well, Captain, would you explain to me the maintenance problems your squadron has with the Shermans?" Without missing a beat, I turned to my staff sergeant and said, "Staff Sergeant Handfield, would you please outline the difficulties that have already shown up for the general." When all regimental officers had to write an examination on maintenance problems I could already see myself back in the re-enforcement depot. To my relief my paper came back with an inscription by Ronnie Morton, our colonel: "Your writing is like the scrawlings of an inebriated spider. I refuse to read this."

Lt.-Col. R.E.A. Morton, later Major-General, had taken over our regiment, the Fort Garry Horse, after having been a permanent force officer and second in command of the Lord Strathcona's Horse. Morton had a distinguished career both during the war and afterwards. He led our regiment into France, became GSO 1 Armour at army headquarters, commanded the army during the Winnipeg flood, and served for Canada on the International Control Commission in Indochina. He had none of the negative attributes that have been unfairly assigned to career soldiers. He had a quick mind and broad interests and was courageous and calm under stress. He was also the most inquisitive man I had ever met; you could not relax a moment in his company because he would constantly be plying you with questions.

The only time I ever fooled him occurred in England when I was his acting adjutant. While waiting to go on exercise with him, I picked up an English magazine showing a large cartoon with the caption: "Find 20 mistakes in this picture. Time: one minute." I gave myself the test and managed to find sixteen mistakes within the time limit. I looked up the answers and found the other four. I had barely finished when the Colonel bounced in, grabbed the magazine, which evidently he had seen before, threw it at me and said, "Go." I quickly rhymed off the twenty mistakes. He looked at me with awe. I shrugged modestly, but to this day I believe this small fraud helped me earn my third pip, which came through a few months later.

The Garrys arrived in England in October 1941 and stayed until the D-Day invasion on June 6, 1944. Like so many other Canadian soldiers, I fell in love with England, Scotland, and Ireland and became a lifelong anglophile, notwithstanding my frequent disagreements with Britain's foreign policy, particularly as it relates to the Middle East. The fortitude and day-to-day courage of the British people from 1940 until victory in 1945 had to be experienced at firsthand to be appreciated. The generosity and warmth extended to Canadians in all countries of the kingdom left an indelible mark on me and on Canadian troops of all ranks.

My British experience and adventures were no different from those of tens of thousands of young Canadian men who had left home for the first time in their lives and gone to fight in a foreign country. I recall the story of Dick Jennings, a subaltern in our regiment. When we were leaving for England, Jennings' father, who had been in the First World War and spent a great deal of time in England, gave him only one piece of fatherly advice: "My son, now that you are going to England, I want to tell you that in Canada fornication is in its infancy."

In 1942, after the Japanese bombing of Pearl Harbor brought the United States into the war, American soldiers started to move into Great Britain in ever-increasing numbers. The U.S. involvement in the war has had far-reaching effects upon the alliance of English-speaking nations — effects that are still being felt today. After some initial acrimony, a mutual understanding and respect were forged among the hundreds of thousands of American, Canadian, and British troops who lived and trained together for two years.

While our troops eventually became very fond of the British people — and particularly of the Scots — up until 1942 they had grumbled about the pervasive influence of the British Army and training schools on the discipline and outlook of the Canadian officer class. There also existed the feeling that our troops should not be subject to the same discipline and military class distinctions as the British (and indeed they were not). When the Americans arrived in the island in large numbers in 1942 with their bigger pay packets, better rations (we were on British Army rations), and less stringent discipline, the Canadians' resentment of the British declined dramatically. The American troops were regarded much less favourably by Canadians than the British were, and deservedly so. During our pre-invasion training, I was in command of the rear party that was turning over a small camp to an American advance party. The Americans arrived and I went to meet with the officer in command. The American troops waiting for their orders broke off, threw down their packs, pulled out large cigars, and started a huge crap game in the middle of the parade ground. Our men were appalled.

The training and leadership of the American troops did not produce as fine an army as the British or the Canadian. This was clearly evident in North Africa, in Italy, and in northwestern Europe. The Canadians, on the other hand, had the best of both worlds: British training and tradition and North American independent initiative. Together these resulted in a strong fighting formation, I believe the best in the world.

The world is much different today. Geography inextricably binds our national defence, and therefore our armed forces, to the United States rather than Britain. Successive Canadian governments have become more non-interventionist, and the lessons of the thirties and forties are remembered by only a few. Conflicts like those in Vietnam and Lebanon, where the troops and the American public did not feel either that their way of life was directly threatened or that a genuine victory was possible, have weakened all democracies' resolve to fight tyranny. Notwithstanding these setbacks, the United States has coura- geously given the world leadership, and it is our democratic obligation to support it.

Prior to our specialized training for our invasion role, the regiment was stationed at Hove on the south coast. Like most Canadian soldiers, I overcame my loneliness by establishing a friendship with an attractive English lady. My friend on the south coast had beautiful green eyes and two children, the youngest being a fine little boy of five. In wartime Britain, bacon was almost non-existent for civilians except when received from a Canadian friend. One Sunday morning, the Fort Garrys were having a formal church parade and I was the acting officer commanding A Squadron. Colonel Morton took over the regiment from the regimental sergeant-major and each squadron leader then went up to report their squadron's readiness. I marched up to the colonel and saluted smartly, when my friend's little boy, who was standing on the sidewalk watching the regiment on parade, piped up in the loudest of childish voices, "That's my Uncle Benny. My Uncle Benny and I had bacon for breakfast this morning." The colonel's moustache twitched as he tried to keep his composure, but finally, like the other four hundred soldiers on the parade ground, he exploded with laughter. Uncle Benny saluted smartly and marched back to his place at the head of the laughing squadron.

My regiment, the Fort Garry Horse, had originally been part of the Fifth Armoured Division when it was formed in Canada. The Garrys eventually ended up on the 2nd Canadian Armoured Brigade, an independent, three-regiment brigade with the First Hussars of London and the Sherbrooke Fusiliers. This brigade was the equal of any among the Allied forces. For this, much of the credit is due to Brigadier Tommy Rutherford, a fine militia soldier from Owen Sound, to his successor, Norman Gianelli, another Strathcona regular, who gave us our basic training, and to Bob Wyman, who led us into battle and of whom we armoured men used to say, "Not a bad soldier for a gunner!" The 2nd Armoured Brigade was chosen to be the armoured support for the Third Infantry Division in the D-Day landings and was part of 1st British Corps for this operation.

By late 1943, the invasion plans were rapidly coming together, and the two lead regiments of our brigade, the Garrys and the Hussars, were to be equipped with one of the great secret weapons of the invasion, floating Sherman tanks that performed like and with naval craft. This amazing invention was achieved by the simple process of attaching canvas sheets and a propeller drive to regular tanks. The tanks could then be driven on water like boats after disembarking from the landing craft several thousand feet from the shore.

The two regiments started training for this exciting role in winter 1943 in Argyllshire near Inveraray. I was in charge of the regimental advance party at the British Army training camp at Inveraray, the very heart of Campbell country. With me was a friend, Jiddy Campbell of London, Ontario, who was my counterpart for the Hussars. On our first evening at the camp, the Duke of Argyll, the head of the Clan Campbell, came over to the small British mess for a drink. The British adjutant introduced me and I in turn introduced Jiddy Campbell. The Duke turned his full attention on Jiddy, saying, "Tell me about your family. I am always delighted to meet Canadian Campbells. What part of Argyllshire did your family come from? When did they go to Canada?" The questions poured out at poor Jiddy, who looked sheepish and mumbled something about knowing little of his family's history. Undeterred, the Duke responded, "Come over to the castle for dinner tomorrow night. Bring your friend Goodman." Delighted by the prospect of a real meal in such baronial surroundings, I accepted the gracious invitation quickly, but Campbell then declined for us both. I knew the reason for his reluctance: Campbell's family weren't from Argyllshire, they were from Greece. His father had come to Canada under the name of Karembelis.

By May 1944, we had finished the massive preparatory exercise for Overlord, the code word for the invasion. The three years of training and frolicking in Great Britain were over. It was time to pick up the cheque and pay for the fun. The regiment moved to Lee-on-the-Solent, the last stop before France. Lee-on-the-Solent was the main centre for the Fleet Air Arm and was packed with attractive WRENS. By some quirk, fellow officer Sandy McPherson and I managed to rent ourselves a small private house, and our last few weeks in England were worthwhile.

On the night of June 3, we left our embarkation area and mounted our tanks to move towards points of departure. On June 4, D-Day minus two, we embarked and moved up the Solent right to buoys. The wind was blowing hard, the barometer was falling, and we remained static. The next day was the same; the wind continued unabated, and the Channel was really in an uproar. Major technical difficulties with the landing lay ahead. Nevertheless, on that afternoon, the great armada began to move.

As far as the eye could see, the water was dotted with warships, transports, and landing craft. I was on the same LCT as Ronnie Morton and, as we passed through the boom, the real maps were issued along with a special message from Monty designed to inspire and encourage us. Ronnie Morton held an O group while, throughout the invincible armada, people were already throwing up their guts. The crossing was a great feat of British seamanship; notwithstanding the rolling seas and high winds, all vessels kept in line. The pounding of the greatest bombardment in history and the constant roar of the fighters and bombers were awesome but of little consequence to my wretched comrades as they heaved the contents of their stomachs over the side of the bouncing craft. I was unaffected by the hurling motion of the ship, and when the midshipman, who was the number two navy man aboard, succumbed to nausea, I found myself in command of the bridge of one of His Majesty's vessels. So much for the discouraging remarks of that naval recruiting officer in Toronto.

The two advance floating squadrons landed at H minus 45, and my squadron landed just before H hour, which had been delayed until seven AM by the incredibly high waves. As our craft hit the beach, down came the ramp squarely on a mine, causing the colonel's wireless truck to become impaled on the ramp and forcing us to pull out and dump the vehicle into the deeper water. When I finally got ashore I encountered an enormous SNAFU on the beach. The 9th Infantry Brigade had somehow taken over the road that Le Régiment de la Chaudière and my squadron were supposed to pull up on. Anxious to reach our objective, I decided to cut across some open fields and circumnavigate the infantry vehicles. I came to one ploughed field and saw a sign reading *Achtung Minen* (Beware of mines). Somewhere in the back of my mind I remembered an intelligence officer saying that often instead of mines the Germans put up signs to slow the enemy's advance. I decided that this was one of those times and went bowling across the field, only to blow up my tank, completely destroying the right track. No one was injured. I grabbed another tank and successfully reached my support position with Le Régiment de la Chaudière.

During the first two days of fighting, one brigade of the 12th ss Panzer division opposing the Second Brigade was commanded by Colonel Kurt Meyer. This was the formation that captured several of the officers of our sister regiment, the First Hussars of London, and then proceeded to slaughter them along with a number of other officers and men. Three of the murdered men were my close friends. My anger and bitterness against the Germans, however, were tempered by an incident that happened in our own squadron on the same day. As we were moving across country, endeavouring to reach our objective near Bény-sur-Mer, we became engaged in trying to clear out some Germans from a large copse. After a few minutes of firing, a group of German soldiers emerged waving a white flag. As more followed, one of our tank's gunners fired upon them. It was a cruel, senseless, and stupid act. Not only because the Germans were surrendering, but also because the survivors immediately went to ground, forcing us to spend another hour clearing them out of the wood.

The extremes of gallantry and cruelty that are displayed in war constantly amaze me. The depth of friendship, the willingness to sacrifice oneself for a fellow soldier, and the anguish at losing a comrade exemplify the best instincts in man. However necessary to survival, the callous disregard for the enemy has a regrettable coarsening effect that some soldiers never get over. I can still remember coming to a village near Caen where there was a huge bulldozed mound of earth surmounted by a hand-lettered sign reading: "Dead Germans, lots of them."

On D-Day plus five, at a little village called Rots, half my squadron were supporting the 48th Royal Marine Commandos, the best unit with which I ever fought. We were cleaning out a strong German pocket in the village when a Panzer hidden up an alley "brewed" my tank from about thirty feet away, killing both the gunner and the loader. I finally extricated myself from the flaming tank only to encounter, not ten feet away in a house window, a machine gunner who was the worst shot in the Wehrmacht. He let loose burst after burst and totally missed me. I fought on foot with the Marine commandos until two of my tanks returned and I took command again. Next day I ended up in the Canadian General Hospital in Watford near London, England, where I was treated for burns and a minor bullet wound.

After three weeks, my burns were sufficiently healed to allow me to leave hospital with Sandy McPherson, who had been injured with me in the attack on Rots. The normal procedure after being discharged from hospital was to report to the Canadian Base Reinforcement Unit in the small town of Fleet, near Aldershot. The invasion was in its early stages and was still confined to a small bridgehead, so that all the reinforcements could do was wait and hope that they could get back to their regiments. McPherson and I also knew that the whole rear echelon of our brigade was still at Tilbury Docks in London under Dick Stapleford, the brigade staff captain, waiting to get over to France on twenty-four-hours' notice. After a thirty-second conference, we decided that waiting at the Canadian base unit in Fleet was not for us and that we would go directly to our unit in France.

On ascertaining that the convoy would not be leaving London until the following day, we decided to spend one last glorious night at Brown's Hotel, Sandy's chief oasis during his four years in England. McPherson stepped up to the desk and asked for two rooms on the top floor. A reliably big spender, he was greeted effusively, and we were told that we had rooms one floor down from the top. In high dudgeon, McPherson demanded rooms on the top floor, whereupon the clerk shrugged and instructed the porter to take us to the top floor. We stepped out of the elevator into a wreckage of bricks, mortar, and plaster inflicted by the v1 rockets just recently launched by the Germans, and were solemnly led to the only two remaining rooms. I turned to McPherson and said, "I hope you enjoy yourself up here alone. I am taking the room below, as I hope to get back to France to inflict this type of damage on the Germans." He quickly followed.

I had cause to exercise the same brand of prudent leadership the following morning when we were at the Tilbury Docks, a major bombing target, situated as they were in the heart of British shipping in the south. McPherson and I were sitting on a bench in the harbour, waiting to board. Suddenly, I heard the peculiar buzzing that heralded the coming of a v1 rocket. The only good thing about the rockets was that you generally knew when they were coming. I jumped up and ran, hollering, "I'm going for the shelter," which was a concrete bunker ten or fifteen feet away. I heard McPherson hurling imprecations of cowardice at my back, then seconds later I felt a hand on my shoulder and a 270-pound body pole-vaulted over me, flattening us both on the floor of the bomb shelter. When we looked up, we saw that the bomb had scored a dead hit on the bench.

On landing in France we hurried to our regiment. Unfortunately, the regimental adjutant had to inform the CBRG (Canadian Base Reinforcement Group) in France that we were back, and we were ordered to report to the Reinforcement Unit some ten miles away immediately. There we and three other miscreants were greeted by a fulminating, frothing Brigadier Warwick Beament, an Ottawa lawyer, in charge of all reinforcements in France. Beament was shaking with rage. He asked me, as the senior officer, what right I had to return to France and I simply said, "Well, I was instructed to report to CBRG and I decided that I had my choice between Fleet and Normandy." "With a travel warrant to Fleet?" he barked and put us under arrest. Fortunately, we were badly needed by our regiments and he had no alternative but to release us from arrest, without prejudice to further rearrest, and send us back to the front.

Three or four weeks later we were ordered to report to General Harry Crerar, the General Officer commanding the Canadian Army at army headquarters. We were marched in individually and I, as senior officer, was first. General Crerar, who appeared to be a kindly gentleman, asked me whether I wanted a general court martial or whether I would take his punishment. Having been warned by my colonel, who had the decency as well as the courage to accompany his errant officers, to accept the General's punishment, I said, "I am quite content to have you try this matter, sir." Crerar went on to say that he was embarrassed that one of his senior officers had put him in this position, but that we were charged first with desertion and secondly with using improper channels to return to our regiment. "The first charge is clearly ridiculous. I find you guilty on the second charge and reprimand you and then having reprimanded you, I congratulate you on what you have done for the army. Good day."

I arrived back with my regiment on July 1 and we began the final stages of the battle for the bridgehead by attacking Carpiquet airfield on July 4. I was in command of the small tank force supporting the second phase of that attack, which was led by the Queen's Own Rifles of Toronto under the command of Lt.-Col. Jock Spragge. Sergeant Charlie Olson's troop captured the German officers' mess and he screamed euphorically over the air, "I have just gone into the officers' mess and there are a thousand bottles of booze in storage." The whole squadron was ecstatic at the news. Imagine our disappointment on discovering that the bottles contained not liquor but Vichy water.

By now I had succeeded to the command of the squadron and was experiencing the heady thrill of being twenty-five and a major with my own command in battle. On July 9, after we finished capturing Carpiquet, we rode triumphantly at the head of the Eighth Brigade through the beautiful city of Caen with its twin-spiraled cathedral. Caen had suffered badly as a result of the bombing by British Lancasters prior to the taking of Carpiquet. Colonel Ronnie Morton warned me, "Now for goodness sakes, young man, get us through Caen or the whole Canadian Corps will be fouled up." I put my best subaltern at the head of the squadron and we were off through the city's winding streets. After about twenty-five minutes of what should have been a ten- or fifteen-minute trip, I called the subaltern to ask, "When the hell do we get there?"

"I'm hopelessly lost," he confessed. So, of course, was everyone behind us. I went trundling up in my tank, visions of squadron disgrace before my eyes. Sure enough, we were at a six-cornered intersection and no one could figure out which way to go. My map was of no help. I took over the lead from the shaken subaltern and set my course up the widest-looking street. Three short blocks later, we reached our rendezvous point, where we were met by dispatch riders who sent us on to our place of deployment. My lucky guess at which direction to take made me an instant hero.

Later in July after a disastrous failed attack on a village called Verrières, I was visited by the infantry brigadier wanting to discuss further tank support. With the brigadier was his acting brigade major, who let out a large bellow when he saw me: "Hello, Benny; how are you doing?" I was delighted to see George Harris Hees, who had been the liaison officer at our 2nd Armoured Brigade on the coast for a period of about six months and with whom I'd formed a firm friendship that has lasted to this day.

My first introduction to Hees had been in 1943 when I was visiting our sister regiment, the First Hussars. I was jawing with Harold Botnick, the adjutant, and Jiddy Campbell, the assistant adjutant, when we heard the noise of a motorcycle. Botnick said to Campbell, "Get in the cupboard," pointing to a steel cupboard. "Here comes the new Brigade LO." In bounced Hees, who briefly introduced himself and sat down. Botnick said, "Campbell, come out, I want to introduce somebody," and Campbell emerged from the small cupboard and shook hands with Hees, who never blinked an eyelash but merely said, "Do you always keep your assistant in the cupboard?"

In battle, Hees proved himself a man of great courage, which he displayed at the battle of the Beveland causeway. The advance company of the Calgary Highlanders was given the ridiculous task of crossing the narrow exposed causeway to get to Walcheren Island off the western coast of Holland when it should have been attacked by water with troops in LCT. All its officers had been killed or wounded when a mortar landed on an order group. Hees, the brigade major of the Fifth Brigade, saw that the whole Canadian advance was being held up. He immediately went up to see the problem, found that the lead platoon had gone to ground in the middle of the causeway, and took command of the company and the platoon and led it to the far side. Though wounded in the elbow early in that action, he carried on until he had successfully planted the leading platoon on the opposite side. He went back to the brigade and from there to the hospital, where he discovered that a pistol he had shoved into the front of his battle dress had been struck by the bullet that got him in the elbow, saving him from a far more serious wound.

After he got out of the hospital, he was shipped back to Canada, where his sense of public obligation induced him to work for the Tories in the famous 1945 Grey County by-election in the Owen Sound area. General McNaughton, a Liberal and former commander-in-chief of the Canadian Army, was defeated by Garfield Case as a result of George's account of the disgraceful mismanagement of Canadian reinforcements by the Mackenzie King government.

My regiment had been fighting continuously from D-Day until just towards the end of July, when we were pulled back for two days' refitting. Our pleasure at having forty-eight hours available for maintenance was promptly diminished when we found out that Lt.-General Guy Simonds, the commander of the 2nd Canadian Corps, would be inspecting the regiment on the second day. Originally a permanent force artillery officer and a general of considerable competence and ingenuity, Simonds was probably the most talented of the Canadian senior officers, although he was certainly not the best liked. He modelled himself on General Montgomery, who was his idol. The regiment was drawn up; I was in command of A Squadron and next to me was C Squadron commanded by Roy Bray. When Ronnie Morton introduced me to the General, I gave him my smartest salute. Our conversation went something like this:

"Well, Goodman, where do you come from?"

"Virden, Manitoba, sir."

"I know Virden. Were you born in Virden?"

"No, sir."

"Work at Virden?"

"No, sir. The truth of the matter is I've never seen Virden, but when I joined the Fort Garry Horse, I was the first easterner. I thought that I'd better adopt a town in Manitoba so I chose Virden."

There was a pause filled by a loud "harrumph." The General strolled over to C Squadron without so much as a glance at my battle-fatigued troops.

"Well, Major Bray, how are your men?"

"Tired, sir."

"I can understand that. By the way, Major, where do you come from in Manitoba?"

"Virden, Manitoba, sir," said Bray, who had been born and raised and had gone to school in Virden and who ran the general store there.

Whereupon the general turned on his heel and walked off the parade ground without inspecting the two remaining squadrons. With his departure went poor Ronnie Morton's chances of becoming a brigadier, even though he was undoubtedly one of the best commanding officers both in battle and out of battle the Canadian Army ever had.

About ten years later, when I was the president of the fledgling National Ballet of Canada, Guy Simonds came on the board of directors. I reminded him of our earlier meeting, expecting at least to get a chuckle from him. He didn't laugh then any more than he had on the battlefields of Normandy. A fine soldier, but a pompous ass.

Next day, we were back in position again, getting ready for still another try at a big breakthrough through the German defences. We were laagered behind a ridge not far from the village of Ifs, and I saw that we were in a farmer's field full of onions and artichokes. It had always been my strong belief that one of the requirements of leadership was to help the men make a decent meal out of the not-too-tasty rations we had in our compo-packs of tinned food. I had started cooking contests between the troops, going from troop to troop every day to taste the various entries, judge a winner, and exchange recipes.

On this particular day, the produce in the field looked especially appetizing, and I asked the corporal commanding the tank next to mine, Paul Charnicki, to go and pick some onions and artichokes, promising him an unbelievable lunch. He obligingly jumped out of his tank and started foraging. There suddenly rained down a horrendous mortar barrage of moaning minnies, which landed right in the area where Charnicki was picking. Charnicki was wounded and whisked back to the nearest hospital unit. I felt guilty as hell until I got a message a few days later from Charnicki thanking me. The wound was not serious enough to cause permanent injury but it was sufficient to send him back to England, for which he was duly appreciative. A few days later I nearly got my own come-uppance when I was visiting the different tanks to try their recipes and got caught in a nasty mortar barrage.

By the beginning of August the German army was standing firm astride the Caen-Falaise road and at times counterattacking westward. It was the job of the Canadians and the British to get to Falaise and close the gap by meeting the Americans in a pincer movement. Every attempt to advance during the daytime had failed. Simonds and his staff came up with the creative idea of pouring the Canadian Army through at night. The attacking force was to line up in three lines, with the infantry in armoured troop carriers supported by tanks, to break through in three straight lines at midnight. This was operation Totalize.

To keep our bearings, we were given extra radios, which would tell us whether we were going too far to the left or to the right. To keep us on course, Bofors were to be fired over our heads in the direction we were to follow. My squadron was on the right-hand flank immediately behind the Sherbrooke Fusiliers. I used my extra radio to get on the regimental network of the Sherbrookes. Things went swimmingly at first and we kept moving ahead until we were certain that we had at least broken through the first line of German defences. Suddenly the radio squawked: "There is an enemy tank moving on our right." I immediately relayed the warning to my squadron over the other set. A few minutes later I heard one of my sergeants say, "I can see him — wham! I've got him," and sure enough, brewing up on the right of the column was a tank. The only problem was that the tank was one from my own squadron that had gotten out of line. Fortunately, no one was seriously wounded, although there were two minor casualties. Until now, I have never told the subaltern who was injured that it was his own sergeant who knocked him out of the war.

A little farther along, the column came to a sudden halt. A German tank gun or guns had brewed up several troop carriers and tanks of the Sherbrookes, who were in the lead. The resultant fires lit up the landscape and prevented us from getting past the guns. I jumped out of my tank to find the infantry commander to arrange for him to muster an attack on the German gun party. The officer in command had with him a whole battalion, and they were a first-class regiment, but when I found him he was in a total funk. Claiming that he was on his objective, although he was clearly two thousand yards from where we were supposed to be, he refused to put in an attack. When I asked for just a platoon to let me lead an attack, he refused. In anger and frustration at not being able to push ahead, I grabbed some grenades to attack on my own. As I crawled along the ground, with Spandaus burping out bullets left and right, I berated myself: "You are an ass, Goodman. There are five hundred infantrymen and they won't attack and you are going to attack all by yourself." For the only time in the war, I was slightly afraid. Suddenly I got my brightest idea of the war. Remembering that I had a bunch of smoke canisters in my tank, I threw a couple of grenades at the nearest German anti-tank gun, then scurried back. I got into my tank and laid down a totally dense smoke screen, which allowed us to get by without loss. An hour later we were on our objective. I had collected so many strays during that attack that I now had twice as many vehicles of all natures and descriptions as I'd started out with.

There followed one of the worst Canadian Corps staff foul-ups of the war. With the German defence temporarily broken, I was now in a perfect position to press the corps' attack. A few miles away a high piece of ground known as Hill 195 dominated the whole plain. This ground, which was unoccupied, was one of the Canadian Corps' major objectives. I called brigade headquarters and requested permission to take my squadron a few miles farther to this spot. The brigadier agreed, but when he requested permission from his higher-ups to send me and some infantry to take up a position on the hill he was told to stay where he was; the British Columbia Dragoons of the 4th Armoured Division were to pass through our brigade to take the hill. We anxiously awaited their passage, but five or six hours elapsed before we saw them starting to pass through on a distant ridge. By the time they had hit the high ground, the Germans had re-formed, and the Dragoons were totally destroyed in the attack on the hill, losing more than forty tanks. The impetus of the Canadian drive was lost, and I was to curse the army staff for years to come.

A few days later, on August 14, operation Tractable, the last phase of the drive to Falaise, began against the withdrawing Germans. The Canadian attack was being led by the 2nd Armoured Brigade at first without benefit of infantry, and the Fort Garry objective was to force a crossing of the Laison River. My squadron was out in front, moving quickly along to take command of the place from which the river could be crossed. As we moved quickly across the rolling open country, German tanks materialized on our right. In the ensuing battle, my third tank was destroyed and large gouges were torn out of both my legs.

The tank, while immobilized, did not brew. I was the only casualty, and I sent a message to McPherson instructing him to take command and concluding, "So long, sucker. I'll be eating lobster in London while you're living in this mud." I bound my wounds with two-week-old underwear and waited patiently for the medical van to arrive. As the doctor's halftrack drove across the field, I started to holler to attract his attention. Fortunately for me, he didn't hear me. The van proceeded three or four hundred yards past me and then, to my horror, was struck by a German shell and turned into a flaming mass, killing several of the wounded passengers. I was then picked up by Brigadier Lewis, who was in charge of our reconnaissance forces, and brought back to a light aid detachment. Lewis was later killed in that attack. I was shipped back by boat to England, lying on a stretcher surrounded by German prisoners of war. I ended up at the same hospital in Watford where I had been two months earlier.

The doctors told me they had never seen such large wounds do so little permanent damage. My injuries prevented me from returning to France, and I took over command of the Canadian Armoured Corps Tactical School and then of the Canadian Armoured Corps Gunnery School. In April of the following year I sailed back to Canada.

Recently I was in Washington, where I visited the Vietnam War Memorial and the John F. Kennedy Memorial, which is inscribed with the following excerpt from his inaugural address:

In the long history of the world
Only a few generations have been granted
The role of defending freedom
In the hour of maximum danger.
I do not shrink from this responsibility.
I welcome it.

I asked myself, "How can I write about a war in which so many were maimed and died to rescue humanity from a beastly tyranny, in terms that are so superficial and anecdotal?" On reflection I decided I owed no apology. The individual combat soldier, once he is in the service, gives little thought to concepts or to territorial imperatives. In the words of the English poet Siegfried Sassoon, "He wars on Death — for life; not men — for flags." What I remember today is similar to what most soldiers remember. In retrospect there are always two wars, the war of the sufferers and the war of the survivors. The war of the sufferers needs far greater historians than I. The war of the survivors, I understand.

Many of us learned important democratic lessons from the war. In a fighting unit you were judged solely on your worth and your contribution to the unit and to your fellow soldiers. You shared an overwhelming sense of comradeship and trust. Gone for the most part were jealousy or anger at officers or NCOs, provided they accepted the responsibility and dangers of leadership. Moreover, in the deep recesses of your heart and mind you were able to judge yourself and know your worth. Much of my own confidence has come from knowing I have been tried in battle and not found wanting.

Time and the appalling horror of a nuclear war are starting to impair this nation's collective vision and memory. The understandable longing for disarmament is causing us to forget that we have had forty years of nuclear peace between the superpowers, the longest period without war for centuries. This nation cannot use *glasnost* as an excuse to abandon its northern vigilance or reduce its all-round defence capability. Fortunately, the Mulroney government appears to be aware of the dangers and for the most part has been taking its own independent defence initiatives, supporting continental defence measures by the United States. The new policy paper issued by Minister of Defence Perrin Beatty is the most important defence proposal since NATO and NORAD. The cause of freedom requires Canadians not to be beguiled by siren calls for unilateral disarmament by left-wing peace movements, many of which are supported by foreign contributions. The recent policy of the New Democratic Party in favour of Canada's leaving NATO is suicidal for the nation. Peace will come only through military strength and careful disarmament negotiations between the United States and the Soviet Union.

CHAPTER THREE

A POLITICAL ANIMAL

With anticipation and excitement mixed with a healthy dose of trepidation, I took my wife of six months, Marjorie, and my two-year-old stepson, Ian, aboard the ship sailing for Halifax. Marjorie, a Yorkshire woman, had been in the WRENS. Her first husband, a glider pilot in the First Airborne Division, had been killed during the invasion of Sicily. Our courtship, like our married life, was rocky; had it been a peacetime romance, it would never have bloomed. The marriage lasted until 1951, when to our mutual relief we separated.

The small ship was full of war brides and troops. I was the second senior officer on board and was appointed the ship adjutant, a thankless job that entailed spending most of my time trying to keep the troops and other soldiers' wives out of each other's staterooms. I was lucky to be able to achieve that with my own wife.

We arrived in Halifax and boarded the troop train for Toronto on the day of Franklin Roosevelt's death. Roosevelt was particularly popular with the Canadian troops, who admired the initiative he had shown in assisting the Allies even before the Americans were at war. Little did we realize the disastrous consequences that would flow from his failure to share Churchill's concern about Russia's intentions. It seemed a double tragedy that after so much blood had been spilled to save Europe from the Nazis, many nations should then fall under Communist domination when the war ended.

For me, as for tens of thousands of other Canadians, coming home to my family and to Canada after four years was traumatic. My mother's hair had been auburn when I left; now it was completely grey. My sister had grown up and was engaged to be married, and my dad, like my mother, had aged under the strain of having a son in action. Nevertheless, I rejoiced in our reunion. Only now, as a father who has lost a child in an automobile accident, do I have some idea of the anguish that millions of parents felt during that war.

My British bride, her son, and I moved into my parents' home on Glenayr Road in Forest Hill Village, where we remained until I finished Osgoode Hall Law School two years later. When I look back and think of what a hellion Ian was, I marvel at my parents' patience and at my own selfishness.

The day after the family reunion, my father informed me that the writs for a provincial election on June 4 had been issued and that Tory headquarters had called him to inquire if I would be interested in being a candidate. They had tried to reach me in England, but I had already left. Alex McKenzie, a former classmate of my father's, was now chairman of organization for the election and president of the Ontario Progressive Conservative organization. He had told my father that the Tories would like me to run in the riding of St. Andrew. I was flabbergasted.

My dad explained, "They are very anxious for you to run. I think Joe Eisenberg suggested your name to Alex."

"What about Osgoode Hall?"

My father replied with typical directness: "I don't think that will be a problem. You are not going to beat Joe Salsberg."

St. Andrew was a central Toronto riding that extended roughly from Palmerston Boulevard on the west to Spadina on the east and from the waterfront on the south, to just south of Casa Loma on the north. I had lived in the area for twenty years before we moved into Forest Hill Village in 1940. Though the southern part of the constituency had been predominantly Jewish between the wars, the Jewish population now represented less than 20 per cent of the riding and was busy migrating northward along Bathurst Street to Forest Hill Village and Cedarvale. Before 1934 the riding had been held by E.F. Singer, the only Conservative Jewish member of the legislature up to that time. From 1934 to 1943, J.J. Glass of the Liberals was its member, until his defeat by Joe Salsberg, a member of the Labour-Progressive Party, as the Communist Party called itself.

The Tories were in power in the province with a minority government under George Drew, who had been chosen as leader in 1938 following Earl Rowe's resignation. I had attended that convention as a student delegate from the Macdonald-Cartier Conservative Club of the university. The war had delayed the provincial election, which did not take place until 1943. By this time the excesses of Mitchell Hepburn prior to his resignation had seriously weakened the Liberal Party. Hepburn was a bright, charming, but undisciplined man given to the weaknesses of the flesh. He feuded bitterly with his federal leader, Mackenzie King, and, for a farm boy from Elgin County, seemed far too willing to listen to his financial advisers from Bay Street. Gordon Conant had succeeded Hepburn briefly to be followed by Harry Nixon, who led a weakened government into the election. Ted Jolliffe was the leader of a strong CCF and Drew led the Tories. The Tories squeaked through the 1943 election by a narrow margin, and the CCF formed the official opposition. The Liberals were in considerable disarray.

The choice of George Drew as leader had been most fortunate for the Tories. Drew was a vigorous, tall, handsome man with a slightly florid complexion and grey hair. He suffered a disability to one hand from a First World War wound. He possessed a good mind, a deep sense of morality, both personal and public, and a highly developed sense of the *noblesse oblige* inherent in the British tradition, of which he was a great admirer. His detractors alleged that he was pompous and arrogant. I found him to be neither, unless voicing strong opinions with conviction is arrogance. He had a habit, when engaging in social conversations, of making a short speech then courteously waiting for you to make one, which was a little disconcerting when all you wanted to do was have a drink and make small talk. Still, he enjoyed a good laugh and his wife, Fiorenza, the daughter of Edward Johnson, a former director of the Metropolitan Opera, was a beautiful, cultivated woman.

Drew had had a distinguished career in public service by the time he was chosen provincial leader. He could boast an excellent war record, having finished the First World War as a lieutenant-colonel in the artillery. A lawyer, he was Master of the

Supreme Court of Ontario, then chairman of the Ontario Securities Commission at an early age. He subsequently became chairman of organization for the Conservative Party in Ontario in the mid-thirties. The only blots on his escutcheon were his having left Earl Rowe in the lurch when Rowe refused to join a coalition government with Hepburn in the mid-thirties and his disagreement with Conservative policy on the best way to handle the Oshawa General Motors strike. This strike issue also split the Ontario Liberals, when Arthur Roebuck, the attorney-general, and David Croll, the minister of labour, broke with Hepburn and left the cabinet. Drew's early views on organized labour were retrogressive, but his record in this field as premier was good.

This incident and his support of a stronger national defence policy gave Drew the reputation of being reactionary. Subsequent events proved that this was most unfair. As Premier of Ontario he pioneered the earliest human rights legislation in Canada in 1946 and 1947 and was an excellent minister of education, a portfolio he held along with the premiership. Indeed, it was Drew who gave the Roman Catholic schools their first fair share of municipal tax revenues. Subsequently, George Drew, John Robarts, and William Davis all helped Catholic secondary school financing, yet the Tories have received little thanks from the Catholic hierarchy and their flock, who keep voting Liberal in large numbers.

Drew attacked the responsibilities of governing Ontario with his usual vigour and brought in an expansionist program. His transportation program opened up the north, his hydro program assisted industry, and in education he greatly liberalized grants. Just shy of two years in office, he called the 1945 election with the hope of obtaining a majority. The one area where the Tories needed to make significant gains was central Toronto, and they were actively seeking returned war veterans as candidates.

The Labour-Progressive leader was Alexander A. MacLeod, the member for Bellwoods, a Nova Scotia Scot. (Later, in the fifties he became disillusioned with Stalin and Communism and left the party.) Joe Salsberg, the Labour-Progressive member for St. Andrew, was a popular and articulate red-headed labour organizer whose wife was a well-known social worker in the

Jewish community. When Churchill and Stalin joined forces, Salsberg emerged and won his seat in 1943. He was convivial and quick-witted but lacked the depth and the grasp of public problems that MacLeod had. He was highly popular both within the Jewish working-class community and to some extent among its middle class. His sense of humour endeared him to the press. It is difficult today with the history of Soviet tyranny in Hungary and Czechoslovakia and the cruelty in Afghanistan to believe what a sizeable constituency the Communists once had in Toronto. But at the time the Russians were our gallant allies and this greatly lessened the opprobrium of being a Communist.

Between 1935 and 1945, the Conservative organization in St. Andrew had fallen into disarray and came to be controlled by a few middle-aged women for whom it was mainly a euchre outlet. My opponent for the nomination was Frank Chambers, a local alderman, a decent fellow but not a strong candidate. Though the feeling in the pit of my stomach as I stepped up to make my speech at the nomination meeting in the basement of the old church on Albany Avenue was far more hollow than it had been at H Hour for the attack on the Laison River, my nervousness was no impediment: as a twice-wounded veteran still on active service who came from a well-known Tory family and was being nominated by Dick Greer, a famed criminal lawyer, I was well placed to win the nomination.

Everyone knew that I was not going to beat Joe Salsberg, and that the point of the exercise was to show that the Tory party could field a variety of strong candidates who had recently served their country overseas. Shortly after I gained the nomination, the nearby riding of Bracondale became available. It was a solidly Tory Anglo-Saxon riding and a safe seat for any Conservative candidate. Party headquarters suggested that I switch ridings, but I refused. I had decided to run against a Communist, I had been chosen by the riding, and I was sticking with St. Andrew.

The change from being a major, in command first of a squadron of tanks and subsequently of the whole Canadian Armoured Corps Gunnery School, to being a political candidate and a supplicant for votes in a Communist-held riding was challenging. In spite of the pessimism about the prospect of a

Tory victory, my combative and competitive spirit came to the fore and by the end of the campaign I was eager to win.

One of the hardest workers in my campaign was Allan Grossman, who brought it some semblance of organization. He subsequently won the riding three elections later and went into both the Robarts and Davis cabinets. He lived to see his son, Larry, become first a cabinet minister in the Davis government and subsequently Tory provincial leader. Allan has never received the recognition that he deserved within the Jewish community. A Toronto rabbi even wrote a history of the Jewish community in Toronto that made a great hero out of Joe Salsberg and barely mentioned Allan Grossman.

My determination to win was kindled by the filthy tactics of the Communist Party, aided and abetted by the Liberals. Their campaign literature was the most scurrilous I have ever seen. It accused George Drew of being a fascist and an anti-semite and me of having betrayed my heritage and become his anti-semitic henchman, a great irony given my family's and my own dedication to the Jewish community. In the Polish and Ukrainian areas, Drew was labelled as hating all people of non-British background. Many of my female workers were threatened, spat upon, and even assaulted by Communist male workers.

The group of supporters I managed to put together was small because the riding organization was non-existent and most of my friends were in the services. My campaign manager, Marion Mehr, decided that she and I had to hire a private secretary. We called up the Jewish employment agency and they sent a girl that I had known and gone to school with. I was delighted to hire an old Harbordite and she was the repository of all our plans and secrets. Throughout the campaign we could never understand why every time we planned to do something, Salsberg seemed to be there first, but we were willing to credit his superior campaign committee. Then, on the Saturday before the election, the *Toronto Daily Star* ran a full-page headline story telling how my campaign committee planned to prevent the various ethnic groups in the riding from voting on election day. The source of the story was my secretary, whose disclosure of these alleged plans was a total fabrication. The final blow was a broadsheet containing yet another slanderous attack on my family, which was delivered to most homes in the riding the day before the voting. On election day, the Communists were successful in raising the dead, who voted for them by the score.

The Liberal candidate emulated Salsberg's tactics. One day he saw my wife and sister canvassing from door to door. Not knowing who they were, he asked jocularly, "How could two nice looking young ladies like you work for a Jew!" The unladylike replies he received are not fit to print.

The role of a candidate in an election is simple. He must meet as many of the constituents as possible. This is accomplished primarily by going from door to door morning, noon, and night. The only time he should cease canvassing is when he is addressing meetings in the constituency or attending receptions and parties in his honour. In St. Andrew meeting the constituents was an incredible experience. The riding is one of the most polyglot in the country with people of every ethnic, educational, and occupational background. Every day was a new experience. The multiplicity of views expressed and questions asked, the understandings and the misunderstandings, often led me to ponder the problems of education and communication in the province. But when it was all over, I remained thoroughly convinced of the soundness of the democratic system.

On Sundays the various Jewish clubs and societies had meetings at which the candidates were invited to speak. Many of the audience spoke Yiddish as well as English. Unlike me, Salsberg was fluent in Yiddish. He used it to advantage in denigrating my youth, my inexperience, and my party, which was not popular with working-class Jews. I eventually learned how to hold my own and used my family background and wartime experience to advantage. My reception was growing warmer and the Communists were starting to get uneasy. The dirty tricks started to increase.

The Communist campaign committee need not have worried, as Salsberg beat me soundly by almost 6,000 votes. He even picked up the majority of the veteran vote, which I found especially galling. My only satisfaction was that I beat both the Liberal and the CCF candidates. Although I had been soundly trounced I was proud that I had run. Democracy requires participants, not just onlookers and critics. Battle had taught me much about the character and courage of my fellow Canadians. Standing for the Legislature taught me about their needs and aspirations. I also learned that for most mortals emotion is a greater force than logic, an important political lesson. If I was destined to become an organizer on the periphery of politics, at least I could always say that once I had had the courage to run. There is no better way to understand the democratic process than to be a candidate for office canvassing in a working-class riding, nor would I have preferred to represent any other type of riding.

The election over, I was no longer a war hero or a public figure. I was back to being a second-year student of law at Osgoode Hall, along with a lot of other ex-war heroes. The class had more than its share of soon-to-be-prominent men: John Robarts, later Premier of Ontario; Sam Hughes, later Mr. Justice Hughes and chairman of the Federal Civil Service Commission; Bill Shortreed, later a senior executive with John Labatt Limited; Doug Bruce, the vice president and counsel of Westinghouse Canada; Vernon Singer, subsequently deputy leader of the provincial Liberal Party; Wally Nesbitt, later an MP for Oxford County and our representative at the United Nations; Syd Robins, now a judge on the Ontario Court of Appeal; Tony Cassels, who was to head up a major law firm and become president of the National Ballet; Dan Lang, a Pearson adviser, now in the Senate; Bob Hamilton, Hutch Gauthier, Jim Kirkpatrick and Hugh Foster, all eminent judges; and Norman Simpson, Canadian head of the international relief organization CARE.

Most of my colleagues were married, some with children. The emolument for a law student was $5 to $7 weekly. Today articling students are paid $15,000 to $25,000 a year, and many lawyers would not dare to send them on menial tasks. I was the highest-paid law student, being articled to my father. Technically, I received $15 a week, but I also had bed and board for my wife, my son, and myself plus whatever else I needed or wanted. Fortunately, the government had a generous system of educational benefits for returning veterans that helped others less fortunate than I through school.

In those days, students articled to their principals for the three years that they attended Osgoode Hall. They attended a lecture early in the morning, went to their law firms and worked a full day, went back for a lecture between four and five, then returned to their law firms to work in the evening. My friends and I would often gather in the New Empress Hotel, on the north side of Queen Street just across from Osgoode Hall, for a few beers and an opportunity to work out our frustrations and exchange stories.

When the time came to have our law school graduation pictures taken, Tony Cassels, Sam Hughes, and Bill Shortreed managed in my absence to have me assigned the responsibility of seeing that each graduate's picture was taken and delivering them the negatives to choose from, a time-consuming and unpleasant duty. I had my revenge by getting the photographer to paint a considerable amount of hair on Cassels and Hughes, who were almost totally bald. Shortreed used to boast that he never sent Christmas cards, so I took the proofs of his picture, pasted them on a maudlin Christmas card and sent them around to his wife and three or four of his closest friends. When I look back on those two years at Osgoode, they seem full of childish exploits unexpected in grown married men with children who had just come through four or five years of searing war. But perhaps it was that experience that made us so eager to enjoy ourselves.

The permanent teaching staff at Osgoode Hall in the period just after the war was undoubtedly the best ever to teach in a Canadian law school. I doubt if Harvard or Yale had a higher standard of professors. The Dean was Cecil Augustus Wright, known as Caesar. A brilliant writer, jurist, and teacher, he became dean of the University of Toronto Law School when it became a graduate school. Bora Laskin, who was Caesar's right hand, subsequently became chief justice of the Supreme Court of Canada; John Willis, undoubtedly the most popular and best teacher I have ever had, went on to work for the International Monetary Fund. Bora, who became a close personal friend, was the least popular of the three because he seemed to make a point of letting the veterans know that they would not be given any special treatment.

Each year there was a dinner for the graduating class a few days before the call to the bar. That evening I gathered with a group of about fifteen friends in my dad's office, where we drank half a dozen bottles of spirits and then trooped off to the dinner. There the hospitality included some exceptional wines donated by the benchers of the Law Society. Also invited to these dinners were the various practising lawyers who gave the practical exams to graduating students. One middle-aged lawyer who was particularly inebriated was bothering one of the young women present. Bill Shortreed admonished the offender and told him that if he didn't quit annoying the lady he'd punch him in the nose. The two then went outside to resolve their differences. Shortreed finished the debate with a right cross to the jaw that broke the solicitor's denture bridge, dusted himself off, and returned to the dinner to finish his wine. Within minutes a stalwart constable appeared to arrest Shortreed. Fortunately, the secretary of the Law Society, Earl Smith, managed to placate the constable and keep Shortreed from being carted off to jail. All he suffered was a few days of torment, wondering whether that right hook was going to cost him his call to the bar.

In June 1947, I received my call to the bar. After the ceremonies, my father and I walked back together to the office. As we approached I saw a glazier and sign painter working on the door. They were scraping off the "David B. Goodman" and painting on "Goodman and Goodman." My father turned to me and said, "We are equal partners," and from that day onward I earned as much as my father, who had been practising for thirty years.

My father was an outstanding lawyer who, by hard work and scholarship, had established himself as a leader, if not *the* leader, amongst the lawyers in the Jewish community. He received his call in 1917 and started to practise with E.W.J. Owens, head of the law firm, which then became known as Owens, Proudfoot, Macdonald & Goodman and later Owens & Goodman. Owens, a big, forceful man with a goatee and a handlebar moustache, took a paternal interest in my father and gave him every opportunity for advancement. There was one drawback. Every Friday he would give dad a signed blank cheque and say, "Take what you need."

After a few years, my father said, "Our present arrangement is unsatisfactory. I want to be a partner at whatever percentage you think is fair."

Incensed, Owens replied, "Have I not treated you like a son?"

"Yes, but now I'm growing up. I have a wife and family." Owens would not budge and my dad left to go on his own. Without my father's steady hand, Owens eventually became insolvent. Many clients left with my father, especially those from the Italian community. I chuckle when I recall how, when my dad left to start on his own, he needed a cable address for his stationery. He initially took the first two letters of each of his first names, DAGO—hardly appropriate for a largely Italian practice. It soon became GODA.

For the next twenty-five or so years, my dad practised either on his own or with the help of a young junior, but never with a partner. His prowess allowed his family to enjoy the comfortable living usually enjoyed by successful professionals. Even during the height of the Depression, my sister and I went to summer camp. I grew up without knowing financial concerns other than when I overspent my modest allowance, and the only time I took steps to augment it was during the summer when I worked as the riding instructor at Camp Arowhon in Algonquin Park. Until the war, life had held few worries for Eddie Goodman; but now it was time to realize my parents' great expectations for me and to begin to support my family.

About a year after my graduation, George Drew, with his eye on a possible future change in the federal leadership of the Conservative Party, called a provincial general election. I was still smarting a little from my defeat of three years earlier and wondered whether I should run in another, safer constituency. The problem was that almost all the City of Toronto ridings that could be won already had a Tory member. My father was much opposed to my becoming an elected member or even running again. He said that I had to make up my mind whether I was going to be a lawyer or a politician, and that, while I could maintain an interest in politics and be a good lawyer, I could not do that if I became an elected member. I consulted provincial president Alex McKenzie, with whom I had remained friendly since the 1945 election. I had joined him and George Drew in helping resuscitate the Young Progressive Conservative Association of Ontario and sundry other chores. McKenzie's advice was exactly the same as my father's. He said, "Don't be a fool. Stay with the law and help me organize." I decided to sublimate this part of my ego once and forever and to follow my dad's sage advice.

There had never been any doubt in my mind since the age of three or four that I was going to be a lawyer. Other children wanted to be firemen, policemen, ball players, or just millionaires. When asked as a child what I was going to do, I always said, "I am going to be a judge." Fortunately for me, I modified that ambition to stay with the practice of law, twice refusing an appointment to the bench. While the bench should be the ultimate achievement for anyone who loves the law, it would have denied me two key sources of enjoyment: politics and money.

I believe that the law is the highest of any calling. It is the framework of civilization and the basis of freedom. The British common law, with its theory of the rule of law, and American constitutionalism and theory of the absolute reign of law are the source of the democratic strength of the English-speaking world. Democracy requires the balancing of conflicting interests, each with some merit, and even requiring some limitation. It is through a strong legal system that this balance is achieved. A free judiciary and legal profession are the greatest safeguards of individual liberty this country possesses.

Politics holds a different attraction. It is an exciting pastime, but, far more important, it is the most important instrument for social change. For many centuries, religion was thought of as being the best — albeit not too successful — means of achieving social ends. The twentieth century, particularly the second half of the century, has clearly established that only through politics and law can we achieve the necessary social changes. Though both careers appealed to me, in the end I felt that as a lawyer I could have the best of both — practise law and still dabble in politics.

No one can successfully dabble in law. It is far too hard a taskmaster and requires too much commitment for a dilettante.

I practised law with my father for twenty-one years, and it was the most rewarding experience of my life. In all those years together, never once was there any acrimony between us. My father allowed me a free hand to run and build the law firm of which he was the foundation and early strength. But in spite of our congenial relationship, practising law with D.B. was no joyride. He was an excellent teacher, but knowing my disregard for detail he was a demanding taskmaster. I remember shortly after graduation showing him a draft contract. He took it home to read; next day he threw the marked-up document on my desk and said, "Some day you may become a highly successful lawyer, but you'll never be a great one. Do that again." The early partners of my firm—such as Norm Schipper, Herb Solway, Lionel Schipper, and Ken Karp—were all indebted to D.B., although he was less critical of them than of me. Probably with good reason.

CHAPTER FOUR
A DYNASTY BEGINS

While George Drew deeply loved Ontario and relished the opportunity the premiership gave him to lay the foundation and establish a structure for its future growth, his ambitions extended beyond the province of his birth. He had shown since youth a strong interest in national as well as international problems, and there can be no doubt that he nursed the dream of becoming Prime Minister of Canada.

In the summer of 1947, at Alex McKenzie's suggestion, I was instrumental in arranging a policy conference for the Young Progressive Conservatives of Ontario at Geneva Park on Lake Couchiching. This lovely lake, which stretches about seven or eight miles north from Orillia, was the site of my family's cottage for fifteen years, and the beauty of Simcoe County is very dear to me. The Drews came up on the Saturday, and in the early evening Fiorenza and George, Mabel and George Hees, and my wife and I motored over to our cottage.

Two conversations from that evening remain implanted in my memory. Early on, Drew told us about a book in which a political scientist by the name of Schwartzenchild put forward his theories.

"Have you read it?" he asked Hees.

"Yes I have, George," Hees replied.

"What did you think of it?"

"Well, to tell you the truth, it was so long ago I've forgotten what he said."

Drew smiled. "That's damn funny. The book only came out six months ago."

Hees, not the slightest bit nonplused, merely laughed. "I usually get away with that," he confessed.

Later Drew and I were sitting in a corner and he started to talk about the great potential of Canada. He was particularly concerned about regional divisions and our failure to weld the country into a strong cohesive force. He saw Canada being the bridge between the United States and Great Britain to strengthen the bonds that the war had forged between the English-speaking peoples. He went on to say, "Many people think that I am anti-Quebec and have no regard for the French-speaking people of this country. Nothing could be further from the truth. I look upon them as a great cultural resource. I do not believe that the difference in language should prevent them from making a strong national contribution."

It was a sentiment that would have appealed twenty years later to Pierre Elliott Trudeau, or thirty-five years later to Brian Mulroney, and it indicated that Drew had strong national ambitions. His timing was astute; the need to appoint a new national leader was becoming obvious.

For twenty-one years John Bracken had been the Premier of Manitoba and the leader of a hybrid provincial party called the Liberal-Progressive Party. In 1942 the Tories, in search of a leader to break the strong hold of Mackenzie King over the country (King had been prime minister for fifteen of the last twenty-one years), persuaded Bracken to run for the leadership. He ran and won, but that was his last win other than in his own riding. In the 1945 national election he failed to make inroads in the western provinces or to do as well in Ontario as Drew had done in the provincial election held a week earlier. As Bracken was advancing in years, a convention for the national leadership would soon be held.

With the move to federal politics in mind, Drew called a provincial election in 1948 just three years after his previous overwhelming win and well before he was required to do so. The ostensible reason for the election was the issue of the conversion of the Ontario hydro-electric system from twenty-five cycles to sixty cycles. This changeover involved a huge expenditure, but the long-term benefits of lower costs and more efficient energy were essential to the province's industrial expansion. Another important issue was the modernization of the provincial liquor laws that Drew had recently implemented, allowing taverns and cocktail lounges in Ontario.

The Tories were returned with an only slightly reduced majority, but ironically George Drew, whose constituency was High Park, the only area in Toronto where spirits could not be sold, lost his seat to a CCF prohibitionist candidate, Bill Temple. The loss was not much of a setback to Drew, however; very soon afterward, John Bracken resigned and the federal leadership convention that Drew had been expecting was called.

(A personal footnote to the provincial election was that A.A. MacLeod, the Communist leader, was re-elected in Bellwoods, the riding I had thought of standing for. His Tory opponent, George Renison, a bright young businessman with a splendid war record, was defeated decisively, and I would have been clobbered if I had run. Joe Salsberg held onto St. Andrew, beating Nathan Phillips, an alderman who was later to become the popular "Mayor of All the People" of the City of Toronto.)

Drew announced his candidacy for the federal leadership shortly after Bracken resigned. In addition to Drew, there were two other candidates for the party leadership, John Diefenbaker, a western criminal counsel, then the member for Lake Centre in Saskatchewan, and Donald Fleming, a Toronto commercial lawyer representing Eglinton riding in Toronto.

John Diefenbaker was first elected to the House in 1940 on his third attempt to win a seat. In that year he had been invited to the nomination meeting to speak and had ended up as the candidate. Two years later in Winnipeg he had unsuccessfully contested the leadership against Bracken. Now he hoped to do better against Drew. Donald Fleming, who was first elected in 1945, had previously served on Toronto City Council. A short, precise man of impeccable personal habits and character, he was combative but pleasant, intelligent but dull, and a prodigious worker.

The October 1948 federal leadership convention took place in Ottawa. It was my first federal foray, and I looked forward to it with keen interest. McKenzie, the head of the Ontario delegation, had me appointed to the policy committee, which was under the chairmanship of the redoubtable Fred Gardiner.

Gardiner, an able, loud-voiced, hard-nosed lawyer from Toronto, later served as the first Metro chairman.

A few other young delegates on the committee were also war veterans. We had seen what military unpreparedness had done to the democracies in the thirties and were determined that it should not happen again. I moved a motion supporting a policy of a year of compulsory military service for every able-bodied young Canadian male. The great body of older delegates on the committee, particularly those from Quebec, showed signs of apoplexy at the very thought. There was much talk about the vestiges of distrust of the Conservative Party that remained among French Canadians from the 1917 Union government's conscription legislation. Finally, after an hour of soul-searching, I was persuaded to withdraw the motion.

George Drew had little difficulty in winning the national convention against Diefenbaker and Fleming. His success was due in part to his special brand of patrician magnetism, and in part to the Ontario provincial Conservative organization directed by Alex McKenzie, who worked closely with the Ontario federal members. Diefenbaker took the strong Ontario support for Drew as a personal affront. A decade later he often said to me, "You people in Ontario have never liked or supported me." I would remind him of the sixty seats he had won in Ontario in 1957 and the seventy seats he had won in 1958, as well as the unparalleled support he had received from Ontario Premier Leslie Frost in the 1957 election. "There hasn't been any federal politician who has received more support to date from the people of Ontario," I would assert. In reply he always repeated the same two complaints: "You drove my father out of the province and he had to go west, and I will never forget how little support I had in the 1948 convention."

With the federal convention successfully out of the way, McKenzie's absolute control over the organizational machinery of the Conservative Party in Ontario was next put to the test with the choice of a new provincial leader. He was firmly of the opinion that the best man to lead the province was Leslie M. Frost, the provincial treasurer. Frost, born in Simcoe County, had practised as a lawyer in Lindsay and had been the member since

1937 for the then predominantly Orange county of Victoria. Frost's brother, Cecil, president of the party in the thirties, had hired Hugh Latimer, a devout Baptist from Northumberland County, as a rural organizer. After a break for war service overseas, Latimer became McKenzie's field organizer outside Toronto. Apart from the premier, Latimer was the best-known Tory among the party workers across the province.

A possible contender to succeed George Drew was George Doucett, the minister of highways, and member for Lanark, but McKenzie had serious reservations about Doucett's capacity for leadership. He believed that Doucett lacked backbone and relied almost completely on the views of Harry Robbins, the party's public relations officer, and a small coterie of friends. The other possible candidates all came from Toronto: Leslie Blackwell, the excellent attorney-general; Dana Porter, minister of education and later chief justice of Ontario; and Kelso Roberts, an MLA from Toronto and a mining lawyer. Though he was close to Dana Porter and Les Blackwell, McKenzie believed Frost would be more acceptable across the whole province than either of the other candidates. The history of both the Liberal and the Conservative parties in Ontario over the past fifty years has shown that they have generally gone outside Toronto for their leaders. The only exceptions have been George Drew, who was born in Guelph, but lived in Toronto, and Larry Grossman, the recently resigned leader of the Tory party.

I was attracted to George Doucett, whom I knew better than Frost and who gave the outward appearance of strength and assurance. I went to see him and asked if he was considering running. Doucett said he had not yet made up his mind and asked me to hang loose. As the weeks went by, and I received no answer, it was clear that he was waffling.

I decided that Ontario did not need a chicken for premier and, following the recommendation of my mentor, supported Frost. While at that time my experience with Frost was superficial, I found him to have an engaging personality. His eyes looked right at you and he had a warm laugh. It was hard to dislike Les Frost. It was also a mistake to cross him.

The convention — which turned out to be more like a

coronation — was held in the Royal York Hotel in April 1949. My friend Sam Hughes nominated Frost and gave the only outstanding speech of the convention. Frost won fairly handily on the first ballot with support from right across the province in almost every riding.

Leadership conventions have greatly changed since the late forties. In those days serious candidates spent ten to twenty thousand dollars. Today candidates spend three-quarters of a million dollars in provincial contests and more in federal fights. Much of the expenditure is wasted. In the 1967 federal convention Duff Roblin supporters spent $8,000 on silver spoons that were never distributed. The goal is to get a well-regarded supporter of your candidate elected as a delegate in every riding, then have him or her woo the other delegates to your side. The best way to use money is to set up a communications system both during the delegate selection period and while the convention is on. Lavish spending during a convention cannot buy a leadership. The delegates have too much personal knowledge of the candidates to be hoodwinked. The hoopla is fun, but nothing more.

Leslie Frost was the possessor of the proverbial iron fist in a velvet glove. With McKenzie's assistance, Frost was to popularize the party with people from all walks of life and lay the foundation for the forty-two-year Tory dynasty in Ontario. He made everyone feel that they were close to "Old Man Ontario." He was a man of excellent judgement, genuine concern for ordinary people, and a belief in orderly progress. Although fundamentally compassionate, he also possessed the most important quality for a successful politician, the guts to slit a throat if he thought it was in the best interests of his government. Without apparent qualm he could walk away from a friend to avoid political damage or even to strengthen his own position.

Up until Frost's ascension, annual meetings of the Ontario Progressive Conservative Association had been cut-and-dried affairs, with preordained results. Not so the annual meeting of 1950, where Alex McKenzie found out almost too late that he was in a fight for his political life. After a dozen years of unassailable and uncontested power—power that he had used with discretion, restraint, and for the benefit of others—he was threatened by the jealousy of those who felt they were on the outside and should be on the inside. Many of these, of course, were delegates who had opposed Frost.

Less than a year after Frost's victory, George Doucett and Harry Robbins decided that they were going to take over the provincial organization and oust McKenzie as president. Robbins, who had been in charge of public relations for the provincial party for more than a decade, was a lifelong friend of Doucett and also, for personal reasons, disliked Fred Gardiner intensely. (Gardiner had made the mistake of acting in a divorce suit against Robbins, earning his undying enmity.) Through his position, Robbins had acquired many press contacts. Stories planted by Robbins started to appear in the press. These said that Doucett was going to run against McKenzie for the presidency, on a platform calling for an end to political patronage. (How many times have I heard that refrain since 1950?) McKenzie's own conduct had always been above reproach, so the attacks centred on his friend Fred Gardiner, who had acted for tavern owners in many liquor-licencing cases. When Doucett had told me of this plans to "reorganize and reinvigorate" the provincial association by running for president, I had replied, "The party appears to be in damn good shape right now. Furthermore McKenzie is the best thing that has happened to this party." That was the end of my relationship with Doucett.

When I warned McKenzie to take this threat to his presidency seriously, he reported that that very week he had received a similar warning from Roland Michener, then a provincial cabinet minister. McKenzie went on to say, "Doucett has not got the guts to risk his standing in the party by running against me himself. It won't be him personally. They will find someone else."

As always, McKenzie was right in his political judgement. Doucett, ever cautious, was not prepared to risk his reputation on an organizational job, but he persuaded Jim Allan, a dairy farmer and the former president of the Ontario Good Roads Association, to run. Allan had dealt often with Doucett as minister of highways, and with politicians, provincial and municipal, across the province. He was well thought of and a good choice. The annual meeting was set for November 1949 and Allan announced his candidacy for president.

It was an occasion of great drama. McKenzie, the original one-man Big Blue Machine with the encyclopaedic knowledge of all things Tory, was in danger of being toppled and thrown to the growling pit bulls. His friends from all over the province rallied to save him, with Hugh Latimer, the provincial party's field organizer, leading the fight. Doucett warned Latimer on the first day, "When this is over, you won't have a job," and Hugh rejoined, "If you're in charge, I wouldn't work here."

The McKenzie forces included all the great names of the provincial party at that time: Elmer Bell of Exeter, Tom Pryde of Huron County, Tip Corey of Lambton, Charlie MacNaughton of Huron, Harry Waisberg of Sudbury, Sam Ault of Winchester, Ben Cunningham of Kingston, Sam Currie of Tweed, Fred Cawthorne of High Park, Toronto. I worked hard with the younger delegates like Bill Archer, Al Lawrence, and Sam Hughes. I remember that Bill Webster of London drove more than four hundred miles in a Jeep just to be able to vote for McKenzie. But the real hero of the occasion was Hugh Latimer, whose loyalty to McKenzie equalled that of Lancelot to Guinevere. In the heat of the second day, just prior to voting, Hugh said to me, "I will beat those liars or die in the trying. Doucett is not fit to polish McKenzie's shoes."

Throughout McKenzie's fight, Leslie Frost didn't lift a finger to help the man who had been responsible for his election as leader. Quite the reverse. On the night before the annual meeting started, when Frost and McKenzie were in Frost's room at the Royal York Hotel, Frost said, "Alex, it would be a great shame if after all your service to the party, you were to be defeated for the presidency. Don't you think that you should consider withdrawing?" McKenzie retorted, "If those bastards are going to take over this party they're going to have to do it by defeating me in a vote and not by me walking away."

After the dust had settled and McKenzie was re-elected, he and Jim Allan became fast friends. Allan was later elected to the Legislature for the Haldimand-Norfolk riding and subsequently brought in to the cabinet by Frost on McKenzie's recommendation. The irony of the story is that in 1953 evidence came to light that, in order to obtain highway construction contracts, certain highway builders were underbidding and then being overpaid by Doucett's ministry of highways for extras such as rock instead of sand. This scam, when added to the occasional minor present from a contractor to highway quality inspectors, resulted in criminal charges and a few brief jail sentences. The scandal forced Doucett not to run again provincially, although he later became the federal member for his riding of Lanark. Allan succeeded him as minister of highways and cleaned up the whole tender system.

As time went by, Frost's hold on the party increased. He was undoubtedly one of the most popular prime ministers the province had ever had. His legislative accomplishments were many and his capacity to bring along able, young members was outstanding. It should be borne in mind, however, that governing Ontario in the fifties was much simpler than governing Ontario in the seventies and eighties. In order to meet the needs of its citizens, government has legislated in many new fields. The complexity of government today compared with thirty years ago is mind-boggling. The problems facing Frost were easier to handle than those facing John Robarts in the sixties. The problems facing Robarts in turn were easier to handle than those facing Bill Davis in the seventies and eighties.

A comparison of the 1950 provincial budget and the 1985 provincial budget speaks for itself. In 1950, the provincial government's gross ordinary expenditures were $238 million. The 1985-86 budget figures for the province showed expenditures of $29,297,000,000. Using the necessary deflators for both years to turn the 1985 figures into 1950 dollars, we still have a 1986 expenditure in 1950 dollars of $4,707,640,000, which means that the expenditures today in deflated dollars are twenty times the expenditures in the days of Frost. In the 1950s there was a small surplus in the budget. In 1985-86, the forecast deficit was about $2 billion.

The cry of most businessmen for less government and more deregulation is of limited validity. Undoubtedly, there have been areas over the last thirty years where government has stepped in unnecessarily and stupidly. For the most part, however, it has responded to the needs of its citizens. The protection of the environment, the regulation of securities markets, the provision of health care and subsidized drugs, legislation on industrial safety, community colleges, human rights, homes for the aged, nursing homes, and town planning are all examples of provincial government intrusion that have improved the quality of life for Ontarians.

No politician in a democratic society, or for that matter even in a totalitarian society, wields anything close to absolute power. Even dictators have to consider what their colleagues and/or the public will accept, and they cannot resist it for too long. In a democratic society, the cabinet, the caucus, the press, public reactions and, ultimately, elections ensure that authority is used cautiously. Even the largest majority—as we have seen in the fifties, seventies, and eighties—withers away like the leaves in fall when the confidence of the public is lost.

Soon Frost had the most absolute control of the reins of government of any politician in my experience. He knew Ontario intimately. As he travelled back and forth across the province, he would recite to his audience the early history of Upper Canada as it applied to their locality. I have heard him tell how a local river got its name or where Samuel de Champlain explored or General Brock encamped or the Hurons fought in his native Simcoe County. Frost served in the 20th Infantry during the First World War. Like me, he came out of the war with a very healthy vocabulary of profanity, which he used effectively. The public had absolute confidence in Frost and believed that he understood their problems. Frost also had the wisest of counsellors in McKenzie and not too swift an opposition in the House. "Old Man Ontario" was clearly in the driver's seat.

A story that illustrates both the relationship between McKenzie and Frost and Frost's style of government concerns the manner in which the Baycrest geriatric hospital came into being. In 1948, George Drew introduced a bill providing small capital grants for non-profit homes for the aged. This encouraged the Jewish community to purchase a tract of land on the west side of north Bathurst Street and to build the first home under the act.

Before the home was built, it became clear that it was necessary to have a chronic care hospital as well as a home for the aged on the site. The most economical way to achieve this was to build the small chronic-care hospital on top of the home for the aged, but Abe Posluns, then president of the home for the aged, and my father, its honorary counsel, were told by the public servants in the ministry of health that the hospital would not be eligible for the normal hospital grant unless it was a separate building.

This made no sense, as the proposal met all the other requirements of the ministry, and the cost of building the hospital as a separate entity would have been prohibitive. Posluns suggested to me that he and his colleagues, supported by the senior board members of the newly built Mount Sinai Hospital, would like an appointment with the Premier to discuss this matter. I spoke to McKenzie, explained the situation, and asked him to set up an appointment with Leslie Frost.

The delegation, which included all the leading shooters in the Jewish community, arrived in Frost's office well rehearsed. The premier walked in with McKenzie. With little ado, he said, "Gentlemen, my friend McKenzie has explained the problem to me. Doesn't seem to make any sense to me to waste all that extra money by having it in a different building. We will approve your application in the manner that it has been made." The delegation were open-mouthed. They couldn't make all the long speeches they had prepared. Frost shook each person's hand and said, "Thank you for the work that you are doing. Goodbye."

Shortly after McKenzie had survived the attack on his presidency, he asked me to drop in to his office. There he said, "Frost feels that the party needs an infusion of young blood from right across the province. Why don't you prepare a list of young, able people? We particularly need them in southwestern Ontario around London."

I suggested a number of names, among them John Robarts, a lawyer in London, who had been my friend at Osgoode Hall; Sam Hughes, then a lawyer in Welland; Allan Lawrence, who subsequently became a cabinet minister in the Robarts government and almost beat Bill Davis for the leadership of the party in 1971; Bill Archer, who became a controller in Toronto and was to run unsuccessfully for mayor; Don Diplock, at that time a lawyer in London, subsequently the city solicitor for Ottawa, and then a vice-chairman of the Ontario Municipal Board; Bob Macaulay, later a provincial cabinet minister, among many distinctions. Macaulay was well known to McKenzie, whose political roots were in South York, which had been represented by Bob's father, Leopold, the house leader of the Conservative Party in the thirties. Nothing much came out of the committee, but it allowed McKenzie and Frost to meet and get to know a cadre of able young people across the province who were sympathetic to the party.

When Frost decided to call an election in 1951, McKenzie called me to say, "Frost would like your friend John Robarts to run in London. He's an alderman there now." The Tories had lost the London seat held by Bill Webster, a great Tory and former Liquor Control Board chairman, to Liberal Cam Calder. "Frost has spoken to Robarts but he seems reluctant to stand, although earlier he showed considerable interest."

I thought I knew the reason for John's reluctance. "It's probably his wife. Norah would hate having him in Toronto, but I will see what I can do." I telephoned Robarts and asked him to come to Toronto with Norah and have dinner with me the following week.

I remember the dinner vividly. We ate at the Town Tavern, now defunct, which was then on the north side of Queen Street just east of Yonge. In those days, it had the best steaks and the best lobster in Toronto. When I approached the subject of running in London, it was clear that John wanted to give it a shot, but that Norah was strongly opposed. I was fond of Norah, a strong-willed woman whose plans did not include a public career for John.

I finally pleaded in total exasperation, "Listen, Norah, I know the legislative scene. With John's ability he will be in the cabinet in a few years with a great chance of becoming premier. You have no right to stand in his way."

She replied with some heat, "I like our life as it is. I do not want to move to Toronto."

I said, "So don't move. Let him commute."

She finally relented and John was able to follow his natural inclination and run, successfully, in the 1951 election.

Bob Macaulay was elected for Riverdale, an east central riding of Toronto. Macaulay possessed one of the most creative minds of anyone I have met, along with the capacity to work diligently. Robarts and Macaulay, as part of the freshmen crop, became fast friends and eventually shared an apartment together. The convivial atmosphere of that apartment during sessions of the Legislature almost ruined both their political careers. A third neophyte was Jimmy Auld, a former alderman in Brockville, elected for Leeds, who, like Robarts and Macaulay, had served in the war. When an additional constituency was added to London, Ernie Jackson, another veteran, was elected and joined the group.

The 1951 election was a high point for the Tory dynasty. With the province falling under the spell of Frost's leadership and McKenzie back in control of the party, the Tories won seventy-nine of the ninety seats in the Legislature. The CCF were reduced to two seats, the Liberals to seven, and the Communists to one. Both Ted Jolliffe, the CCF leader, who possessed a good intellect but little practical judgement, and Walter Thompson, the Liberal leader, were defeated in their own ridings.

Frost repeated his electoral victory in 1955, and the Tories received a slightly higher popular vote and elected eighty-four out of ninety-eight members. The only problem faced by Frost and McKenzie was finding enough intellectually demanding tasks for the surfeit of able backbenchers like Macaulay, Robarts, and Auld. When these ambitious men were not given enough stimulating tasks they would start prodding and criticizing the party leadership for opportunities to challenge their energies, giving Frost more headaches than the Liberal or CCF parties ever caused. Frost would occasionally jest that he didn't know whether Farquhar Oliver, who had reassumed the leadership of the Liberal Party, or Macaulay was the leader of the opposition.

Frost's term of office was a period of expansion for Ontario. The fifties saw the conversion of the hydro-electrical system from twenty-five to sixty cycles as had been promised by Drew; the creation of dozens of new water and sewage systems under the aegis of the Ontario Water Resources Commission set up by Frost; and expansion of both the health care and the municipal grants programs; the growth of the highway system, including the construction of Highway 401; and a host of other improvements.

In the spring of 1958 Frost suffered the second of the few scandals that occurred during his tenure. Northern Ontario Natural Gas Company had obtained a series of municipal franchises in northern and central Ontario to assist in the financing of necessary gas lines. Three of Frost's ministers, Phil Kelly, Bill Griesinger, and Clare Mapledoram, had each received a few hundred shares of Northern Ontario Natural Gas just prior to the sale to the public. While the purchase of the shares was not in any way linked to any privileges or benefits given to the company, Frost insisted that all three ministers resign.

These resignations and that of Fletcher (Tommy) Thomas, the ailing minister of agriculture, left plenty of room in the cabinet for the young hawks. Macaulay was brought in to the Frost cabinet in the spring of 1958, together with John Yaremko. John was an undergraduate law school friend of mine whom I had helped in his successful bid for the Tory nomination in Bellwoods riding. He was the first Canadian of Ukrainian extraction to hold a cabinet post in Ontario. One of the greatest satisfactions I had in politics was the occasional success in breaking through the Anglo-Saxon monopoly that still existed in the fifties and helping Canadians of European extraction to make a mark. When Yaremko wanted to run in Bellwoods against the hand-picked candidate of the riding, Harold Fishleigh, I went to McKenzie and made a strong case for Yaremko. Open-minded as he was, McKenzie immediately saw that John was given a fair opportunity at the nomination meeting, which provided the party with one of its finest members and cabinet ministers for a period of many years.

I told Macaulay that I thought Frost had put him in the cabinet because he was getting fed up with the constant flow of letters and memoranda from Macaulay offering new ideas for running various departments. Macaulay's elevation to the cabinet also benefited me when his junior, Lionel Schipper, left Macaulay's firm and joined Goodman & Goodman, where he became a tower of strength and one of my closest friends.

Unfortunately, the partying prowess of John Robarts became exaggerated as the stories of young backbenchers carousing spread through the Legislature to the Office of the Premier. That office's rather puritanical tone was set not only by the Methodist background of Gert and Leslie Frost, but also by the stuffy approach of Colonel Young, the Secretary of the Cabinet, and the other members of Frost's senior staff. These advisers had serious reservations about Robarts' entitlement to a cabinet post, despite his obvious ability.

At this time — 1958 — my lovely second wife, Suzie, and I were living in a modest little stone house on Cortleigh Boulevard in North York. The house had been chosen in 1954 by Suzie, who, after nearly a year of living with my parents on Glenayr Road, was eager for us to establish our own domicile. The Glenayr Road house was quite large, but my mother had appropriated the master-bedroom bathroom, and Suzie and I shared the other bathroom with my father. Suzie never quite recovered from the day when my father gently told her that he wished she would put away her towel after she was finished using it.

To make the new house suit our purposes we made some changes. My wife retained Herbert Irvine of Eaton's as our interior decorator. He walked into the house, looked around and said in a voice that dripped with distaste, "What a perfectly horrible house." Suzie was devastated. This incident followed fast on the heels of my mother's comment after her first tour of our new premises: "I hate it." Yet we were happy in the house and both our daughters were born there during our seven-year residency. Eventually, when a house became available not far from my parents' home, we moved back to Glenayr Road, where we have remained to this day.

(I later had my opportunity to get even with Herbert Irvine.

When John and Olive Diefenbaker were moving into 24 Sussex Drive, Olive retained Herbert Irvine as decorator. She invited me to accompany her to see Irvine, who greeted us like royalty. He started to show various chesterfield and sofa coverings as well as draperies to Olive, who turned to me repeatedly for comment. I kept on saying, "I'm not much impressed by that. I really don't like that piece. Surely you must have something else." By the time the morning was over, I felt that I had compensated for the anguish that Herbert had caused my wife.)

It was while we were living on Cortleigh Boulevard that the question of John Robarts' "suitability" for a cabinet post was an issue. In late 1958 Robarts asked for a meeting with me, and we arranged that he would come to my home. On that wintry weekend, John sat himself down in my small library, morosely accepted a double Scotch, and then confided, "I think I'm going to have to get out of politics and devote myself solely to law." I asked him why. He replied, "I've done a good job for Frost on every responsibility he has given me and I certainly feel I have as much ability as some of his recent appointments. Yet he has given no indication to me that I might be going into the cabinet. I have to earn a living, and politics constantly interferes with my practice and prevents me from doing the type of work that I like to do. Unless I go into the cabinet I am not going to run again." He stared into his glass.

"What the hell goes on at these wild parties that everyone keeps talking about? And why haven't I been invited?" I joked.

He sighed. "Unfortunately, I am getting the name without the game."

On Monday, I visited McKenzie in his office. "I think Frost is nuts if he doesn't appoint Robarts into the cabinet," I said. "Furthermore, if he doesn't do it pretty quickly, Robarts will announce that he is not running next time in order to give London time to find a replacement for him."

McKenzie's response was the predictable one: "Stories keep on reaching Les about the partying that goes on with the backbenchers, and Robarts figures prominently in them."

This gave me an opening to pass on Robarts' denial. "Most of these stories are exaggerations. It all comes from Les not giving them enough to do. I don't think you have so much capacity in the cabinet that you can afford to waste anybody as bright and able as Robarts."

McKenzie took the point immediately. "You tell your friend to hold his shirt. I'll get back to you in a few days." He was as good as his word, and soon called to say, "Tell John just to relax and things will be all right before too long."

Sure enough, in December Frost announced that Robarts was going into the cabinet. Initially he was minister without portfolio, with special responsibilities for the Ontario Water Resources Commission, of which he became a member.

In April 1959, Frost called his third election. Once again the Conservatives maintained a strong majority, winning seventy-one of the ninety-eight seats, and Robarts won very big in London North. Shortly after that election, Frost recognized Robarts' value to the party and made him minister of education.

Robarts was fortunate, both in the timing of his appointment and in the portfolio he was given. His predecessor, William Dunlop, had held the portfolio for eight years and had gone into politics late in life. Because of his age and his health problems, Dunlop's department had received little leadership in the latter part of his tenure. By comparison Robarts appeared to rocket on to the horizon. A new federal initiative for technical schools provided a good part of the monies for much-needed capital expenditures, creating an expansion and acceleration of skills training for high-technology job needs. Under Robarts the department developed a secondary school system that was "streamed" according to academic achievement and a program of scholarships to Ontario universities for the best students. Those of us who knew Robarts were surprised by the reputation he earned as a dynamo. Careful and cautious, but determined to achieve his goals, he usually reserved his "let's get moving" attitude for a fishing or shooting trip or for repairing to his hotel room for a drink of Scotch.

Although he was not the wild party animal that Frost had feared, Robarts loved a good time. He, Jim Auld, and Ernie

Jackson used to take annual boat trips in a medium-sized power boat, usually through the Rideau-Trent canal system. In the year of Expo 67, while Robarts was premier, they decided to go to Montreal in this manner. Unfortunately, they got behind a freighter going through the locks, and the trip dragged on interminably. The heads of the Ontario pavilion and of Expo were waiting patiently for their guests' arrival, but it was late in the evening when the trio reached their destination, and they were in no shape to be received.

On another occasion, when Robarts was staying at the Westbury Hotel in Toronto and Ernie Jackson went in to wake him up for an important meeting, Robarts did not want to get up. They fell into some good-natured but heavy wrestling and were on the floor rolling over and over when Dick Rohmer, a friend and advisor of Robarts, walked in. The sight of the two 220-pounders pounding each other put Dick into a state of shock and, speechless, he left them to their antics.

In the summer of 1961, Leslie Frost started to feel the strain of twenty-four years in the Legislature, thirteen of them as premier. His wife, Gert, was ill, Alex McKenzie had died the previous year, and Harry Price, his chief fundraiser, was in failing health. It was time to retire and Leslie Frost knew it. On August 3, he wrote to Elmer Bell, president of the Progressive Conservative Party of Ontario, announcing his resignation and asking Bell to call a convention.

The scramble for the succession was immediate. Attorney-General Kelso Roberts, who had run against Frost in the previous election and was only slightly younger than the premier, immediately announced his candidacy. He was a well-motivated, genial lawyer, whose main fault was that he would occasionally go off half-cocked. As the race gathered momentum, he attracted many of the malcontents within the party, who felt their abilities had not been recognized. John Robarts, of course, was a candidate, as were Jim Allan, Bob Macaulay, Matt Dyamond, the health minister, Wally Downer, the former speaker, and George Wardrope, who was also in the cabinet.

The leadership race posed a real problem for me. Macaulay and Robarts both expected my support, which was valuable to them because I was prominent in the federal organization. Macaulay had the best intellect and was the most creative thinker of all the contestants. In addition, he possessed an amazing amount of energy and was a natural leader. On the other hand, Robarts had abundant common sense and a conciliatory nature, two of the most useful qualities for a politician. I felt Robarts was safest for the long haul and regretfully told Macaulay that I was unable to support him. It was one of the most difficult decisions I have made in politics. Ten years later, I was faced with the same dilemma in choosing between Bill Davis and Darcy McKeough.

The first organizational meeting of the Robarts group was held in my library, but Ernie Jackson and the rest of Robarts' friends in London soon took over the management of his campaign. Elmer Bell, the party president, had asked George Hogan and me to become co-chairmen of arrangements for the convention. The job was to provide great training for me for the federal leadership convention that was to take place six years later. For the 1961 convention, held in the Varsity Arena, I managed to convince the CBC to put together an Ontario regional network. Don MacPherson, later a vice-president of CTV, was in charge and made it all work. It was the first provincial convention to have substantial television coverage.

The night of the retirement of Leslie Frost was a warm nostalgic evening that left many people in tears. Frost had changed the whole outlook and composition of the Ontario Progressive Conservative Party. He had quietly made it a caring party with a strong sense of justice, and the result was a government in the same mould.

The federal leader, John Diefenbaker, was scheduled to speak on the following day and I was having great difficulty in getting Allister Grosart, the executive director of the party, to give me the details of his timing, so that I could make arrangements to meet him. On Monday afternoon I got in touch with Allister again and said, "For Christ's sake, what in the hell's going on? When is the leader coming?"

"I'm having quite a bit of trouble with the leader," he replied reluctantly.

"What do you mean you're having trouble?"

He blurted out, "He doesn't want to come. He's angry at Frost."

"Angry at Frost! What in the hell for?"

"I don't really know. It's some slight that he's imagined during the past month and now he says he isn't going to go."

At this stage of his career, John Diefenbaker needed all the help he could get, as things were not going well federally. Not to show at the Ontario convention would have been disastrous for him. I said to Allister, "I sometimes think that he is really nuts. I would like to tell him to go screw himself. He can't afford to miss this opportunity to speak to the strength of the Conservative party in Ontario." I finished by giving my favourite aphorism: " 'Whom the gods wish to destroy, they first make mad.' What in the hell are you going to do?"

Allister said, "I'll call you back in an hour."

About two hours later he called me to say that Diefenbaker had agreed to fly in, but that he insisted on Frost's coming out to the airport to meet him. With considerable indignation and some unprintable expletives, I agreed, although I didn't know how I would explain the arrangement to the premier. Honesty was the best policy, I decided, so I told Frost exactly what the situation was. He let out a stream of oaths, but then said, "We can't spoil the convention to choose a new leader and premier·just on account of that old reprobate. I'll go. Sometimes I really do believe he's crazy."

"Why only sometimes?" I retorted, and we both had a good laugh.

When Diefenbaker's plane arrived he was as genial as he had been when he badly needed Frost's help to win the leadership. I never did find out what Frost's alleged slight to Diefenbaker had been.

On the first ballot Kelso Roberts was in the lead by seven votes but among the first four candidates only twenty ballots separated first from fourth place. I had a little office in the arena, from which Leslie Frost and one or two of his cronies watched the convention. After the third ballot, when Robarts was in the lead but Kelso Roberts was hanging tough in second position, Frost, who wanted either John Robarts or Bob Macaulay to win, began to get nervous. He had maintained strict neutrality throughout the campaign, but he now turned to me and said, "Eddie, Kelso is a fine fellow, but he should not be the premier of this province. Do you think I should make it clear that I'm supporting Robarts or Macaulay?"

With great force I replied, "Les, that would be a huge mistake, for you, for the party, and for the ultimate winner. At this stage you will have very little effect on the voting and, frankly, to come out now would do more harm than good. Besides, Robarts has got it made." Frost took my advice, which was seconded by his wife, Gert. John Robarts went on to win the leadership on the fifth ballot.

There were now five vacancies in the Legislature, and in January 1962 Robarts called the necessary by-elections. Since the Tories had taken power in 1943 they had never lost a by-election. George Hogan and I worked the two Toronto constituencies, and Ernie Jackson was responsible for the others. We squeaked through in the two Toronto seats. In the three other seats, two in northern Ontario and one in central Ontario, we lost, the first losses since George Drew had been elected. Clearly, the new leader had not yet made his imprint on the province. He wisely appointed Ernie Jackson to review the whole party organization, a strategy that paid off. By 1963 the province decided that it liked John Robarts' type of government, and he was elected with almost 49 per cent of the popular vote.

CHAPTER FIVE

THE POLITICS OF REVIVAL

One day in September 1956, my secretary interrupted me in a meeting to say, "Mr. A.D. McKenzie is on the line and would like to speak to you for a moment." I excused myself from the meeting. I might not have been taking calls from paying clients but I always took a call from Alex McKenzie. Alex had just had a slight heart attack and was in Wellesley Hospital. His tone conveyed urgency. "I have something important I'd like to discuss with you. When can you come down to the hospital?"

"I'll be over in about forty-five minutes," I replied. "Make certain they will let me up to your room."

When I arrived McKenzie was lying on his bed, and I sat down to listen to the oracle speak. He got to the point quickly. "George Drew is about to resign the leadership of the party." Drew had been in and out of hospital for a period of several months, and it was clear that he was losing much of his vigour and boundless energy. It was also becoming evident that, his undoubted ability notwithstanding, he was too patrician for the tastes of most Canadians. While Drew had been a highly successful prime minister of Ontario, federally his unpopularity in Quebec and his failure to obtain any real gains in the 1953 general election had convinced the party that he was not likely to be successful in the next national election, even though the country was tiring of the Liberals. Drew himself knew that without good health he could not hope to win.

"What will you be doing in the leadership convention?" McKenzie asked.

"I will probably run George Hees' campaign for the leadership." George and I had discussed this on several occasions.

"Do you really think Hees can win?"

"No, but I believe that he can give a great account of himself. There is an outside chance that he could pull it off if it's properly organized and you help me."

"Tell George to hang loose and not to make up his mind too quickly," McKenzie responded. "Les Frost and I are going to be talking about this. Les will have some pretty definite views, which could become an important factor in the choice."

I promised to relay the message and beat a fast path to the nearest telephone to call George.

On September 20, Frost, McKenzie, and Hugh Latimer met to discuss the upcoming federal convention. Despite Latimer's objections, Frost and McKenzie decided they should support Diefenbaker. The meeting ended with McKenzie saying, "People want John Diefenbaker and there is no use kicking against the pricks." Shortly after this meeting McKenzie called me to say that Les and he both felt that the best interests of the party would be served by electing John Diefenbaker as leader. Latimer was opposed to Frost's decision because he did not trust Diefenbaker's dedication to the party or his personal integrity.

Diefenbaker's popularity throughout the country had been strong for many years. Within the party, he had not been noted for his loyalty to previous leaders, and he had the unfortunate reputation of marching to his own drummer when the party would have been better served by unity. This had made him unpopular with the "establishment" members of caucus. Diefenbaker had two main character flaws: an overweening ego and his suspicion of the motives of almost everyone except a few very close friends and admirers. On the other hand, he was a brilliant parliamentarian with a reputation as a supporter of the underprivileged.

There could be no doubt that the Tories were suffering from their image as an Anglo-Saxon, upper-middle-class, Ontario-centred party. These perceptions, plus the party's historical unpopularity in Quebec dating from the Riel Rebellion, had resulted in only three Tory administrations since the turn of the century. Of these, only Borden had been re-elected, and his government had been part of the First World War coalition. The election of Diefenbaker as leader would go a long way to changing the party's image everywhere except in Quebec, where he was viewed as anti-clerical. He would be a particular asset in the west, where he was much admired and the Tories historically were weak.

I told McKenzie to tell Frost that I would certainly pass on their thinking to George, but that in my view it was in Hees' best interests to run. I also warned that while Frost's logic might be sound, electing Diefenbaker as leader was not without its dangers. I worried that Frost was trying to enhance his own populist image and that of the provincial party by electing a federal leader who, in the minds of the public and the press, was looked upon as a supporter of the underdog. Worthy as this objective might be, stability is a critical factor in a leader and I wondered whether Diefenbaker had the necessary stability. In retrospect, McKenzie and I were both right in our assessments.

In the meantime, Drew's announcement of his decision not to run again was made and leadership fever quickly overtook Ottawa. Later that week George called me, saying that he was under tremendous pressure from a large number of the caucus to support Diefenbaker. Indeed, Diefenbaker had indicated that he would like George to run his national campaign and had asked George to persuade me to run his Ontario campaign (the chairman of his provincial organization, Clayton Hodgson, his friend and a fellow member, had suffered a serious injury). I was not particularly flattered, because I knew that it was my relationship with McKenzie and Frost that they were interested in rather than my stellar organizational abilities. To argue with Hees was futile. The caucus had done their work on him well, and the lobbyists for Diefenbaker included several of those on whom Hees had been counting for support. He said with his usual modest nonchalance, "I have got to go along with the gang, Benbo."

It was generally expected that Don Fleming would be Diefenbaker's chief opposition, although subsequently Davie Fulton ran as well. While I admired both men, neither was the proper choice for leader. Fleming, who was favoured by the party establishment, was a man of industry, intelligence, and sober Christian virtue, but he was uninspiring and sometimes inflexible. Fulton was a man of intellectual depth and a creative thinker, but he was too conservative both for his age and for the era and he lacked flair. In Hees' view, if Fleming succeeded, the Tories would continue in exactly the same mould as in the past and would lose the next election. He felt our only chance of winning was with John Diefenbaker. Both Fleming and Fulton later became outstanding ministers in the Diefenbaker cabinet, Fleming as minister of finance and Fulton as minister of justice.

Diefenbaker never did fully appreciate the contribution that Don Fleming made to his government. Late in the regime, when Don left Finance and took over Justice, Diefenbaker made a firm promise that Don's services to the country would be rewarded by appointment to the Supreme Court of Canada — a promise he later reneged on. Also Diefenbaker never forgave Fulton for not supporting him, but running against him instead. Even two and three years later, he said to me on several occasions, "Fulton promised me his support, but ran anyway, thinking it would help his chances the next time. For him there may not be a next time."

A few days after my discussion with Hees, I received a telephone call from Diefenbaker, who said he would like to come down the following day to meet with me in Toronto. His arrival caused considerable excitement among my small office staff. To them, indeed to the whole country, Diefenbaker was almost a folk hero — the man who had constantly been rejected by the Tory party because of his progressive ideas. I walked to the reception area to greet the great man. He put out his hand, looked at me with all his famed intensity, and said, "I am pleased to see you again. I really need your help. Unfortunately, Clayton is making a very slow recovery from his accident and everyone tells me that in any event you should be the head of my organization in Ontario. I would like the two of you to work together."

I replied, "I'll certainly do what I can. It shouldn't be too difficult in this province, since everyone other than a few of the old establishment seems determined that you should be the leader. In Ontario the strength of the organization lies in the provincial party, and both Frost and McKenzie believe you're the person the party needs."

"Are you certain of that? I have been fooled before."

"You have never before had a commitment from Frost and McKenzie," I reassured him.

The campaign, while it seemed exciting at the time, was really no contest. It was run under the national co-chairmanship of George Hees and Gordon Churchill, an ironic contrast to the previous party presidency election, when the establishment had unsuccessfully tried to defeat George by running Gordon Churchill against him. For all practical purposes Allister Grosart was the campaign manager, and to him belonged the credit for the superb organization.

The Diefenbaker organization in Ontario had everything going for it. While Frost, as befits a premier, did not take an announced position, his whole organization supported my efforts to elect Diefenbaker. Even though Don Fleming was from Ontario, the great majority of Ontario provincial members supported Diefenbaker. I received a great deal of help with the federal caucus from Clayton Hodgson and Gordon Fraser, the federal member for Peterborough. To organize the provincial members' support, I chose Wally Downer, a somewhat roguish but absolutely delightful Anglican minister from Grey County who was later to become the speaker of the Legislature. His clerical collar covered a multitude of slightly off-centre ideas, and keeping Wally and his cohorts supplied with spirituous beverages was a major expense. Mabel Hees still tells the story of the night Wally came to her room at 2 AM during the convention in Ottawa, crying, "Where is another case? I need it now. I'm working on some wavering delegates."

The convention, which took place in December 1956, started off rather badly when Diefenbaker laid down the rule that no liquor would be served in his hospitality suite. On the first day, Diefenbaker's suite was conspicuously empty, while the Fleming and Fulton hospitality rooms were full to the brim. I knew something had to be done. The Diefenbakers' personal suite in the Château Laurier was next to the hospitality suite. I moved them to a corner suite beside my own bedroom and away from the din. I then called a meeting of the campaign committee, which only I attended, as no one else had been notified, and passed an amendment to the no-drinking rule. The result: a full hospitality suite. I did not fool Diefenbaker—one seldom did—but he bowed without comment to political necessity.

The only region where there was any real opposition to Diefenbaker's leadership was in Quebec. Even there, with some help from newspaper owner John Bassett and from Ivan Sabourin, the leader of the almost non-existent party in Quebec, he managed to obtain a reasonable nucleus of strength. Diefenbaker won on the first ballot, with 744 votes to Fleming's 393 and Fulton's 117. Ontario voted overwhelmingly for Diefenbaker.

The convention over, I returned to Toronto determined to devote myself totally to the law and to my family. In December 1953, I had married a dark-eyed beauty, Suzanne Gross, the daughter of Anna and Selig Gross, who had come to Toronto from Belgium in the very early twenties. Both Suzanne's parents' families had been engaged in the diamond business in Holland and Belgium for several generations. They were also devout Orthodox Jews, as were her brother, Mark, and his wife, Helen. Coming from Belgium, however, they were westernized and more sophisticated in their outlook than Central and Eastern European Jews. We had decided that we would strictly observe the laws of the Kashreth in our house, not because my wife was Orthodox, but because we wanted her family to be able to dine with us and to feel comfortable in our home. It was a change for me, as I had been a Reformed Jew since birth, and religion played a minor role in my life. I was so fond of both my in-laws that I was delighted to be able to please them in this manner, although if they had both continued to vote Grit instead of becoming Tories, I might have been less accommodating.

My first-born daughter, Joanne, was now two and receiving too little attention from me and too much from my wife. I had been at the bar for almost ten years, the firm was flourishing, and I was getting the occasional good brief, as well as spending a great deal of time on our development clients, particularly Cadillac

Development Corporation. I was ready to let politics take a back seat to these other interests for a while.

Too much professional dedication and political involvement had taken their toll on my family. One Saturday morning my wife and I took Joanne for a walk along Eglinton Avenue. When we dropped into a restaurant for a plate of ice-cream and a Coke, my wife took advantage of the opportunity to berate me for my lack of attention to our daughter.

"Listen, Eddie, you're not spending enough time with Joanne. Between your office and politics, there is no room in your life for your family." It was downhill from there.

I defended myself vigorously, laying claim to the high quality of what small attention I was giving, and even arguing that I was perhaps the best father in the city. We finished our ice-cream in stony silence and resumed our walk along Eglinton Avenue. Suddenly Joanne, who was holding my hand, broke away and started to run toward the densely trafficked street. I ran after her in a panic. In a regrettable lapse, her name escaped me for the moment and I called out, "Little girl, little girl, stop!"

After the few minutes of parental panic had passed, my wife said icily, "You don't even know your own daughter's name." Needless to say, my credibility as a paterfamilias was destroyed. I knew I had to clean up my act and started to come home more often for dinner. In 1958 my second daughter, Diane, was born. She fared better in paternal care.

In the early part of 1957, I received a call from the ubiquitous McKenzie with his usual request to "drop over for a moment." The provincial party was humming along in fine style. Les Frost used to have breakfast with Alex McKenzie on most mornings in a corner of the Venetian Room at the Royal York Hotel, where Frost stayed and where McKenzie himself had a room on the eighteenth floor, although he had a large house in Forest Hill Village. To that breakfast table, they would often invite Hugh Latimer, and occasionally me, or a cabinet minister whose problems or jurisdiction they were discussing. At these breakfasts, political decisions would be made and government policy would be set. They were the forerunners of the famed Tory breakfast meetings of the Davis regime, although in both cases the matters in question always also got a full airing at the weekly cabinet meetings.

Once again I went to McKenzie's office, where he lay down on the couch while I waited to hear what he had in store for me.

"Frost has been speaking to Diefenbaker and they have sort of worked out a plan of federal organization for Ontario," he volunteered. "We thought that we should leave Harry Willis as chairman of the organization because he knows the history, the background, and all the players on the federal scene and will keep the old guard happy. Also, we should add Bill Brunt, because he is so close to Diefenbaker and has his total confidence. It's better for him to be part of the official organization, or he'll be advising Diefenbaker on the side." Brunt, who was fifty-five, came from Hanover in Grey County, and had worked for Alex in the 1943 provincial election. "We thought that you could join the two of them, to add your understanding of the provincial scene along with a little youth and vigour." I was thirty-eight at the time.

From an organizational point of view, it was a rational, intelligent plan and, as events were to show, it worked well for everyone, especially Diefenbaker. I told McKenzie that I had reservations about taking a federal role and wanted to talk to my father and to my wife before I made a final decision. The proposal was glamorous enough, but I knew that my involvement would interfere with my law practice and my family life. Also, from an organizational point of view it would be difficult to be the third man on the Willis-Brunt team. Above all, I could foresee the problems of working with an erratic, albeit compelling leader. By this time, I had come to know John Diefenbaker well and had developed a fair appreciation of his strengths, weaknesses, and foibles. I respected him but was still troubled by both his unpredictability and his paradoxical mixture of ego and lack of confidence. I didn't think he was going to be prime minister, although I was beginning to believe that he had an outside shot at it. I discussed the offer with my father and my wife, but deep down I knew the result was pre-ordained. Throughout my life, my eternal quest for excitement, together with my own demanding ego, have gotten the better of my rational outlook.

Just a few months after Willis, Brunt, and I took over, we were into the election of 1957. It had been agreed, largely on our committee's strong recommendation, that Allister Grosart would be the national campaign director. With Diefenbaker's popularity low in Quebec, and the party in Saskatchewan and in Alberta in such bad shape that a western sweep was not in the offing, the election would be won or lost in Ontario. In the Maritimes we hoped only to increase slightly our share of the vote.

The Ontario provincial organization extended total support. One of my jobs was to visit as many constituencies as I could and check on their election organization. Hugh Latimer, the provincial field organizer, was most active in the campaign, going with me to dozens of ridings. He knew everyone and increased my store of knowledge tenfold. Frost himself took part in the 1957 federal campaign with a vigour that was not seen again until Bill Davis became premier. The importance of Ontario in the campaign strategy and the confidence that John Diefenbaker had in Bill Brunt, which was translated into confidence in the committee, enabled us to remain close to Diefenbaker throughout.

It was decided that the campaign would commence in Toronto, and the first meeting was set for May at Massey Hall. I was given the rather dubious honour of being responsible for the organization and success of that meeting. My plan of attack was simple. I would convince the party that a Tory was a Tory was a Tory, whether he be provincial or federal, and would fill Massey Hall to the rafters with the faithful. The media would report on the enthusiasm and momentum of the meeting and the public would perceive the party as undergoing a dynamic revival. With the widespread popularity of Leslie Frost and the growing popularity of Diefenbaker in Ontario, this impression would not be difficult to achieve. I wanted the public to see that Leslie Frost and the Ontario organization were four-square behind John Diefenbaker. To this end, I met with McKenzie. I put my case to him strongly. "Listen, you got me into this and now you have to help me carry it through successfully."

"What's the problem? Can't you handle Willis and Brunt?"

"No, that's not it, they are behaving just fine. But I am responsible for the opening meeting and I want Frost to participate in a big way. No perfunctory remarks. I want a twenty-five-minute speech lauding John Diefenbaker's record of caring for the ordinary Canadian of every background."

"I'll speak to Les at breakfast," he promised. I knew that with McKenzie behind me, my job was half done.

The meeting was to be chaired by Joel Aldred, then in his bloom as a television announcer and a longtime friend of Bill Brunt. As a show of unity, we arranged for all the federal candidates and members from across the province to sit on the platform with the leader.

The evening was a great success. The place was packed. Enthusiasm was high and, as requested, Frost made an important and lengthy speech asserting his total confidence in Diefenbaker. Indeed, Frost spoke longer than Diefenbaker, who for once sensed that this was not an occasion for pettiness. He mumbled something afterwards about "Whose campaign is this anyway?" but took it in good part. My strategy worked, and the press, the provincial members, and the public got the message that there was to be an all-out, united Conservative campaign in Ontario.

Diefenbaker's unusual generosity of spirit did not extend to everyone that night. After the evening was over, there was a crush of well-wishers around the leader. On the fringe was Earl Rowe, then the federal member for Dufferin-Simcoe, who said to me, "John does not want to be bothered by me now. Tell him that I wish him luck," and departed.

After the meeting, while Brunt, Diefenbaker, and I sat in a room backstage at Massey Hall reviewing the night's events, Diefenbaker said petulantly, "Earl Rowe did not come over to speak to me." I relayed Rowe's message and assured him that Rowe was most supportive. Diefenbaker was hurt and would not be placated. Earl Rowe, the only member in caucus who had been in the Bennett cabinet and an able parliamentarian, was not appointed to Diefenbaker's cabinet, though some years later Diefenbaker relented and, on Brunt's urging, made Rowe lieutenant-governor of Ontario.

The campaign was now on in earnest, and we set about co-ordinating Ontario's efforts with those of the national office. The national office would control the general thrust of advertising and party pamphlets and the co-ordination of the overall campaign in the various provinces. In Ontario, however, the leader's campaign was to be the exclusive property of Willis, Brunt, and Goodman. We decided where he went and made certain that one of the three of us was with him whenever he toured Ontario. The arrangement worked reasonably well. Allister ran a good campaign, with valuable help on the media and publicity side from Dalton Camp, whose advertisements, particularly the one on closure, were brilliant. The campaign centred on the arrogance of the Liberal government and its contempt for Parliament and disregard for the needs of senior citizens.

For the most part we travelled by car around the province, but for longer hauls we took the train — with splendid results. John Diefenbaker had had a long association with the railway unions and had acted as their lawyer on numerous occasions, so they were great supporters of his. Wherever we went, there were always railway men on the train clustering around him and encouraging him.

I was scheduled to accompany Diefenbaker on one of his trips to the Windsor area. To make sure that there was nothing back at my law office that would interfere, I went over to see Alf Preston, the clerk of the Court of Appeal. I had a case that was soon to be heard in that court. Preston told me that he merely had to make a slight shift to the court list to accommodate me without causing anyone else an inconvenience. A few days later, Diefenbaker and I were sitting having a cup of tea in his railway car in Windsor when the telephone rang. My partner Norm Schipper was on the line saying, "The Reimer case is on tomorrow's list for the Court of Appeal."

"That's impossible," I spluttered. "I've personally made the necessary arrangements with Alf Preston to keep it off till next week."

"Preston told Mr. Justice Laidlaw [then Acting Chief Justice of

Ontario] of the arrangement, but Laidlaw said there is to be no changing in the order of the list. He said, 'Tell Mr. Goodman that he is expected to appear and that politics have no priority in this court.' "

I telephoned Alf, who confirmed that he could do nothing for me. To say that I was furious was to put it mildly. I told Diefenbaker, "I'm sorry, but I'll have to leave at once to get back to Toronto for tomorrow's hearing in the Court of Appeal." Visibly surprised, he asked, "Are you ready to proceed? This would never happen in Saskatchewan where the bench look upon one of their priorities as conveniencing and assisting the bar." He then added cryptically, "But these are the things we will remember."

Remembered it was. When the election was over and Diefenbaker had the obligation to appoint the chief justice of Ontario, the acting chief justice's name was never on the short list. Although Mr. Justice Laidlaw was an able hard-working judge, he had a tendency to arrogance. Indeed, the whole Court of Appeal bench at that time, though it contained some good jurists, did not believe in conveniencing counsel, or indeed at times even in being courteous. When the chief justice appointment was made it went to the then attorney-general for Ontario, the Honourable Dana Porter, on strong urging from Leslie Frost.

As we toured the province, John Diefenbaker's skill on the hustings became increasingly evident. One day in Simcoe, in Norfolk County, the centre of the tobacco-growing region, Diefenbaker spoke to a large audience, among whom were many tobacco farmers. He dealt at some length with hardships caused by the excessive tobacco tax. At that time, smoking was not held in the disrepute that it is today and the onerous tax on tobacco was considered by many to be unfair. In words not unlike these, Diefenbaker told the crowd, "One of my first obligations when I am prime minister will be to take under serious consideration a review of the tax on tobacco with a view to ameliorating the present hardship of the tobacco farmer."

While we were driving back to Toronto, I said to Diefenbaker, "A lot of people left that meeting feeling that you had promised to make drastic changes in the tobacco tax."

He whirled to face me, finger jabbing the air. "I never said any such thing."

"I know exactly what you said, but I am telling you that is the impression you left and that is the impression you meant to leave."

He merely chuckled and said, "I will examine the issue."

Most politicians, indeed most people, endeavour to say what they think the people they are addressing want to hear, but none did it with such consummate skill as John Diefenbaker. In the long run, his deftness would have disastrous consequences, as people came to feel that he had failed to honour his commitments.

The final meeting of the campaign took place in a large old movie theatre in Hamilton. Largely a labour town, Hamilton was not a Tory bastion, but for once the palpable optimism of the party's supporters appeared justified. We knew that there was going to be a fine Tory vote. The meeting was chaired by Joe Sweet, an able, difficult lawyer who eventually became a county judge for Wentworth. There had grown up during this campaign a group of Tory lawyers who worked hard to put on a fantastic meeting: Bill Parker, subsequently chief justice of the High Court of Ontario; John Agro; Dave Duncan; Ted Okuloski; Lincoln Alexander, who years later became a federal minister of labour and is now Ontario's lieutenant-governor.

John Diefenbaker was at his best at that meeting, helped by the presence of a couple of hecklers whom he dealt with briskly and entertainingly. Whenever he answered a heckler, a supporter would yell, "Give 'em hell, John." He would reply, "No, I only tell them the truth and to them it sounds like hell." Whether in the House or on the hustings, there has been no politician in the second half of the century who possessed oratorical skills comparable to Diefenbaker's. His only rival was Liberal Paul Martin. Others, particularly Arthur Meighen, were fine orators in a rational, logical way, but Diefenbaker's capacity to move an audience was superb. The evangelists of today, such as Oral Roberts and Jimmy Swaggart, would have envied his hold on audiences. (Some credit for his success must be given to Merril

Menzies, an accomplished economist and writer, who prepared most of the leader's speeches.)

There can be little doubt that the major issue in the 1957 election was leadership. On the one hand there was the respected, but aging and tiring Prime Minister St. Laurent — "Uncle Louis." On the other, there was the eloquent Baptist who spoke like a biblical prophet, a Tory who thundered against the establishment on behalf of the underprivileged and forgotten people who had been neglected by a party too long in power. A Liberal party that would only raise the old age pension by "six bits," that had forgotten its British heritage at the time of the Suez crisis, that wanted to turn over control of our oil riches to the Americans, and that had made a mockery of Parliament with closure during the critical pipeline debate.

After the Hamilton meeting, Diefenbaker asked me, "How many seats do you think we will win?"

"Not fewer than ninety and not more than a hundred," was my estimate. "I think we will end up with about ninety-six seats. Certainly the Liberals will not get a majority. If we could win a few in Quebec we would beat them." That was my honest assessment. Diefenbaker was more optimistic. He pierced me with his magnetic gaze and said slowly and deliberately, "No, I am going to win. I am going to get the largest block of seats in the House. I feel it every place I go, and while I know that other leaders have believed this in the past, I am sure that the support I am getting from people who are not Conservatives will project itself into seats."

Two days later the moment of electoral truth arrived. My wife and I had arranged to spend the evening with Alex McKenzie in his room at the Royal York Hotel. As we drove down to the hotel, the results started to come in. Our spirits rose: it was clear that, in Ontario at least, we were having a remarkable sweep. When Suzie and I got to McKenzie's room, he too was caught up in the thrill of victory, and showed an unusual excitement. "I never thought I would live to see the day that the Tories were again in power in Ottawa," he exulted, "but it looks like this might just happen." And happen it did. In Ontario, which had 85 constituencies, we won 61 seats out of the 109 that we carried in the country. To my surprise, we won 9 seats in Quebec. Two independent conservatives in Quebec who thought they would have a better chance of winning without the official party label were also elected and joined our caucus. We did not do well in the prairies, winning only three seats in Saskatchewan, one of which was Diefenbaker's own.

The next question was what would St. Laurent do now that he was in the minority. There were those within the Liberal Party, particularly Jimmy Gardiner, the Saskatchewan minister, who wanted him to fight it out and try to enlist the support of the CCF, which had taken twenty-five seats. However, after such a startling rebuff it was clear that Mr. St. Laurent had lost the confidence of the people. First and foremost a gentleman, albeit a somewhat autocratic one, he submitted his resignation. The governor-general called on John George Diefenbaker to become the twelfth prime minister of Canada, living proof that ambition, perseverance, and demagoguery do have their rewards.

Skeptic that I was and remain about John Diefenbaker, it was my belief at the time, and it is my belief today, that in its own fashion democracy made the right choice and that he was the best person to be prime minister at that stage in the development of the country. Although his faults were glaring, his accomplishments more than compensated for his weaknesses. Canada is better off for having had him as prime minister, and he has had a long-term influence on unifying the country and its disparate ethnic groups.

Diefenbaker now began the business of selecting a cabinet. Willis and I decided that the best way for us to get our ideas across to the Prime Minister was through Brunt, who was with him constantly. Hees badly wanted to be minister of trade and commerce and was under the impression that the job was his. He was wrong, of course. It went instead to Gordon Churchill. Hees was given Transport, a challenging portfolio, in which he did extremely well. The seasoning he got in Transport stood him in good stead when in 1960 Diefenbaker appointed him trade minister, a portfolio he handled with great skill.

The morning he got the call from Diefenbaker to fly to Ottawa to discuss his cabinet position, George Hees, his wife, Mabel,

Suzie, and I were sitting outside his stately red brick house on Dunvegan Road, Toronto. He excused himself to get ready to fly to Ottawa, later emerging with a very thin attaché case. I said to him, "Well, George, hang tough for a decent portfolio and if you want me to call Diefenbaker, I certainly will." As an afterthought, I asked, "What's in the briefcase?" He opened it and there was a carton of Dentyne chewing gum, a toothbrush, and toothpaste.

Shortly after Diefenbaker was sworn in as prime minister, he invited me to come down to Ottawa. He had not yet moved into 24 Sussex Drive and we had lunch in the main floor dining-room of the Château Laurier and then walked over to his office. It was amazing to see the change that had taken place in the public's attitude toward the government. The election of a new prime minister is greeted with the enthusiasm and optimism that used to greet the ascension of a new monarch to a medieval throne. The change in courtiers (or cabinet ministers) creates a charged atmosphere of energy and anticipation. During his initial months in office, the new prime minister may even come to believe that he is ruling by divine right. The wise, democratic leader, however, quickly learns the restraints on power, and the need to maintain public support.

The Diefenbaker government was the first Tory government to be elected in twenty-seven years. As expected, there were legions of the faithful who were prepared to step up to the bar and explain their entitlement to office. The Grits had not for a moment thought that they were going to lose the election and had not troubled to fill many of the important vacancies with their own supporters before they were defeated. There were appointments to the Senate, judiciary, various commissions, boards, and Crown corporations all to be made — and ten people applying for every job.

While the media love to characterize patronage as the enemy of democracy, it is simply not a significant factor in politics. Most people are in politics for the fun and the sense of being at the centre of power, or at least close to it. For every appointment that is made, there are legions who think themselves more deserving than the recipient, and the envy and rancour that result do cause distress within the party ranks.

The strangest aspect of patronage is the lack of appreciation of those who do receive an appointment. They always feel that they were entitled to it, and indeed that they are honouring the government by accepting it. Furthermore, they develop a strange hostility to their benefactors. This is best illustrated by a story about Sir John A. Macdonald. When one of his colleagues told Macdonald that a well-known Tory was bad-mouthing him all over the country, Sir John paused, reflected, and said, "That is really strange. I do not recall having done anything for him lately."

An important indication of how well a government will be administered is the type of personal staff the prime minister and the various ministers are able to gather around them. There is an unfortunate tendency for ministers to choose as executive assistants and special assistants very bright but very young people, who are fascinated by government and by being near the levers of power. A far better practice is to hire older people who have been involved in either government or business in the past and who will apply some mature judgement.

With the government formed and in office, I returned to Toronto to earn a living and left Bill Brunt to be Ontario's *éminence grise* in Ottawa. One day a few months later, Hugh Latimer and I were having lunch and we came to the mutual conclusion that the Ontario vacancy in the Senate that existed should be filled by Alex McKenzie. There could be no doubt that more than anyone McKenzie deserved the appointment. Since 1938 he had spent his life strengthening the Conservative Party in Ontario. He had been a source of excellent advice for Willis, Brunt, and me. Indeed, we did little without consulting him first. He was a man of great principle whose sagacious presence in the Senate would have benefited the Tories. Latimer asked me to go to Ottawa to speak on Alex's behalf. Over lunch with Diefenbaker, I pressed McKenzie's case. Diefenbaker was, for the present, non-committal, but a few months later he appointed Bill Brunt to the Senate. While there is no doubt that McKenzie deserved the appointment ahead of Brunt, Brunt had been a tower of strength to Diefenbaker in the years of adversity and if he wanted the appointment he was going to get it. A decent man of occasionally erratic judgement, Brunt continued to assist Diefenbaker until Brunt's premature death in 1962.

In 1958 I was in Ottawa on a professional matter and dropped over to pay my respects to the Prime Minister. He greeted me with, "I was just going to telephone you to get a little advice." Things were going well in the House and he was in a buoyant mood. "When should we call an election?" he asked ingenuously, as if my opinion were the deciding factor.

I replied without hesitation, "When you have met every major commitment that you made during last year's election."

"You are absolutely right and I am about to reach that stage very shortly."

Very shortly was in two or three weeks, when he telephoned again and asked me to be in Ottawa the next day, the first of February. That was all I could get out of him. I had the good sense not to speak to Brunt to see if he knew what the secrecy was all about. I knew that when John Diefenbaker wanted matters to be kept quiet he did not want you to be prying around.

When I walked into Diefenbaker's office unannounced I was greeted with, "You always say that I never take your advice. This morning you will see that I have done so. In a short time I am going into the House to announce an election call for March 31."

I was not vain enough to believe Diefenbaker was taking this course of action because of my views. His game was to call you up, ask you about a course of action that he had already decided upon, and then endeavour to make you feel that it was all your sagacious advice. After a couple of years in office he did not bother going through this sham.

The Liberals were in total disarray. Pearson, their newly elected leader, had made a disastrous beginning in the House and Diefenbaker had torn him to shreds. Nineteen of their 105 members would not run again. The momentum was totally with the Tories. Pearson had had no time since assuming the leadership either to rally his troops or to plan a policy strategy. At the convention at which he was chosen leader he had said, "Government is more than a give-away program," but during the

1958 campaign he rained promises on the electorate: a tax cut of $400 million, a municipal loan fund, a farm development bank, increased family allowances, and above all a promise of "peace," although Canadians did not think they were at war except against a recession. He might as well have stayed in his riding in Algoma East. The voters were determined to give John Diefenbaker the opportunity to fulfil his "vision" for Canada to allow all citizens to enjoy the benefits of "its vast resources" and to create a "new sense of national purpose and national destiny."

Wherever we went in Ontario during the 1958 election, we were greeted by thousands who literally just wanted to touch the hem of Diefenbaker's garment. In Leamington, a lovely small town in southwestern Ontario, more than four thousand people lined up to shake his hand. By the end of the night his hand was so tender that he could not touch it.

Time and time again Diefenbaker would give evidence of his incredible memory for people. As they pressed through the line, many would say, "Do you remember me, John?" Without hesitation, he would reply, "Certainly I remember you. Your name escapes me, but you were my prize witness at the murder case in . . . " and he would name some small town in northern Saskatchewan.

Or, "John, do you remember when we first met?"

"Of course I do, Harry. It was at a party that Betty Henning had in Prince Albert. You're a cousin of Mabel Connell."

I have never seen such adulation before or since in political gatherings in this country. While Pierre Trudeau drew huge enthusiastic turnouts in the 1968 election he did not establish the same type of rapport with the public. Ordinary people never felt that Trudeau was one of them, but Diefenbaker's admirers certainly did. It was small wonder that their affection touched him. When we would arrive back on the railway car or in the hotel room, he would turn and say, "Did you see them? Did you see them? They believe in me. They have confidence that I will carry out my promises." He would shake his long finger and swear solemnly, "I will not let them down. I will not let them down."

I recently read an interview with I.F. Stone, the American

philosopher and political scientist, in which he said that some people become radical out of hatred for the establishment, while others do so out of love and sympathy for ordinary people. While I am not saying that John Diefenbaker did not have genuine sympathy for the less fortunate members of society, I believe that he became a populist and a radical in Tory terms out of hatred for what he believed were the oppressors both of his family and of the west, the eastern financial establishment.

In the election of 1958, however, Diefenbaker's come-uppance was not easy to envisage. When he asked the people to "catch the vision this kind of Canada can be," they responded by giving him 208 seats. The Liberals elected 48, the CCF only 8 and the Social Credit none. The 53.3 per cent of the voting public who chose the Tories would now see what the messiah had to offer.

CHAPTER SIX

THE BOMARC DEBATE

For a politician, victory on the strength of a vision rests on quicksand: all visions are ephemeral, and the visionary must turn them into hard facts or face rejection. John Diefenbaker did not prove capable of this achievement between 1958 and 1962.

There cannot be any doubt that most of the steps taken by his government in the fiscal budgetary field, under Don Fleming as minister of finance, were sound and careful. Even killing the Avro Arrow aircraft, which was Canada's pride and joy in the field of aeronautical engineering, was prudent, although very harmful politically, especially in the Metropolitan Toronto area. In 1960 the budget deficit was kept to less than half a billion dollars, but 1961 was a year of rising unemployment, and instead of enjoying the promised glorious future, people became worried and pessimistic. This loss of faith was accentuated when the government was forced to peg the Canadian dollar at 92.5 cents U.S. in 1962. Although the step was sound, for years the Canadian dollar had been worth more than the American, and the country felt disgraced. Relations with the United States were also at a low ebb, largely because of the mutual dislike between President John F. Kennedy and Diefenbaker.

In addition to the problems of unemployment and low monetary reserves, provincial support for the Tories in Quebec and New Brunswick had evaporated. Paul Sauvé, the talented Union Nationale premier in Quebec, had died suddenly, and Jean Lesage, the Liberal leader, gained power in 1960. The Liberal victory in Quebec seemed to have a spill-over effect into New Brunswick, with its large Acadian population, and Tory Hugh John Flemming lost to the Liberals under Louis Robichaud in the same year.

Overall, the public's disillusionment centred less on specific issues than on the government's appearance of bumbling management, as exemplified by their mishandling of the deserved firing of James Coyne, the governor of the Bank of Canada, who for several years kept taking public political positions contrary to government policy. More than anything else, however, the disenchantment with the government was based on a countrywide feeling that John Diefenbaker was not the humble underdog they thought they were electing in 1958. What happened to Dief in office is best illustrated by the story of a meeting between him and his close friend Clayton Hodgson. One day Hodgson was in the prime minister's office sitting on his desk and talking to him. He led off, "The way I see it, John—" Whereupon Diefenbaker interrupted with, "Mr. Prime Minister, Clayton."

Without drawing a breath, Clayton rejoined, "John, you could sit on your hands until they become attached to your ass before I call you Mr. Prime Minister."

John Diefenbaker called an election for June 18, 1962, even though the polls showed his party eight percentage points behind the Liberal party in popularity. The 1962 election campaign was the only time I saw John Diefenbaker perform poorly on the hustings. He was petulant and seemed determined to antagonize the press. In stark contrast to the 1958 campaign, travelling across Ontario with John Diefenbaker in 1962 was agony. He regaled me with a constant litany of the faults of others. Not once did I hear him later suggest that any blame for his precipitous fall from public grace belonged to him. It was always "they": the press, or Bay Street Tory malcontents, or political enemies envious of his success, or the mistakes of his own ministers. When the votes were counted, the Tories won 116 seats, down from the 208 following the previous election. The Liberals won 100, up from 49. The NDP had 19, up from the CCF's 8, and the Social Credit had 30, 26 of these in Quebec, where they had previously held no seats. It was a major rebuke, but Diefenbaker was still prime minister. For many Canadians even Diefenbaker at his worst was better than the wimpish Lester Pearson.

Unfortunately for the country, the Tories took most of the

rural areas and the Liberals won the urban seats. Montreal, Toronto, Vancouver, and Hamilton were overwhelmingly Liberal. In Toronto, where we had won every seat in 1958, only Fleming, Hees, and Frank McGee held on. One of the fallen, in spite of intensive campaigning, was my friend John Bassett, who had taken the plunge in Spadina. George Hees' riding, Broadview, had a large working-class electorate that was very loyal to George. It also had, however, a growing Catholic community who were attracted to the Liberal party. If I had not insisted Hees come back from a cross-country speaking tour to work in his riding, he would have lost his seat.

The annual meeting of the party following the election was set for mid-January 1963 and I was the chairman of the Policy and Resolutions Committee. The meeting was bound to be contentious, as the government was hanging on to power by the skin of its teeth through Social Credit support. At meetings where there was not a full-fledged policy conference, the party's procedure was for the various ridings to send in whatever resolutions the riding executive felt merited consideration by the Policy and Resolutions Committee. I as chairman would then cull them and present a series of recommended resolutions to the committee. The committee would meet for several days before the annual meeting to finalize the resolutions to be presented to the meeting for public debate. Anthony Westell, then of the *Toronto Daily Star,* wrote that the policy of the Conservative Party was written on Eddie Goodman's coffee table, and there was some truth to the statement.

When a party is in power with a precarious minority, it is only on matters of great principle that the rank and file should embarrass the government. A matter of principle was part of the policy debate at the 1963 annual meeting, and the ensuing conflict was a memorable exercise in party democracy, even from my point of view as a loser. In the fall of 1958 the government had announced an agreement with the United States to install a series of Bomarc anti-aircraft missiles. When the time came for these missiles to be fitted with nuclear warheads, the

Diefenbaker government backed down from accepting them. Canada's reneging on the deal, combined with the antipathy between Kennedy and Diefenbaker, further soured Canada-U.S. relations and polarized the public. In the weeks leading up to the 1963 annual meeting, I received numerous telephone calls from Conservatives and many constituency resolutions requesting that Canada honour its international obligations and accept the nuclear warheads as part of our commitment to NATO and NORAD. People expressed their beliefs that strong continental defence required mutual trust and confidence between Canada and the United States and that we were dangerously weakening this crucial relationship. Our delayed and hesitant support for the United States during the October 1962 Cuban Missile Crisis had also exacerbated the situation.

In 1961 the Liberals had taken an anti-nuclear position, to the dismay of many both within and outside that party. This position was of particular concern to our NATO allies, as it appeared that Pearson might soon become the next prime minister. Diefenbaker feared being outflanked by Pearson, who always posed as the advocate of peace. What the prime minister did not grasp was that, in the eyes of many, the Bomarc debate was not primarily about Canada's stance on nuclear arms. That decision had already been made by the government when it agreed to accept the Bomarc missiles. The issue now was whether we would or would not live up to our commitments to our most important ally. Most Canadians simply did not want to go back on their word to a friend.

Meanwhile across the street, the Liberal opposition was not misreading the feeling within the country. A few weeks before our annual meeting, I received a telephone call from Flora MacDonald at national headquarters. She had just come by the information—I don't know how—that Lester Pearson would be addressing the first Canadiana Conference, a Liberal think-tank to be held in York-Scarborough. She also had intelligence that Pearson was going to swallow himself and the Liberal Party alive by reversing their 1961 policy and advocating the acceptance of nuclear warheads on the Bomarc missiles. His justification for the reversal was to be the necessity of living up to our commitment to the United States. The Liberal defence critic, Paul Hellyer, had recently returned from a NATO tour and reported to Pearson that our NATO allies were most critical of the Canadian government's position, and that the morale of our troops stationed in Germany was low. Pearson was about to act on Hellyer's advice.

The consequences for the Tories of this Liberal reversal would be disastrous. I said to Flora, "This will deal us a devastating blow. The party core, many if not most of whom served in the war, will be furious if we end up on the wrong side of this issue, and the public generally are already upset about our relations with the United States. This is not the time or the issue on which to portray a peace-loving stance, and Pearson obviously understands that."

She agreed. "The Prime Minister is going to be in Toronto tomorrow to address a meeting and he's coming down in his private railway car. You must go and see him and convince him to take up a position before Pearson makes his Scarborough speech."

The next day I went down to Union Station, searched among the maze of platforms, and boarded the Prime Minister's car. I was greeted by Bunny Pound, who was, as always, typing furiously. Bunny was a long-time secretary to John Diefenbaker and one of his most loyal admirers, but today she was distraught.

I tried a cheery opener. "What's new, Bunny? How's the Great Man?"

Without acknowledging my greeting, she urged breathlessly, "You must do something. I don't know what is wrong with him, but the speech that he has given me to type cannot be given tonight. He must come to his senses about the United States. Read this." Her voice shook. She was visibly upset about criticizing her revered boss.

When I read what the Prime Minister had drafted, I was appalled. It was clearly not the speech of someone who was pre-pared to meet his commitments to arm the American missiles with nuclear warheads. I went into Diefenbaker's sitting room and said to him after the usual pleasantries, "I have it on absolutely impeccable authority that Pearson will be speaking tonight at Scarborough and that he will advocate living up to our commitments to the United States. I think it is essential that you come out with something before him."

"The Liberal Party has clearly adopted an anti-nuclear position. How can Pearson have any credibility if he changes that position?" Diefenbaker asked querulously.

"He will have lots of credibility when he simply says that you made the commitment to the United States and it must be met. He will argue that he will negotiate himself out of these agreements when he is prime minister."

He was unmoved. "I certainly hope he reverses himself and does that."

He got his wish. That night Pearson made the address in which he said, "As a member of the NATO coalition we accept the nuclear deterrent in the hands of the United States as essential for our defence."

In his book, *The Rainmaker*, Keith Davey, at that time national director of the Liberal Party, states, "It was an exceptionally important move for Pearson but for an altogether different reason than simply nuclear arms. Defence and external affairs have never in any of the polls I have seen been major issues of concern for the people of Canada. The Grit breakthrough occurred because Prime Minister Diefenbaker had been waffling for weeks about this matter and seemed chronically unable to make a decision." While I agree with Senator Davey that external affairs matters never appear high in the public opinion polls, Canadians look upon the relationship with the United States as a quasi-domestic matter and are far more sensitive regarding issues between our two countries than they are toward other international problems.

As the time for the Tories' annual meeting approached, the issue was heating up both in the press and within the party. I called Doug Harkness, the minister of defence, and said, "Doug, I am chairman of the Policy and Resolutions Committee at the annual meeting and I cannot fail to bring to the floor a resolution dealing with arming the Bomarc missiles with nuclear warheads."

"By all means, go ahead," he replied. "It might give me the support I need to persuade the Prime Minister to live up to our commitment to the Americans. There's no doubt the great majority of the cabinet are in favour of fulfilling our commitment, but the Prime Minister and Howard Green refuse to make the decision." Green was the secretary of state for external affairs and was counselling Diefenbaker that through Canada's mediation some sort of disarmament agreement could be reached between the United States and the Soviet Union, which would bring great credit to the Prime Minister and challenge Pearson's reputation as the apostle of peace.

The annual meeting took place in the Château Laurier starting on January 17. For two days beforehand the Policy and Resolutions Committee composed of representatives from all the provinces met to discuss what resolutions we should present to the plenary sessions. The only controversial issue was the question of arming the Bomarc missiles with nuclear warheads. The committee passed a clear, but mild resolution, which I had drafted some weeks previously for circulation. The resolution commended the government's peace effort, lauded the Prime Minister, then in the final clause called for the fulfilment of our obligations to the Americans, including accepting the nuclear warheads. The committee gave me the authority to hold discussions with Diefenbaker and the secretary of state for external affairs, if necessary, and delegated to me the further authority to modify the resolution by deferring the warheads' installation until a later date, if required, to obtain government support.

When all my resolutions were approved by the committee, I sent them over to be finalized and put into the delegates' kits, which they would pick up the following day. I then received a telephone call—I cannot recall whether it came from Allister Grosart or from the Prime Minister's Office—that the Prime Minister was perturbed about the resolution and would like a breakfast meeting with me the following morning at 24 Sussex Drive.

When I arrived I found Dalton Camp, who was soon to take over national headquarters, and Gordon Churchill, minister of veterans affairs, both known by Diefenbaker to be friends of mine. The atmosphere was strained, but cordial. We sat down to breakfast and Mr. Diefenbaker said flatly, "The resolution on the Bomarc warheads is not to go to the meeting."

I have never reacted well to bullying. "Mr. Prime Minister, I have absolutely no alternative but to present that resolution. It was passed by the committee and they are now functus and the resolution must go. I do, however, have authority to make certain time amendments in that resolution if we can come to some agreement."

"I do not believe," he retorted icily, "that the prime minister of the country requires your permission or agreement on the country's policy."

"You don't require my permission on the country's policy. However, I am the custodian of the resolution committee's position and of what will be presented to the plenary session as a recommendation for the party's position. I don't intend to take that responsibility lightly on a matter of international importance such as this."

Diefenbaker could sense that I was not going to budge on this issue. Finally, he sighed, "You go over and discuss it with Howard and I will accept the amendments he agrees to."

It was arranged for me to see Howard Green in about forty-five minutes. As Dalton Camp and I walked out of 24 Sussex Drive, he commented, "That is the first time I have ever seen anybody within this party stand up to John Diefenbaker and not back away." A few years down the line he was to become the second.

I admired Howard Green. A true gentleman and a devoted public servant, he was principled, courteous, and an especially loyal supporter of the British Commonwealth. When I arrived at his office he explained his position. "We are making great progress in our disarmament talks and I would not want anything to happen this weekend that would interfere with that."

I responded, "Read this resolution. It is very laudatory of the government's efforts. However, we have been holding disarmament talks for quite a while now and it is my belief that Canada's unwillingness to back up the United States doesn't help the

American position in the disarmament talks."

"You'll have to take my word for it. We require more time."

"I would be prepared to agree that the acceptance be deferred for six months to allow further discussions on disarmament to take place."

"It might take a year," he warned.

"That castrates the resolution, but all right. Now do I have your support?"

"Yes."

"Then I will make the necessary amendment. Will you please tell the Prime Minister."

I left the East Block and went over to party headquarters to have the resolution printed for distribution to the delegates. Imagine my shock when I said to Flora, "Well, it's settled. Let's get started," and she replied, with obvious embarrassment, "I can't. I've been given instructions by Mr. Grosart that I am still not to do any work for your committee."

I was aghast. "I cannot believe this. Green has agreed. The Prime Minister said that if Green agreed then it was OK. What in the hell goes on?"

"Mr. Grosart met with Mr. Diefenbaker and those are my instructions. I think that the Prime Minister is furious with Green for accepting the amendment."

My descriptions of both the leader and Allister left absolutely nothing to the imagination. I called up Grosart and said, "I settled this matter with Howard and compromised more than I should have. What authority do you have to refuse to prepare the material for a duly and properly appointed committee of the party? What more in hell does the Prime Minister want?"

"I run the party's headquarters," he answered haughtily.

"You don't run the fucking party. We have a president and executive for that purpose. You are merely an overpaid executive director who has forgotten his place. Let me speak to Diefenbaker."

"He is occupied," came the reply. Whereupon I banged down the phone and said to Flora, "I am going to have a press conference and get these resolutions out to the public and the delegates over their heads. If they refuse to put them in the packages for each delegate, I'll get them in the newspapers. Will you please type them for me?"

Flora went outside the office so as not to be in breach of her instructions. She typed the resolutions and mimeographed about forty copies. At the press conference I assiduously avoided any criticism of the government or the leader, but I was most voluble about the policy and picked up enough coverage for the delegates to know that a fight was at hand.

When Grosart and Diefenbaker saw that I had foiled their attempt to keep discussion of the resolution off the annual meeting agenda, they promptly juggled the agenda and arranged for Diefenbaker to speak immediately before my report was presented. He made a most impassioned speech to the meeting imploring them "not to tie my hands in my quest for peace." I had to admit ruefully that it was one of his better efforts. As he was winding up, I said to Flora, "At least we made the s.o.b. go all out to beat us."

When I presented my report, the opposition were ready; they moved an amendment that the resolution, instead of being approved, should be forwarded to the government for its "consideration and decision." I fought against the amendment, arguing that the time had come for "Canada to regain its self-respect by meeting its international obligations." I went on to say that we were losing the trust of our NATO allies and that the resolution met the prime minister's need for time to negotiate. To no avail; the amendment was passed by a vote of approximately three to one. The ultimate irony is that, in his memoirs, Diefenbaker said that he agreed with my position completely and quoted my amended resolution as justifying his position.

After the policy session, the press asked me whether I was resigning. I informed them that ours was a democratic party and that I accepted the decision of the majority. I said I would work for Diefenbaker as long as I was convinced that the party would meet its obligation and accept the warheads. In retrospect, I was probably unfair to Grosart, who had given yeoman service to the party. We both later saw to it that this incident did not lessen our friendship.

Two weeks later there was good reason for me to resign, as
Diefenbaker kept taking a stronger and stronger position against
the warheads. On February 4, Doug Harkness resigned from the
cabinet because of "irreconcilable differences" with the leader
on defence policy. On February 5 I wrote to Diefenbaker to say
that because we were not meeting our obligations I was resigning
from his Ontario organizational committee. That night the
government fell.

I received a telephone call the morning after my resignation
from Edward Dunlop, who was George Hees' brother-in-law. He
said, "George must resign today."

"I agree, but the decision is up to him."

"We will have to go down and see him and make certain that
he resigns."

I replied, "I won't take the initiative. I will go with you if you
want me to, but it's his life and he will have to decide."

A few hours later the two of us were on a plane to Ottawa. At
the Hees house, we found George and Mabel with Léon Balcer,
minister of transport, and his wife, Geneviève. Léon was also in
the cabinet and was the strongest of the Quebec ministers. There
followed a long and rambling conversation about what was in the
best interests of the party, the country, and George and Léon.
After about two hours it was finally agreed that both should write
to Diefenbaker and resign their portfolios.

When Edward and I returned that night to Toronto George's
ebullient parting words were, "Listen to the news tomorrow
morning, fellows." We listened all right, but the news was not
what we had expected. George's resignation did not occur.
Instead, there was a report that George had emerged from a
caucus of the federal members arm in arm with Diefenbaker
saying, "We are united and we are going to win this
election."

When I finally got him on the phone that afternoon, I asked
with more than a tinge of anger in my voice, "What in the hell
made you change your mind? You look like a fool after all the
machinations you fellows have had in Ottawa."

"Ben, you had to be there to understand. First of all, Senator
Grattan O'Leary [the former publisher of the *Ottawa Journal*]

made one of the most eloquent speeches about the need for unity at this time. When I got up to say that I was resigning from the cabinet and not running again, some of the members were crying and they would not let me leave. The members pleaded with me, Diefenbaker promised me that he would consult me on defence and our relations with the U.S. There was just no way that either Léon or I could resign."

"George," I said wearily, "there's no point in arguing, but you, my friend, have been had. It's too late now, but you are going to regret this decision. Besides you don't resign at a caucus meeting. You resign from the cabinet by letter to the leader."

It didn't take long for my prediction to come true. Within two weeks Diefenbaker had reneged on his promises to Hees. Hees resigned and did not contest the next election, a wise decision, as it was unlikely that even as popular a member as George Hees could have held Broadview in 1963 – a year in which no Toronto Tory candidate was elected.

On election day, April 18, 1963, my father and I walked over to Holy Blossom Temple, where our polling subdivision voted. As we walked into the auditorium where voting was taking place, Dad said, "Here goes the first Goodman Liberal vote in eighty-two years." When he came out of the polling booth, I said, "Here goes the second." I made my first, last, and only Liberal vote for Marvin Gelber, who was elected. Many other people who usually voted Conservative must have made the same decision. The Conservatives lost to the Liberals, 95 seats to 129. It looked as though John Diefenbaker's star had finally burned out.

Léon Balcer ended up running in his riding of Trois-Rivières and was elected along with seven other Quebec Conservatives in that election. He had set the record, after fifteen years, 1949-65, for holding a Quebec seat longer than any Conservative since the turn of the century. Just prior to the 1963 election, Balcer had been appointed Quebec deputy leader. After the election, Diefenbaker denied that there was a deputy leader in Quebec. The members from *la belle province* started to feel increasingly alienated from the party and from certain aspects of party policy that clearly showed a lack of understanding of the needs and aspirations of Quebeckers.

On January 15, 1965, Balcer sent a letter to Dalton Camp, the party president, on behalf of the Quebec members. In the letter, Balcer accused the party under Diefenbaker's direction of being "so misguided as to indulge in the political luxury of nourishing an anti-Quebec backlash," which in his opinion menaced "the very foundation of Confederation." He went on to say that the Quebec Tory MPs were "ill at ease and uncomfortable within their own party," and charged that the responsibility was Diefenbaker's, claiming, "it is our firm conviction that the Conservative party can no longer carry on as a great national party under its present leadership and the policies which that leadership has engendered." He requested the president to have a meeting of the national executive to discuss the issues that he had raised, before Parliament resumed on February 16.

A meeting of the national executive was called to consider Balcer's allegations and to decide whether or not a national leadership convention should be called. The evening before the meeting, Dalton called a meeting of the senior officers of the association, and I was asked to attend. It was agreed that Balcer would be asked to speak at the national executive committee meeting. A ballot would then be presented to the executive committee for them to vote upon Balcer's demands. The ballot was to be drawn up by the senior officers including Dalton Camp, Finlay MacDonald, Dorothy Harrison Smith, and one or two others.

When the meeting opened the next day, I found myself seated opposite John Diefenbaker at a narrow table. Camp called on Balcer to speak about his letter to the president and explain the basis of his concerns. Balcer was very nervous and made a poor presentation. The president then presented the four-point ballot he and the others had drawn up. The ballot, among other things, called for a vote on the holding of a leadership convention and for Diefenbaker's resignation. Diefenbaker was incensed. Erik Nielsen challenged the jurisdiction of the executive committee.

I rose and moved a simple amendment that would satisfy both Diefenbaker's and Nielsen's technical objections and would still have allowed a ballot on a convention to go to the meeting. A vote on my amendment was called and, according to my count, it was only two votes short of carrying. Four senior officers, including Camp, seated at the head of the table did not vote. In view of the fact that the ballot had been presented by the senior officers and that they had indicated their desire to proceed in this manner, I assumed that with their vote my amendment was carried. I rose to my feet and said, "Mr. President, the vote cannot be decided without the senior officers' votes."

"We are not voting," Camp replied. I was dumbfounded. More than a hundred people had come from across the country for what was described by many observers as the most serious crisis in the recent history of the Conservative Party and the four senior officers would not vote on allowing the executive committee to express its opinion.

I said, "How can you not vote in favour of your own ballot when you got us here and presented it to us?" Dalton gave no answer either then or after the meeting.

Léon Balcer resigned from the caucus in April 1965 and sat as an independent. When the election was called a few months later, he subsequently declined to run again.

CHAPTER SEVEN

"GIVE THE OLD BUGGER
ANOTHER CHANCE"

On September 8, 1965, Lester Pearson, after spending months wringing his hands and asking his colleagues "should I or shouldn't I go?" finally followed the strong recommendation of Walter Gordon and called an election for November 8. In his statement he announced that the decision was "mine and mine alone." Two or three days later, I received a telephone call from Elmer Bell, that great Tory warrior from Exeter, Ontario. "Are you going to Ottawa to the organizational meeting of the Campaign Committee on Thursday?" he asked.

Although I was entitled to be present as the national vice-president for Ontario, I replied, "It seems pointless to me when I am almost at the top of the leader's hit list." Apart from my attendance at the meeting of the national executive earlier in the year, I had been totally out of politics since 1963. Diefenbaker would not even nod to me after the support I had given Léon Balcer earlier that year; he was certainly not going to be interested in my views.

Bell kept after me. "Listen, young man, you owe it to this party to come to this meeting and work in this campaign. You have more federal experience than any of us good guys and we must be represented."

"Thanks for the compliment, Elmer, but at forty-six I'm not young. You can't contribute if you're not wanted, and I'm busy in the office. Let the leader's loyal retainers run this one."

"No damn way. You're coming," he insisted and hung up.

I succumbed and went.

Underneath my protestations lurked the knowledge that while the country was not enamoured of either Lester Pearson or his accident-prone government, they preferred him as prime minister to John Diefenbaker. I did not share the popular view. I had little respect for Lester Pearson and was convinced that he was the most overrated prime minister of the century. His distinguished career in external affairs under Louis St. Laurent gave him the strong support of many of his former fellow civil servants and of the academic community, and he enjoyed an uncritical media. His enviable reputation in Ottawa distorted the country's view of his performance as prime minister.

My personal dislike dated back to 1956 when Pearson was the author of Canada's Suez policy, for which he received the Nobel Peace Prize. The Canadian government strongly supported President Eisenhower and the U.S. government in opposing the invasion of Egypt by Britain, France, and Israel to open the Suez Canal. This rare example of co-operation between Great Britain and Israel appealed to my pro-British and pro-Israeli emotional attachments. I believed firmly that Egyptian leader Gamal Abdel Nasser was a menace to the West and that the Suez Canal must remain an open waterway. While it was undoubtedly unfair of me to dislike Pearson on this account, subsequent events justified my feelings.

When St. Laurent resigned after his 1957 defeat, and the Liberal Party rejected Paul Martin as leader in 1958 and turned to Pearson, I was considerably relieved. I did not believe that someone whose whole career had been in international diplomacy would be tough enough to handle John Diefenbaker in the House. For my money, Paul Martin was the only person in the Liberal Party who could have stood up to Diefenbaker. As Diefenbaker once said to me, "Paul is the only parliamentarian the Grits have." Pearson's first speech as opposition leader in the House of Commons in January 1958 was a total disaster. He merely stood up and suggested that Diefenbaker should resign and give the government back to the Liberals, as they were the only party who knew how to govern. The speech was as arrogant as the adviser who helped write it, Jack Pickersgill, and was drowned out both in the House and in the press with derisive laughter and hoots of disdain. In 1963, Pearson acceded to power largely because John Diefenbaker allowed himself to lose touch with the country and his own cabinet.

From the outset, Pearson's regime ran into trouble. During the election campaign of 1963 they had promised "Sixty Days of Decision," including a budget from Walter Gordon, the minister of finance, within sixty days. In order to achieve this, the existing deputy minister of finance, Ken Taylor, was to be replaced by Bob Bryce, the clerk of the Privy Council. After Taylor was informed that he was being supplanted, Pearson then selfishly refused to give Bryce to Gordon to help him prepare his budget. It was a mistake for which Pearson and Gordon were to pay dearly.

Gordon was left in an unenviable position. The previous government had not presented a full budget for close to two years, and he was obliged to bring one in within sixty days. The deputy minister had just been informed that he was being dismissed, leaving Gordon with four assistant deputy ministers, each of whom had his own ideas. None of them supported the nationalistic policies that Gordon had committed himself to both as financial critic in opposition and during the election campaign.

Gordon then made what might appear to be a common-sense decision that was in fact a fatal error. He called in David Stanley of Wood Gundy; Geoff Conway, who was at that time at Harvard; Martin O'Connell of Harris and Partners, and Rod Anderson of Clarkson Gordon. Gordon and his private-sector advisers then set about fashioning a budget designed to increase Canadian ownership in industry and to encourage existing foreign owners to seek Canadian partners. All these measures were opposed by the four assistant deputies and by most finance officials. To this bureaucratic stonewalling was added the opposition of Louis Rasminsky, governor of the Bank of Canada, who was concerned that Gordon's withholding-tax proposals in the budget would anger the Americans.

The technical difficulties of some of the budget's sweeping proposals required Gordon to amend his resolutions after presentation and seriously impaired his credibility as minister of finance. Most of these problems would have been avoided if Pearson had lived up to his commitment to release Bryce, who enjoyed great respect throughout the public service and could have brought the disparate forces together.

It was in connection with the Lucien Rivard affair, however, that Pearson appeared at his very worst. Lucien Rivard, an unsavoury character on his good days, was being held in the Bordeaux jail and the U.S. government was seeking his extradition to face charges of smuggling dope. A Montreal lawyer, Pierre Lamontagne, was acting for the American government. Allegations were made that Rivard's underworld connections had leaned on Raymond Denis, executive assistant to René Tremblay, the minister of citizenship and immigration, to bribe the U.S. government's counsel not to oppose the granting of bail to Rivard. In addition two members of Minister of Justice Guy Favreau's personal staff had also been pressured and, in their turn, had telephoned Lamontagne, putting additional pressure on him. The most serious revelation was that Guy Rouleau, a Liberal MP and Pearson's parliamentary secretary, had also made strong representations to obtain bail for Rivard while the Americans were endeavouring to extradite him.

In the House of Commons Pearson was asked by Doug Harkness when he had been informed by Guy Favreau of any of the circumstances of the Rivard case. Pearson stated, "Mr. Speaker, I think I was informed the day before Mr. Favreau's estimates were brought into the House." This would have been the previous week. In fact, when the opposition finally forced an inquiry under the chief justice of the Province of Quebec, Frédéric Dorion, Favreau gave evidence and the judge found as a fact that Favreau had informed his prime minister three months previously. When Favreau's evidence came to light, Pearson did not have the courage to apologize to the House for misleading them but instead wrote a letter to the chief justice "clarifying" his previous statements.

It became clear that Pearson had not just misled the House, he had also hung Favreau out to dry. Favreau was left to defend himself against charges of having failed to investigate the fact that government officials, including the prime minister's parliamentary secretary, were involved in a serious attempt to subvert justice, and of having failed to inform the prime minister, when in fact he had.

In short order after assuming power, Pearson had seriously impaired the careers of his minister of finance and minister of justice.

The campaign committee meeting to which Elmer Bell had summoned me was held at the Château Laurier. After the first morning's discussion of the coming campaign Dick Thrasher, national secretary of the party and a former MP from Windsor, asked to speak to me privately. Thrasher had been parliamentary secretary to Diefenbaker, and the Prime Minister had told me that he was slated for a cabinet position when we were defeated in 1963. He was an intelligent, likeable fellow and loyal to Diefenbaker without being blind to his foibles. We went to a small anteroom, where he asked, "How would you like to run this election campaign?"

I was thunderstruck. "You've got to be joking. How can you run an election campaign when the leader doesn't speak to the campaign chairman? Dief would never agree to this."

Then came the real shocker. "We have already discussed it with Mr. Diefenbaker and he is quite prepared to have you as chairman. Besides, we don't have anybody else who could really do the job. We have tried several who have refused."

The last statement came as no insult; I knew I would have been the leader's last choice. I said to Thrasher, "I'll have to telephone Suzie and my partners and discuss this bombshell with them. I'll get back to you later in the day." I repaired to discuss this novel turn of events with Elmer Bell and with Flora MacDonald, by far the most knowledgeable person at national headquarters. They both urged me to accept. "I can only do this with superhuman help from you, Flora," I warned.

When I told my wife, she was incredulous, but supportive. My partners were less enthusiastic, but accepted the inevitable. Pointing out that I was taking on a hopeless task, Herb Solway jokingly admonished that I would probably end up looking "like the bum you are."

Diefenbaker was at the lowest point in public esteem that he ever had been or ever would be. The first poll we did showed that only 19 per cent of the public preferred him to Pearson or Douglas as prime minister. The party was clearly split between the Diefenbaker loyalists and those who believed that he should have resigned earlier in the year. The strong divisions within the party had affected the whole organizational apparatus across the country. In Quebec the party was almost non-existent. Tory coffers were low, while the Liberals, notwithstanding business's concern about Walter Gordon, were well heeled. On the other hand, there were a few pluses. The public had never taken to Pearson. There had been a series of lesser scandals among his cabinet, particularly in Quebec, scandals that Diefenbaker was to use most effectively during the campaign. The Liberals were far too confident of victory. Pearson was a poor campaigner while Diefenbaker was to prove again that he was the greatest of this century.

In his book *The Distemper of Our Times*, Peter C. Newman accurately described the 1965 Tory campaign as "not a campaign in the accepted sense. It was a guerrilla war fought along a four-thousand-mile front in treacherous circumstances with unreliable troops and intriguing generals. Victory was impossible; success would be measured by mere survival."

After I had decided to accept the job, I arranged to meet Diefenbaker. It was the first conversation we had had for almost two years. One of the qualities that made me a reasonable appointment was that, apart from Bill Brunt and Dalton Camp, I was one of the few people who were not overawed by John Diefenbaker and who would stand up to him. Being able to be frank with the leader is a vital prerequisite for a campaign chairman. Loyalty consists in telling him not what he wants to hear but what you honestly believe—as a good lawyer does for his clients.

I went to Diefenbaker's office in the Centre Block. With a mixture of amusement and trepidation I entered his office and said, "Good morning, sir."

The leader looked at me intently for a long time, as if he were reviewing our erratic ten-year association, then replied curtly, "Good morning."

"Dick Thrasher tells me that you wish me to assume chairmanship of the campaign," I volunteered.

"I would not have put it exactly that way, but I accept his advice that you are the best man under the circumstances."

"Mr. Diefenbaker, I must tell you that it is a big mistake for you to agree to my appointment unless you are prepared to repose absolute confidence in me throughout the campaign, both in my loyalty and my judgement. If you can't, you would be better off with someone else even if they have less experience."

"I have always found you forthright if sometimes mistaken, and I certainly accept your promise to do your best." Pause. "I want Arthur Burns at headquarters."

I really exploded at that. The only reason for Arthur Burns, an advertising executive, to be at headquarters would be to report directly to Diefenbaker. I said, "Mr. Diefenbaker, there will be only one person reporting to you at my headquarters. Me. In one breath you tell me you trust me and in the next you ask for a personal agent."

He acquiesced and said, "I have one condition that I absolutely insist on and that is that Lowell Murray does not set foot in national headquarters." Lowell Murray had been executive assistant to Davie Fulton and Wally McCutcheon, both former ministers who were totally out of favour. "Lowell could be very helpful but you have my undertaking that he will not come into headquarters." Nor did he. Instead, I met with him regularly at my suite at the Château, usually around midnight. He was helpful with both strategic and policy advice.

Diefenbaker then pulled out a transcript of confidential evidence given by one Elizabeth Bentley, a Soviet agent in the United States, to the House Un-American Activities Committee, during the period in the fifties when Americans were busily engaged in looking for Communists under every rock. The tenor of the evidence was that Lester Pearson was a Communist agent.

It was all guilt by association and consisted mostly of old circumstantial inferences from Pearson's relationship with Herbert Norman, a Canadian diplomat with Communist sympathies. It was clear on reading that Bentley had absolutely no direct evidence to bring against Pearson.

I told Diefenbaker that in my opinion any reference to this evidence would do more harm to the campaign than good. Furthermore, it would be most detrimental to the office of prime minister. I also made the more telling argument that we had quite enough material to make Pearson's leadership look bad without resorting to this type of scurrilous innuendo. I was no admirer of Lester Pearson, but the suggestion that he was a Communist was scandalous and unfounded. Diefenbaker never mentioned the evidence again.

The day I accepted the chairmanship of the campaign, Gordon Churchill told me that he had had several conversations with Duff Roblin, the Manitoba premier, who had almost made a commitment to him to stand for the federal house in one of the Winnipeg ridings. I told Gordon that I would do anything he wanted to finalize this decision, but he assured me that he had it under control. He would keep the pressure on Roblin, who would announce within the next two or three days. I returned to Toronto to set my office in order and then came back to Ottawa for the duration of the campaign. I took a small suite in the Château Laurier, had the hotel move in a large refrigerator, and stocked it liberally with food from Nate's Delicatessen. Come what may, I was ready.

Flora and I had decided that the number one priority was to unite the party and bring back the dissidents of 1963 and 1964. The return of Davie Fulton as a federal candidate after a disastrous stint as the leader of the provincial party gave us some British Columbia momentum. Dalton Camp decided to run in Eglinton against Mitchell Sharp. George Hees was running in Northumberland against Pauline Jewett, and George Hogan in York West against Bob Winters. My friend newspaper publisher John Bassett was delighted I had taken the appointment, and the Toronto *Telegram* was back in the Tory fold. Though Léon Balcer would not return and the situation in

Quebec was not promising, John Robarts promised me Ontario support, and Bob Stanfield of Nova Scotia was the loyalest of the loyal.

The first news I received on the day of my arrival in Ottawa was from Gordon Churchill: Roblin had decided not to run and would make an announcement to this effect the following day. I quickly got on the telephone to Roblin and said, "Duff, you can't make a decision on whether to run without speaking to me face to face. I'll fly down tonight." He agreed to wait. I grabbed a pillow from my bed in the Château and took a cab to Montreal to catch the last plane to Winnipeg.

I arrived early the following morning and went straight to the premier's office. The forty-five-minute session with Roblin was among the most frustrating discussions I have ever had in my political life. I told him that the spirits of the party were rising with the return of many of the dissidents: Hees, Fulton, and Camp all were going to be candidates. I emphasized that the impetus we were gaining would be lost if he didn't run. I then said, "Duff, I am confident" — which was far from the truth — "that we can keep the Grits in a minority position if you run, and we might even get the largest number of seats" — which I didn't believe.

Clearly flattered, he asked, "How many seats' difference do you think I would make?"

This put me in a quandary. I had to give a high number of seats to show how important I felt he was in the public's esteem and yet I couldn't be ridiculous about my estimate. "Fifteen to eighteen seats," I replied, which was the maximum my elastic conscience would allow me to go.

"I would only mean fifteen to eighteen seats across the country?" Roblin retorted peevishly. To me that was a tremendous number. I pointed out that it meant thirty to thirty-six seats' difference in the relative standings, but to no avail. I tried a different line of attack.

"Mr. Diefenbaker is most anxious for you to run. He told me how important your candidacy is."

Roblin's response finished me off: "That was not the impression he gave me when I spoke to him last week." I was appalled to realize that Diefenbaker, who was supposed to have encouraged Roblin to run, had done quite the opposite. The interview ended with Roblin categorically refusing to run but agreeing to go to Quebec for a short speaking tour. He was popular there and spoke excellent French. My disappointment equalled what I felt at twelve when my mother refused to buy me a bicycle.

I grabbed my pillow and flew back to Ottawa. I had learned a lot about Roblin. While he was an intelligent man, he was indecisive and far too cautious to become a strong national leader. Furthermore his ego required as much feeding as John Diefenbaker's. These two qualities were to cause him to lose the federal leadership of the Conservative Party when he ran two years later.

The great human resource of the national headquarters was Flora MacDonald, who knew everything about the party and everyone in it. Her advice was almost invariably first class. Her only fault was that her frequent mistreatment by the leader had made her overly sensitive, and she would occasionally sulk if not stroked. Flora was indefatigable; she would be up and working by no later than six o'clock every morning, occasionally even by five. Another worker active in the campaign was Jim Johnston, who was in charge of advertising, and later became the national director of the party and a close ally and confidant of John Diefenbaker.

The next minor catastrophe concerned the election platform. Prior to the election call and immediately thereafter, Alvin Hamilton, the former minister of agriculture, and Roy Faibish, who had been his executive assistant and was then working in the leader's office, put together an election platform for the party. I wasn't thrilled at having an election platform written by two people — unless I was one of them — but these were both inventive, intelligent Tories whose outlook on policy and approach to matters was not too far from mine. That helped me accept the situation.

The source of my dismay was the manner in which the leader handled our secret campaign program. During his flight to the opening meeting at Oakville, fog prevented the plane from landing. Diefenbaker then held a press conference on the plane. For want of anything better to say — a rare occurrence for John Diefenbaker — he dumped out half the policy in one hour without having discussed it with me. The usual practice is to allow it to be unveiled item by item.

We decided that the official opening of the campaign would stress party unity and support for Diefenbaker across the country, so I invited all the Tory provincial premiers and leaders. The meeting was held early in September at Varsity Arena. I walked the one block from the Park Plaza Hotel to the Arena with Roblin and Stanfield, during a mild drizzle. Roblin was whining because we didn't have a limousine laid on; Stanfield looked at him as if he were crazy.

The evening was a great success. Even John Robarts, who liked to put a fair amount of distance between the federal party and the Ontario party, as well as between Diefenbaker and himself, got caught up in the emotion of the evening and came out strongly for the leader, promising us the full backing of his organization. He lived up to this commitment, at least until the last ten days.

At the onset I tried to put together a team of young enthusiastic persons at national headquarters. Doug Bassett helped me find a group of student volunteers for the period of the campaign. One volunteer I enticed was Darcy McKeough, then a backbencher and subsequently the treasurer of Ontario and a politician who played a prominent role through both the Robarts and the Davis eras. McKeough's main job was to get a solid poll worked out to help us know where the party and the leader stood in the eyes of the voters. McKeough ably handled the job, but the news was disastrous. The poll showed Diefenbaker's approval rating third behind those of Pearson and Tommy Douglas, the NDP leader.

The challenge facing us was how to turn the leader into an asset as opposed to a liability. At an early meeting in the small living-room of my suite at the Château, Lowell Murray, Flora MacDonald, Jim Johnston, and I had searched desperately for an appropriate campaign slogan. In 1957 Dalton Camp had come up with "It's time for a Diefenbaker government," a great inspiration because in one short sentence it wiped away all the public's misgivings about the Conservative Party and took advantage of their affection for John Diefenbaker. In 1965 that sentiment was virtually extinct. After we all made a couple of dozen bad suggestions, Jim Johnston said, "I've got it." We turned to him breathlessly. "Give the old bugger another chance," he intoned with a straight face.

We all had a good laugh, but Johnston's prankish suggestion turned out to be prophetic, when with no prompting from us Diefenbaker more or less took up the same theme. His pitch to the public was that he already had all the honours and prestige that the country could bestow, and that he was only running again because of his humble desire to serve the people one more time and to rid them of the evil Liberal government. After I heard these sentiments delivered a few times in Diefenbaker's inimitable style, I even came to believe them myself. I know that by the campaign's end, Diefenbaker had even convinced himself of their sincerity.

While the Tory leader was going in the direction that his campaign workers wanted him to go, though perhaps a little too far and too fast, the Liberal leader seemed to have a death wish. Pearson was making our fantastic objective of preventing the Liberals from getting a majority suddenly seem attainable. When he announced the election, Pearson had bravely said, "The decision is mine and mine alone," words that would come back to haunt him two months later. He stated his intention to carry on the business of running the country during the election. Except for a few major appearances in large centres, his campaign was to be limited to discussing the issues with the people via television because, as he grandiosely put it, "My first obligation is as prime minister."

Lowell Murray, Flora MacDonald, and I met immediately to consider how we should handle this arrogant pronouncement. Murray reminded us that some weeks earlier, during the crisis of a possible war between Pakistan and India, Pearson had grandiloquently offered his famed services for peace to mediate between India and Pakistan. Here was our stick. I issued a press release saying, "A short month ago Mr. Pearson was ready to go to India or Pakistan. Today he doesn't have time to go to Lévis or Kelowna." The press lapped it up and immediately went to Pearson for comment on my statement. Pearson retorted: "Who is Mr. Goodman? I am the prime minister." While I understood Pearson's disdain for me, a mere campaign chairman, contempt is a luxury that no elected politician can afford during an election campaign. The next step in our strategy was to have Diefenbaker met at all his famous whistle stops by young people carrying home-made placards saying, "He cares enough to come."

Determined to add to his own troubles, Pearson kept on reminding the public how important it was for him to be given a majority. All his speeches made reference to his wish for a "clear mandate" and the country's "need for a strong government." Gradually, Pearson's petulance became visible under the stress of campaigning. He was asked one day during a radio interview at the Toronto airport what he would do if he didn't get his wished-for majority. He replied that he would call another election.

Pearson's reply was relayed to me within an hour by our radio bureau, which collected all the broadcasts about the election. I then arranged for him to be asked, when he landed in Vancouver, whether he had said a few hours earlier in Toronto that he would call another election if he didn't get a majority. By that time cooler heads had gotten to Pearson and told him the dangers of the tack he was taking. When he was asked the same question in Vancouver he denied ever having made the statement. I had the tapes of the two interviews broadcast side by side as part of our nightly distribution of news to all radio stations across the country. The ploy was a huge success and caused untold embarrassment to the Grits.

As the campaign livened up and the Liberals began to realize that they were in a fight, I noticed in the paper that Pearson had appeared at a meeting in Lévis. I sent a wire to Liberal campaign manager Keith Davey, for whom I had the highest regard, saying, "Congratulations on getting the prime minister to Lévis. Now try for Kelowna."

Meanwhile, back on the whistle-stopping Diefenbaker campaign, the leader was making the most of the scandals that had plagued the Pearson government. He would start many of his speeches with, "It was a warm summer evening and Lucien Rivard was watering the prison skating rink," a reference to how Rivard had escaped from the prison with the aid of a watering hose. By the time Diefenbaker had finished conjuring up a skilful mixture of facts and inferences, all done with humour and irony, his listeners would almost get the impression that Pearson and half a dozen of his cabinet were cosy with the Mafia. Many members of the press came to me with complaints about Diefenbaker's hyperbole. On several occasions I urged the leader to be careful and warned of a backlash. All he would do was chuckle. The backlash never came. Towards the end of the campaign I pleaded with him to switch to discussing our program, which was getting a warm reception for our candidates. He responded with a series of rhetorical questions: "Am I not attracting people to our meetings? Are they not interested in my message? Is the country not behind me?"

About half way through the campaign I had a call from John Robarts, telling me that Dick Rohmer would like to be of some help in the campaign. Rohmer, a Toronto lawyer, was an adviser and close friend of Premier Robarts. I had first introduced Rohmer to Robarts in the middle of the 1961 Ontario leadership campaign. Dick has a creative mind, which he has turned to the writing of several successful commercial novels. His high opinion of himself made him ideal for the role I was to find for him.

When Rohmer called, I asked him how he thought he could best contribute to the campaign. He replied, "I think that I should travel on Mr. Diefenbaker's train and give him some of my ideas."

"I'll see if that can be arranged, Dick. The leader will be in Ottawa for a few hours tomorrow. Why don't you fly down and I'll arrange for you to see him." I hung up the phone whistling to myself.

Diefenbaker arrived early the next morning and I told him that Rohmer would be in to meet with him in about an hour. Dick showed up on time. I took him to the room where Diefenbaker was relaxing and said, "I'll just introduce you and then you two can have a discussion alone." There was no way I was going to be trapped in the drama that was to follow.

I went in later to discuss several matters with Diefenbaker. Right off the bat he said, "That young man wants to come on the train."

"Yes, sir. Mr. Robarts thinks that he could be helpful. He is a very bright fellow and he has been very helpful to the premier."

"I think you might tell him that the train is full," he growled. "I have enough people telling me how to handle myself without adding to the number."

"The original suggestion came from John Robarts. I don't want to alienate the whole Ontario organization when we have succeeded in drawing them into the campaign, but I'll see what I can do."

That night I telephoned Dick. "The leader was pleased with your offer, but the sleeping arrangements on the train are very tight. He will be in Toronto tomorrow. You'll have to get there and somehow find yourself a place."

"Don't worry, I'll get on. Then what should I do?"

"You'll have to fit yourself into the tour schedule, but you should take every available opportunity to discuss your ideas with the leader. Just push your way in."

Three days later I received a plaintive call from Rohmer from somewhere in eastern Ontario. "I have been on this train for seventy-two hours and I haven't been able to get in to see the leader for a minute."

"I can't believe that. All you have to do is to walk into his living-room. Just tell his aides that you are coming in."

The next morning in my usual early morning discussion with Diefenbaker, he complained, "That fellow Rohmer is still on this train."

"How would you know? You haven't seen him in the three and a half days he's been there." I heard some throaty chuckles. "All I want you to do is to spend half an hour with him and listen to his ideas. He is a creative fellow." Diefenbaker grunted and hung up.

The following day I got a telephone call from Dick in either

Montreal or Quebec City. "The train went off without me," he whined.

"How could that happen? Catch a plane and pick it up again in Moncton. Are you going to let this thing beat you?"

The next morning Diefenbaker reported that Rohmer was back again. "He'll be there until you have your discussions with him," I said. Finally Rohmer's persistence prevailed, and he had a couple of meetings with Mr. Diefenbaker to express his views.

As the campaign moved ahead, to our surprise we noticed that we were getting newspaper support. Four times as many papers supported us this time as had in 1963. While we were not making large inroads into Ontario, particularly Toronto, we were stronger in the Maritimes than the Grits, especially in Nova Scotia and Prince Edward Island, and we were holding on firmly to the west. It was just possible that Mr. Pearson's arrogant campaign for a majority, in which his advisers had assured him of 170 seats, was going to fail.

I had reserved two final gambits for the last week of the campaign. More and more in his speeches John Diefenbaker was taking the position that this was his swan-song, although none of us believed him. For the final full-page daily newspaper ads, Jim Johnston, Flora MacDonald, and I put together various excerpts from his speeches with a picture of Diefenbaker surrounded by children. The way we combined the excerpts made it sound as if he undertook to resign a short time after the election when he had achieved a few of his policy objectives and cleansed the government. Diefenbaker had told me he wanted to see this ad and I sent Johnston to Stratford to get his approval. Johnston left in fear and trepidation, for which I did not blame him. There was no way that you could tell how the leader would react to this advertisement. Diefenbaker took the copy, sat down with a pencil on a bench, and with a few deft obliterations and skilful additions changed the whole sense of the ad to foil our purpose.

My other idea was to print a short pamphlet for wide distribution in Ontario during the last week of the campaign with a picture of Robarts and some excerpts of his speech at the opening meeting in which he had praised Diefenbaker highly. It was a simple ploy to ride in on Robarts' popular coat-tails. Unfortunately for me, Dorothy Downing, the provincial women's organizer, was working at my campaign headquarters. When she heard about my scheme, she immediately telephoned Robarts. An hour later I got a message that he wanted to speak to me. He was in a towering rage. "What the hell are you doing down there?" he roared. "I have heard about your pamphlet. Why didn't you call me for my approval?"

I replied casually, "What was the point of calling for your approval, when I know you wouldn't approve? There was nothing in the pamphlet that you didn't say, and I need your strength to help us in Ontario."

Robarts became even more agitated. "If you print that pamphlet I will make a statement withdrawing my support of the federal party."

"Oh come on, Jack, don't get your shirt in a knot for nothing. You know you won't do any such thing." I was certain he would not carry through his threat, as it would have hurt him provincially. He could still do me a lot of harm, however, by telling the MPPs privately not to help as the campaign went down the stretch. I decided not to risk the open break. "Okay, I'll withdraw the pamphlet, but I thought that I personally was entitled to your help."

"You'll have it, but not this way." He hung up abruptly.

I was more than a little annoyed because I felt that Robarts owed me quite a few, but I decided to laugh it off. Instead I did a special Ontario advertisement showing Diefenbaker standing with all the Conservative premiers. The ad featured Robarts prominently, including his quotation in support of Mr. Diefenbaker.

The one person to whom John Diefenbaker was truly indebted for his efforts in the 1965 election was Robert Stanfield. In the middle of the election, it began to appear that the Liberals were making headway in Nova Scotia. The press, particularly the influential Charles Lynch of Southam, prophesied losses for us. I called Stanfield and told him that unless he injected himself vigorously into the campaign, as though it were his own

The author at six with his mother, father and sister, Cecily, 1925.

Clinton Street Public School, circa 1927.

Goodman on exercises in
Surrey, England, 1943.

he author as a lieutenant about to party in Sussex, England, with (third from left)
eutenant Colonel, later Major General R.E.A. Morton, 1942.

Suzie and Eddie on their honeymoon in Mexico, December 1953.

Goodman as Chairman after his presentation to John and Olive Diefenbaker at the
leadership convention in September 1967 in Toronto. John Robarts and George Drew are
also on the stage.

Left to right: Bob Stanfield, Heward Grafftey, Marcel Faribeault and young Brian Mulroney in Montreal early in Stanfield's 1968 campaign.

Stanfield and Goodman still happy in the 1968 campaign.

Presenting Celia Franca to Governor General and Mrs. Vanier.

With Bill Davis and Ambassador Lee chatting with Prime Minister Yitzhak Rabin in Jerusalem. Kathy Davis and Suzie Goodman at end of the table.

The Goodman family in 1968.

Daughter Joanne.

Daughter Diane in Quetico.

George Hees and John Bassett on the Aegean Sea, 1963.

Peter Hardy and Lionel Schipper on safari in Kenya.

The Goodmans and the Worthingtons in San Francisco.

Gerry Sheff, Goodman, Peter Widdrington, Cliff Lax, Joe de Pencier, Vicky de Pencier, Michael Halpert on the South Nahanni River, Northwest Territories.

Mike Prentis, Goodman, Peter Widdrington, Tom Kierans, Bernie Ghert, Pertemba the Sherpa and Gerry Sheff on the Annapurna trek, Nepal.

'ith Queen Elizabeth II at the Royal Ontario Museum, September 1984.

ith Margaret Thatcher, Tom Kierans, Bill Davis in Toronto, 1982.

Quetico, Ontario, 1987.

provincial campaign, we ran the risk of losing several seats. He immediately responded. The result was that we won ten of the twelve seats in Nova Scotia and came very close in the two remaining seats.

When the votes were counted, the Liberals had 131 seats, two short of a majority, the Tories had 97, the NDP 21, the Social Credit 5, and the Quebec Créditistes 9. The Liberals and the Conservatives had each gained two seats. In Quebec, the Tories had won 8 and the Liberals 56. Outside Quebec, the Tories led the Grits 89 to 75.

Diefenbaker was exultant. He knew he had made the most of his limited opportunities and had redeemed his reputation as being the most effective Canadian on the hustings since the days of Wilfrid Laurier. He also knew that while he was not going to be prime minister this time, the failure of Pearson to win a majority might well be a mortal blow. John Diefenbaker still had his eyes on the distant vision of confounding his detractors by becoming the Prime Minister of Canada again.

CHAPTER EIGHT

HOW THE MIGHTY

In the early summer of 1966, Dalton Camp threw into the public arena the question of the leader's right to continue without a clear endorsement from the rank and file of the party. During the acrimonious debates of the next six months, the issues and views were twisted and distorted beyond recognition. Camp's original position, put simply, was that in a democratic party the constituency members should have the right to decide whether a leadership convention should be called after an election in which the party had not gained power. This right would be exercised through a ballot at the next annual meeting. If the leader were endorsed he would carry on into the next election. Today, the right to put confidence in the leader to a ballot vote is taken as a matter of course in all parties, but it was not then the protocol of either the Liberal or Conservative parties.

While I had great sympathy for Camp's position, both philosophically and practically, at the outset I did not form part of the group that began to mount a campaign for the question to be decided at the annual meeting in November. I had two reasons for staying on the sidelines that summer and fall. The first was that I had just finished running a campaign for John Diefenbaker during which the leader and I had re-established a good relationship. I had worked to the point of exhaustion on his behalf and that of the party. Indeed, I suffered slight permanent damage to my eyes from a virus acquired during the campaign. I thought it would be unbecoming to turn on him immediately, notwithstanding the validity of the Camp position. The second reason was that in addition to being the party's national vice-president for Ontario, I was chairman of the Resolutions and Policy Committee. I would be in the chair when the issue came to the plenary session, and I preferred to appear at least slightly objective at that time.

Camp made two very effective speeches to start his campaign, one on May 19 at a private meeting at the Albany Club in Toronto and the second similar address on September 20 to a large public meeting of the Toronto Junior Board of Trade. He outlined thoughtfully and articulately the mutual relationship and obligations between a leader and his party: "The leader should give at least as much loyalty to his followers as he demands from them. This is not a matter of personal loyalty alone, but rather loyalty to the party, to its continuing strength, best interest and well being. This common sense of loyalty must be shared by leader and followers alike if unity and harmony are to be enjoyed by both." The *Globe and Mail* wrote an excellent editorial supporting this position, entitled "Mr. Camp's Courage," and indeed Dalton exhibited courage throughout his campaign, along with a rare conceptual understanding of party politics.

In between these speeches he went across western Canada to marshal support for this position. He strengthened his hand by playing an important role in the June 1966 Manitoba provincial election in which Duff Roblin was re-elected. Slowly his campaign started to gain momentum in the press, but it was not yet making overwhelming headway in the party.

In early October, I received a telephone call from George Hees in Ottawa.

"Hello, Benny. It's your old friend George. Listen, I was talking to some of the fellows down here about this campaign that Dalton is waging against the leader —"

I interrupted. "He says it is not against the leader, but for the principle of a vote by ballot on whether or not Diefenbaker enjoys the party's confidence."

"I know that, but you and I both know he wants to get rid of the son of a gun and so do a lot of people here. But the guys are worried that this could turn the annual meeting into a shambles. Gordon Churchill suggested I call you and see if you can't intercede to straighten all this out."

"How, George?"

"That's up to you, Ben, old boy. Call Churchill and discuss it with him."

I called Churchill, who voiced the same concern about the damage to the party. Still hesitant to insert myself into this no-win situation, I called Senator David Walker, a long-time close friend of John Diefenbaker who had served in his cabinet. I inquired whether he thought there was any point in my speaking to Diefenbaker, in the event that I made some arrangement with Camp to hold off. He urged me in the strongest terms to do so.

I told Dalton that I had had these conversations and that, if he agreed, I was prepared to meet with Diefenbaker, to propose what I thought was an obvious compromise: the vote of confidence in the leader would be taken by secret ballot, as would the vote on the presidency, as it always was. If Diefenbaker agreed, there would be no overt campaigning against his leadership. Camp agreed, insisting that he was primarily, although not totally, fighting for a principle. If the majority of the party wanted John Diefenbaker as their leader then they were entitled to have him. It has always been my view that if a leader cannot carry more than 70 per cent of a party with him, he clearly has an obligation to resign, which Diefenbaker would never have done. It was not my intention, however, to muddy the waters with my personal views. I made an appointment with John Diefenbaker and flew to Ottawa.

The leader greeted me cordially and I wasted no time in getting down to the subject at hand. I said, "Mr. Diefenbaker" — I could never call him Chief; usually I called him Mr. Prime Minister, sometimes John, sometimes Mr. Leader, but never Chief — "the campaign that Camp is waging will do a great deal of harm to the party if not settled."

"Tell that to your friend Camp," he grumbled.

"I have a simple solution that will solve everything. You will call for a vote of confidence in your leadership to be taken by ballot. It will take the wind out of your opponents' sails, and you will win in a landslide if you ask for the vote yourself. You will lose if it is forced on you."

He paused for a long time and gave me his searing look.

"What happens to Camp?"

"He will run and probably be re-elected president."

He said, "No deal. I will never lead a party of which Camp is president."

I pleaded, "Mr. Diefenbaker, please don't be stubborn. You are making a mistake of heroic proportions." I repeated my argument that if he took the initiative and called for a ballot, there was no doubt he would have overwhelming support from the rank and file of the delegates.

He seemed quite taken by this point. "There is no doubt that I can win a ballot." He paused and I held my breath. "But I will not accept Camp as president of the party."

I argued vigorously that he was reversing the roles, that it was the leader, not the president, who was in charge and that the vote would not impair his leadership, but strengthen it. I also reminded him how loyal Camp had been in 1963 when he ran Diefenbaker's campaign. I was spitting against the wind.

The annual meeting of the Ontario provincial party was to take place from October 30 to November 1. Dalton called to find out whether or not some encouragement for his position might flow from the provincial meeting. I called John Robarts and discussed the question with him. He was most sympathetic to Camp's position, but quite properly was not prepared to allow a federal fight to weaken the provincial party, which would be going to the polls in a year to fifteen months. He said, "This is the last annual meeting of the provincial party before I call an election. This divisive matter should not be allowed to dominate." While I had some sympathy with Robarts' position, I pointed out that everyone would be talking about it privately and that an end to federal divisiveness would help us provincially. Robarts agreed to attend the federal annual meeting and to have further discussions at any time. At every provincial annual meeting there was always a pro forma motion of confidence in the federal leader. I deleted it to prevent having the matter come to the floor and nobody noticed.

I reported Robarts' position to Camp, who was disappointed, but accepted the premier's reluctance to become involved. Camp was not getting any overt indication of support from his two buddies Roblin and Stanfield, and he didn't expect it from Robarts. In the final analysis, though, Robarts and his representatives at the annual meeting were more helpful to Camp than the other two. The anti-Diefenbaker feeling was strongest in Ontario.

In late October Arthur Maloney announced he was running for the presidency against Camp and as a Diefenbaker loyalist. Maloney was an Ottawa Valley Irishman with whom I had gone to law school. He had an outstanding career at the criminal bar and had been a leader in the fight to abolish capital punishment. His brother had been a cabinet minister in the Frost government. In 1957 Arthur had been elected as the MP for Parkdale riding in Toronto. Most of us thought he should have been put in the cabinet after the 1958 election, but he was not a Diefenbaker favourite and was merely a parliamentary assistant in 1957-8.

The national conference opened with a meeting of the national executive on November 13, which I attended as vice-president for Ontario. Two bitterly tough items were at the top of the agenda. The first was a resolution censuring Dalton Camp for his actions, moved by Erik Nielsen. The second was the conference agenda. This had been prepared by Jim Johnston, the national director, without consultation with the president, or anyone else. He had placed the discussion of the resolutions before the election of officers. The best interests of the Camp supporters would be served by having the election for president first, as there would be many people who would be prepared to vote for Dalton who might not be prepared to vote against John Diefenbaker. Furthermore, Camp's re-election as president would have a significant effect on the leadership vote.

The Camp forces alleged that Jim Johnston was using his position as national director to stack the meeting in an effort to prevent a fair expression of party opinion. The vacancies in the Quebec delegation — which were quite a few, due to the weakness of the Quebec organization — were being filled by national headquarters with Diefenbaker supporters. Many of these replacements had only very tenuous ties with the party. The Diefenbaker loyalists countercharged that Paul Trépanier, the Quebec president, was substituting Camp supporters.

While I had come to the national executive meeting determined to sit quietly and watch, I could not contain myself when I
saw the tactics that were being used against the president of the
party. I led the fight against the censure motion and the manipu-
lation of the agenda, saying, "The party is indebted to the president for endeavours to give Conservatives across the country the
opportunity to express their views in a democratic fashion."
Camp said later that my intervention was critical, as his
supporters were either unprepared for the manoeuvres of the
Diefenbaker loyalists or hesitant to take a public position. Stan
Randall, a member of the Ontario cabinet, was attending as a
representative of Robarts. He backed me up forcefully, and we
were successful in preventing both the censure motion and the
changing of the agenda.

In the corridors and rooms of the Château Laurier, the
campaign between Camp and Arthur Maloney for the presidency was increasing in intensity and bitterness. Maloney was a man
of deep loyalties, and when he decided on his course he went at it
with vigour. He had many friends, particularly among the
members of the House. He was also a great friend of Hugh
Latimer, who did not like Dalton and who worked hard for
Arthur, especially in rural Ontario. It was going to be close.

The agenda on the evening following the executive committee
meeting included the opening speeches and the speeches of the
presidential candidates. First, however, Joel Aldred gave a
lacklustre introduction to John Diefenbaker. The audience
behaved badly according to their given views, particularly the
Camp supporters, who had grabbed all the front seats early and
who heckled loudly when Diefenbaker spoke.

Camp spoke well, but was too cerebral for the occasion.
Maloney made an emotion-charged speech that started with,
"When John Diefenbaker walks into a room, Arthur Maloney
stands up," a reference to the poor manners of Dalton's young
supporters earlier in the evening. The speeches made little
difference to the outcome. On the following day's vote Camp
defeated Maloney 564 to 502. The battle lines were clearly
drawn.

After the vote, Dalton collared me. "From here on in it's up to you. You will be taking over the plenary sessions tomorrow as chairman when we reach the presentation of the resolutions. I do not intend to appear on the platform from here on."

I asked what arrangements had been made about the procedure to be followed on the resolutions. I also wanted to know how he had planned to decide the vital issue of the meeting on whether the resolutions of confidence in the leader would be done by ballot or open vote. What would we do in the event, as now seemed possible, that there was a vote of non-confidence? How would a decision be reached on whether to hold a leadership convention? Dalton's answer was shockingly simple: "We have not discussed any of those problems." I could not believe that no thought had been given to these crucial matters. The Camp forces had come well-prepared to re-elect their candidate, but not prepared to effect the reforms that he wished to achieve.

I had come to the conference hoping only that the wishes of the majority of the party would prevail. While I felt that the time had come for John George Diefenbaker to retire as leader, I did not want the party for which I had toiled so long to fragment. Dalton's view was that if Diefenbaker did not go the party would either split apart or be decimated in an election, perhaps never to recover.

To go into that meeting without some plan of action would be to invite chaos, and it was not my intention to preside over chaos. I then did what I always do when I want to get a job done and turned to my friends in the Ontario party. I called Elmer Bell, Ben Cunningham, Lionel Schipper, and Flora MacDonald up to my room to decide how the matter should be handled. To add to my troubles, I had had a cold, which had settled in my throat. This, aided by the tension of the meeting, rendered me, for once in my life, almost unable to speak.

The strategy we agreed upon was that I would outline the rules of procedure for the afternoon and ask for a mover and a seconder. The procedure was simple. The meeting would decide by a standing vote whether or not there should be a ballot on the vote of confidence in the leader. In the event there was to be a ballot on the vote of confidence there would be two resolutions on the ballot. The first would be a vote of confidence in the leader and the second would read that in the event the meeting did not have confidence in the leader, a leadership convention should be held no later than December, 1967, of which the terms and conditions would be set by the national executive committee. To move the resolution, I had Elmer Bell. To second it I had Ben Cunningham. In reserve, I had my partner, Lionel Schipper, whose job was to fill the gap if a special resolution were required to ensure an orderly discussion of the issue.

Early in the afternoon, I received a telephone call that Dalton wanted me down on the platform right away. The Diefenbaker forces were assembling in the lobby to march on the meeting and take it over: a sort of shoot-out at the OK Corral. I got out of bed, dressed, grabbed a shoe-tree to use as a gavel and, with my heart pounding, went down to the convention hall in the Château Laurier. When I reached the main floor, there was a large crowd gathering around the leader in a room next to the lobby yelling, "We want John." I went to the convention hall to take over the chair while they paraded around the lobby and various anterooms, never entering the main meeting. I mounted the podium and pounded for order with my shoe-tree. It banged almost as loudly as my heart. Interrupted by the occasional catcall, I then outlined the procedure I proposed to follow. My prearranged mover and seconder moved the necessary motion approving the procedure. There followed about twenty minutes of preliminary technical scuffles, but then the anti-ballot pro-Diefenbaker group collapsed like a leaky balloon. The motion to vote on confidence in the leadership by ballot was passed by a large majority on a standing vote. The meeting adjourned to vote. Lincoln Alexander, the election officer, came in to announce the results several hours later. The count was 563 to 186 to hold a leadership convention. The mighty had finally fallen.

A day or two later, the great majority of the caucus signed a pledge of loyalty to John Diefenbaker. The separation between the rank and file of the party and the elected representatives appeared to be total. In fact, however, the pressure from Diefenbaker loyalists on the MPs to sign the pledge had been strong and few took it seriously. The pledge mattered not: under the constitution of the party, the vote of the annual meeting prevailed.

Early in January of the next year, 1967, Dalton Camp asked me to be chairman of the convention and of the convention committee. The office included full responsibility for the planning and operation of the leadership convention. The job was an interesting challenge. There would undoubtedly be a considerable number of candidates; furthermore, there were many wounds to heal and there was a strong possibility that some of the diehard Diefenbaker supporters would press their stated intention of challenging the constitutionality of the convention in the courts. This did not concern me as much as the possibility that the convention committee would be unmanageable.

First I had to consider my obligation to George Hees. After our decades of friendship, I felt duty bound to take an active part in his leadership campaign if he ran, as I was certain he would. I discussed the matter with Hees. We decided that if we could get an outstanding organizer to run his campaign, I would take the convention chairmanship. Fortunately, there was an obvious choice for a Hees organizer in Bob Macaulay, the former provincial member and cabinet minister from Riverdale, the provincial counterpart of George's former federal riding of Broadview. Macaulay had held a series of cabinet positions in the Frost and Robarts governments before going back to the private practice of law. His deputy chairman was to be Lionel Schipper, who had practised law with Macaulay before Schipper came to Goodman & Goodman.

One matter remained to be settled before I could accept the chairmanship. I had to speak to Robarts and find out his intentions. He had told me on several occasions that under no circumstances would he stand for the federal leadership; he was going to remain provincial leader for one more election and then go back to law. I met with him at the Westbury Hotel and told him that I was considering taking the appointment of convention chairman. Then I added, "John, obviously if you run that requires rethinking the whole matter. I am assuming you are not interested."

"I have no interest whatsoever," he answered firmly.

"If you are not supporting anyone, I will become convention chairman," I told him. "If you are supporting Duff, I will not become chairman but will work for George." The basis of my reasoning was that a combination of Robarts and Roblin would be very difficult to beat. I would want to exercise whatever influence I had among the delegates in Ontario on Hees' behalf to counteract to some degree Robarts' support of Roblin.

Robarts said, "I assure you I will not support Duff or any other candidate." As always, he lived up to his word.

I went back to Camp a few days before the meeting of the national executive committee, which was taking place in Toronto on January 28, 1967, and agreed to accept the chairmanship with two conditions. The first was that while I would not in any way use my office as chairman to further Hees' chances, I was free to speak to my friends in the Tory organization, tell them of my preferences and ask them to help. The second was that, as convention chairman, I was to have wide executive powers to choose staff and make the arrangements, subject only to the committee's approval on matters of importance.

At the meeting of the national executive committee, I was confirmed as chairman of the convention committee and rough guidelines were set for its formation. The caucus representatives were Bob Coates of Nova Scotia and George Chatterton of British Columbia, both of whom had been Diefenbaker supporters, but who were certainly co-operative after they saw that I had no hidden agenda. Jim Johnston was also on the committee as national director. We had always worked well together and he provided a line of communication to Diefenbaker, who was still, after all, the leader. Gene Rheaume, the former member for the Northwest Territories, was to be the executive secretary. I liked Rheaume, who was well connected in caucus and a great wit. In 1964 he had attended a thinkers' conference the party held in Fredericton, where I had arranged for Marshall McLuhan to be the keynote speaker. McLuhan explained to listeners the many ways communications occurred, including subliminally. The next night Diefenbaker was to arrive, and a group of MPs wanted Rheaume to come to the airport. His reply was, "Don't bother me. I learned from McLuhan today how I could stay right here and have a beer and still kiss the Chief's ass out there."

Roger Régimbal, the member from Argenteuil-Deux Montagnes, was subsequently appointed as my co-chairman, and a more intelligent co-operative colleague I could not have found. Not only had he accomplished the considerable feat of getting elected as a Tory member in Quebec, he was genuinely respected by his parliamentary colleagues and maintained the confidence of Diefenbaker. I was absolutely determined that this convention was going to be successful and that no one could legitimately complain that it was tilted in favour of any group or candidate. I persuaded the committee to appoint Lincoln Alexander, who in 1965 had run unsuccessfully in Hamilton West for Diefenbaker, as the elections officer for the convention.

In 1966 the day of packed riding conventions had not yet arrived. I am totally opposed to the present-day practice of allowing candidates to sign up members in an effort to win a riding convention. It plays havoc with riding associations and causes resentment among long-time party workers. If you aren't a party member on the day a convention is announced, you should not be entitled to vote. Members who sign on just for conventions melt away like the snow in spring.

As the September 7 date for the leadership convention drew nearer, I became increasingly convinced that the party needed to devote some attention to policy. The Tories had lost ground in the urban centres and among the intellectual-professional community. Régimbal and I convinced the committee that we should plan a serious policy conference to which leading thinkers from across the country would be invited as participants and delegates. We chose Vic Valentine, an ethnologist at Carleton University, as academic adviser, and Montmorency Falls, Quebec, as the site for the mid-August meeting.

I thought that Tom Symons, president and vice-chancellor at Trent University, a known Tory and a friend of Leslie Frost, would be an ideal chairman. I met with Symons at the Park Plaza Hotel, and after a long discussion he agreed to accept the post; but at the last minute, weeks later, he backed out, claiming Camp had advised him to do so. I saw a newspaper story that Don

McDougall, one of the executives of Labatt's, was leading a "Bill Davis for national leader" movement. Davis was the provincial minister of education in Ontario, and his reputation and stature had grown greatly in this office. He was an able and knowledgeable minister, but a candidate for leadership of the federal party at that stage he was not. I had known him well since the 1961 provincial leadership convention. I immediately telephoned him and arranged to have lunch. When we met I said, "I see that you are contemplating running for the federal leadership. For what earthly reason?"

"Don McDougall is after me. He has put together a group of good people across the country to form an organization and he thinks I can pull a respectable vote."

I sighed. "Bill, this would be a major mistake in your career. You will not do well. You may pick up 100 to 150 votes and that will do your future a great deal of harm. You are far better off to stand pat. John Robarts certainly will not fight more than one more election and you have a first-class opportunity to become the next premier of Ontario. Being premier of Ontario, first of all, is a much better job than being leader of the opposition in Ottawa. Secondly, if you run and only get 150 votes, it is highly unlikely that you will ever be premier of Ontario, because people will feel that you are just using it as a stepping-stone to federal politics. On the other hand, if you *are* interested in federal politics, a much better way to get exposure would be to become chairman of the policy committee and come to Montmorency with me."

He was obviously intrigued and agreed to get back to me in forty-eight hours, when he accepted.

The Montmorency Falls conference was almost a resounding success. The surroundings were delightful, the delegates were the best group of thinkers the Conservative Party had ever put together, and the discussion was stimulating and thoughtful. The only blot was the controversy over the resolution concerning the status of English and French Canada within Confederation. The conference accepted the concept of *deux nations* not in the sense of two political states, but as a recognition of the country's two founding peoples: an English community and

French community with distinct cultural and linguistic back-grounds. It was an effort to show Quebec that the Progressive Conservative Party was sympathetic to its legitimate aspirations to maintain the existence of Canada's French culture. Unfortunately, these ideas are difficult to express, but easy to distort. The accusation was made by some of the delegates at Montmorency, led by Dick Bell in a spirited debate with Marcel Faribault, that we were advocating two sovereign states, or separate political status for Quebec. This was the beginning of an issue that was to be shrewdly manipulated by Pierre Trudeau and the Liberals to defeat the Tories in 1968.

In order to avoid the allegations that the party was too élitist, we devised a two-part procedure. The proposals that had been discussed for several days at Montmorency Falls by party supporters, academics, and business and professional leaders would then be forwarded to the leadership convention. Prior to the opening of the convention in Toronto, a group consisting of one delegate for each riding would consider the Montmorency resolutions and would forward a report to the plenary sessions.

When the convention opened on Thursday evening, Maple Leaf Gardens was a splendid sight. Between the broadcast booths, the press arrangements, and the candidates' quarters every available space had been used. The podium was well designed and the press were seated at its rear, which added an atmosphere of immediacy and excitement. Rheaume and I had journeyed to Washington to pick the brains of both the Republican Party and the Democratic Party for ideas on how to increase the efficiency — and the excitement — of what was to be the largest and most democratic convention ever held in Canada, with 2,429 accredited delegates.

I was as tight as a violin string as I awaited my debut on national television. While a barber was shaving my locks in my hotel room, I chewed a toffee to calm my nerves. *Crack*: the cap on the front tooth had broken, leaving only a gaping hole. While I am not particularly vain (it is difficult to be vain when you have to deal with my physical features), I had no intention of appearing across the country looking like a gap-toothed hill-billy. I feverishly tracked down my dentist, who did the necessary repairs in the directors' lounge at the Gardens just before showtime.

Almost daily for the past month I had been hearing rumours that the validity of the convention would be attacked. If this was to happen, it would have to happen at the outset. This time I had prepared a detailed report of the convention procedures, a report I gave after my short welcome. I had my mover and my seconder for the procedures and for the ratification of everything that the convention committee had done during the past nine months. If all that passed I was home free.

I gavelled the meeting to order, then gave my historic opening, "Good evening, sports fans." Emboldened by the audience's laughter, I tried a sentence of welcome in French. Some wag in the audience heckled, *"Parlez en français,"* in response to my pitiful accent, and I decided to leave the French to Roger Régimbal. Ratification of the committee's actions was given without a murmur of dissent and the convention was under way.

Our keynote speaker was Peter Lougheed, who was then the newly elected leader of the Conservative Party in Alberta. Rheaume had suggested that the convention would be an excellent opportunity to give Lougheed some important national exposure. Régimbal was the French-speaking keynoter. The evening ended with my making a presentation to Olive and John Diefenbaker, who still had not announced whether or not he was going to be a candidate. Olive was warm and gracious. Diefenbaker spoke well but said not a word to me throughout the convention, not even when I greeted him on arriving or made the presentation.

The following morning, just prior to the close of the nominations, Diefenbaker's name was put into candidacy, testimony to the stupidity of his friends and advisers. In addition to Diefenbaker, the list of candidates included two provincial premiers, Robert Stanfield and Duff Roblin; six former cabinet ministers, Davie Fulton, Alvin Hamilton, George Hees, Donald Fleming, Wallace McCutcheon, and Michael Starr; and two forgettable nonentities. I soon received a telephone call from Dief loyalist Gordon Churchill that Joel Aldred and he wished to meet with Bill Davis and me. When we met that afternoon in my hotel suite, Churchill started the conversation. "Benny, I want you to know that when Bill Davis puts his report to the plenary session Dief and his supporters are going to vigorously oppose the *deux nations* resolution."

I knew that such a show of division within the party would be calamitous. "Why are you doing this to the party when we are on an outstanding upward surge in public acceptance?" I asked.

Davis said, "Gordon, you know damn well that the resolution doesn't mean there should be two political states in this country. What is the basis for Mr. Diefenbaker and his supporters being so vehemently opposed?"

Churchill and Aldred replied that the resolution would be the beginning of a special status for Quebec, which had always been opposed by the party. I knew that was only half the story, that Diefenbaker was using the issue to create a crack in party unity in order to obtain control. After fifteen minutes of discussion, it was clear that we were going to make no headway. I finally said, "I have no intention of letting you fellows destroy this convention and the party. I suggest that Davis will table the report of the policy meetings and we will then move on." Churchill, a man of good, if often mistaken, intentions, agreed.

The next day when Davis tabled his report at the plenary session, the meeting was prepared to accept it, except for Charlotte Whitton, the former mayor of Ottawa. I had been warned that she would insist upon her right to debate the issue even though the report was merely being tabled. She took the microphone in hand and started in the most strident of tones to make her point. I turned to Rheaume, who controlled all the microphones scattered around the floor, and barked, "Turn off that bank of microphones." After a few minutes of silent harangue from Whitton the crowd started to boo. I made a point of order, stopped the discussion, Whitton screamed "Fascist" and the crisis was averted.

The candidates' speeches on Friday night had little effect upon the audience. The policy addresses two days earlier had been far more important. The voting commenced on Saturday. In my eagerness to present the image of the party as contemporary and up-to-date, I had arranged for the voting to be done on voting machines like those used in the United States. To help the delegates learn to use them I had placed several of the machines on the floor for trial during the convention, but few delegates had bothered. On the first ballot, most of the delegates were either so intrigued by the machines or so inept at using them that the voting, instead of being quicker, was interminable.

Stanfield led on the first ballot, Roblin was second, Fulton was third, and Hees was fourth. John Diefenbaker was fifth, receiving just 271 votes, 12 per cent of the total. It was obvious after this ballot that the question was which of the two premiers would be the new leader. When I announced the withdrawal of George Hees after the third ballot showed he couldn't win, my voice broke. To this day I wonder what would have happened if I had not taken the convention chairmanship, but had run Hees' campaign instead. I voted for Stanfield on the next two ballots.

In the final ballot between Robert Stanfield and Duff Roblin, the Nova Scotia premier who had so often lent his support and loyalty to John Diefenbaker was elected his successor by 1150 votes to 969.

CHAPTER NINE

A DEBTOR TO HIS PROFESSION

When I walk into the Cadillac Fairview Tower at the south end of Toronto's Eaton Centre where Goodman & Goodman is housed, I often think back to the day in June 1947 when I received my call to the bar. After convocation, my father and I walked back from Osgoode Hall to our modest offices at 85 Richmond Street West. I had no early visions during that walk of leading a "prestigious downtown law firm." Young lawyers do not think in those terms, nor should they. They dream in terms of personal career success: of being a fine counsel; of becoming a leading tax consultant; of advising on sophisticated corporate or real estate matters; not of building institutions. That is the reason why managing a law firm is the world's most unpleasant job: you are dealing with scores of personal egos.

How then did Goodman & Goodman grow from two lawyers to more than eighty lawyers, from two employees to more than three hundred and forty, from fifteen hundred square feet to five floors of office space? The early members of the firm were good lawyers who worked hard, but there were better lawyers who worked just as hard with less success. The reasons for our success are numerous and varied, and not the least of them is luck. Our early growth was probably due first to the high professional standards set by my dad and to the fact that the early members of the firm were all close friends who together built an environment of mutual trust and deep affection.

Our growth is also an example of what has happened to the legal profession all over North America since the war. Economies grew, businesses expanded, the tempo of business increased, and the law became much more complex. All this activity required greater legal specialization and larger law firms. When I graduated just after the war, there were just under one hundred lawyers called to the Ontario bar that year in Ontario. Now more than one thousand lawyers are called to the bar year in and year out.

The first rule of any profession is that you must put your client's interests before your own. That edict applies to all professionals, be they lawyers or prostitutes (sadly, too often in the mind of the public little distinction is made between these two professions). Lawyers should not practise to get rich, although they are entitled to be well paid. Their advice should not depend on the size of fee or whether their reputation will be enhanced if the matter proceeds. The corollary to this philosophy is that a good lawyer doesn't tell clients what they want to hear but what he or she believes is true. If clients don't like what they're paying you to tell them, show them the door.

In my first year of practice, my dad gave me two vivid examples of his philosophy. In one day he told our two most important clients that if they were not prepared to accept his advice they should get another lawyer. I pleaded, "Dad, at least limit your ultimatums to one client a day."

The second incident occurred in court. My father had been retained by another lawyer as counsel in a trial before Mr. Justice Schroeder. Schroeder had the reputation of having a good legal mind but an extremely autocratic manner. For at least three days he kept interrupting and hectoring my father. On the fourth day Dad was well into his cross-examination of the other side's most important witness when at a crucial moment Schroeder interfered again. Father stopped, folded his brief, put it into his case, told me to gather up the rest of the papers, and started to walk out of the courtroom. In great surprise, Schroeder said, "What are you doing, Mr. Goodman?" My father replied, "My Lord, my clients retained me because they had confidence in my ability and my capacity to run this case. Clearly your Lordship does not share this opinion, as you have been taking the case away from me for three days. Therefore, I am going to withdraw from this matter because I cannot continue in this way." The courtroom fell into a deafening silence as everyone waited for the famed Schroeder temper to explode. Instead he merely chivvied my father, saying, "Come, come, Mr. Goodman, do not be so sensitive; carry on." The interruptions ceased and Dad went on to win the case.

What else assists a firm to grow and to maintain high standards of excellence? Obviously it requires outstanding lawyers and successful clients who bring it sophisticated work. But what attracts these two precious commodities? I knew from the beginning that the key was close and warm relationships, first among the lawyers in the firm and then between them and the clients — not only on a professional level, but socially as well. In addition to my political associates my circle of friends has to a large extent been composed of members of my firm and my clients. I would not hire lawyers I did not like or try to keep clients who were difficult and obnoxious.

Respect must extend also to non-professional staff. Far too many lawyers think they are a superior breed. Our firm has refused to accept as partners lawyers who could not keep a secretary. Kay Schmidt was my friend and secretary from 1958 until 1980. She and her husband, Dan, remain close friends. When she left, Shirley Hodgins, who had been with the firm for more than twenty years, took Kay's place, and we have developed equally good relationships both with the Hodgins family, and with Carol Brophy, our accountant.

The first associate taken into the firm in 1954 was Norman Schipper, who started as an articling student and who to this day remains a solid rock for our commercial practice. The following year we were joined by another student, Herb Solway, who is today the head of the firm. Two years later Lionel Schipper, Norman's cousin and Solway's closest friend, moved to Goodman & Goodman when Bob Macaulay left McLaughlin Macaulay to enter the Frost cabinet. Lionel was with us for twenty years, until he went into business, and he is still sorely missed. These first three additions to Goodman & Goodman were not only able lawyers, but also outstanding individuals who were to become close and lifelong friends.

Though my career at the bar has absorbed me for forty years, it has not always been one that would make an absorbing tale for the general public. Stories of the success and failure of a client group of developers, brewers, manufacturers, or financial institutions do not keep people turning pages the way crime and sex do. My involvement with newspapers and broadcasters may strike some as glamorous. My career at the traditionally more colourful criminal bar has been limited to prosecuting drug peddlers in the late fifties and defending bookmakers, stockies (unprincipled sellers of stocks), and the occasional prostitute.

In my first criminal case, I defended a prostitute charged under the vagrancy section. I decided not to have her testify, as I felt that my stellar cross-examination of the Crown's witnesses had already won the case and that she would do more harm than good. Over my protestations, she insisted on taking the stand to tell off the police. When the magistrate gave his judgement he said: "Until the accused went into the box I was going to convict her, but now that I have heard her evidence the case is dismissed." My client walked out of the box, came over to me and said, "You young jerk, get lost." On another occasion I assisted in the defence of a fellow who attempted to murder his wife. My defence was no more successful than his pistol shot.

I soon realized that I was no Perry Mason and turned my attention to civil litigation. I appeared at every court level and later before a variety of administrative tribunals: the Ontario Municipal Board, which deals with planning, property assessment, and expropriation; the Canadian Radio-television and Telecommunications Commission and its predecessor, the Board of Broadcast Governors, which deal with broadcasting and communication matters; the Liquor Licence Board of Ontario; various highway transport boards in Ontario, Quebec, and Alberta, which regulate trucking and buses; farm boards that oversee the production and sale of eggs, milk, and chickens; the Canadian Transport Commission when it dealt with aeronautics; royal commissions such as the one to inquire into the Gerda Munsinger espionage scandal; and legislative committees, both federal and provincial. These were the adjudicators that I tried to persuade, charm, or hector according to the circumstances.

Early in my career I was retained by two clients who, with my dad's previous loyal commercial clientele, became the foundation on which we grew. These were John Labatt Limited and

Cadillac Development Corporation Limited, later the Cadillac Fairview Corporation. In 1947 on graduation Bill Shortreed, my classmate at Osgoode Hall, joined Labatt's. The head office of the company was in London, Ontario, but he felt that the company needed some solicitors in Toronto, so I received my first retainer. Forty years later, Labatt's is still a major client, and I have been a director of that company for more than twenty years.

Just after Shortreed retained me, Hugh Mackenzie, the general manager of the company, hired Peter Hardy, who resigned as Toronto manager of the Brewers' Warehousing Company and became the Toronto plant manager of Labatt's and the person from whom I received my instructions. At that time Labatt's was a struggling regional brewery. Hardy, a teetotaller, was only thirty-one, a soft-spoken but tough-minded executive with strong corporate loyalty. For him it wasn't enough for me to be Labatt's Toronto lawyer; everyone who worked for Labatt's had to sell beer. Thus I was conscripted into Labatt's army of foot soldiers who flogged suds across the province.

At that time, Hardy was married to a most attractive woman, while I was separated and on the way to being divorced from my first wife. The allocation of duties, therefore, was that Hardy would deal with the public house and tavern owners and I would persuade the waitresses to push Labatt's products. To me it seemed like a fair division of labour. The Town Tavern, the Holiday Tavern, the Brown Derby Tavern, the Orchard Park Tavern, the Chateau Dufferin, the Edgemore, the Black Knight Room — all were on our beat. The job was not without risks. You might say that my enthusiasm "cooled" when Frenchy, an attractive waitress at the Holiday Tavern, and I were locked into the beer cooler by another waitress and almost froze to death. Another time I barely escaped without injury when I neglected to find out that Emma, who worked at the Town Tavern and to whom I was busily giving my strong Labatt's pitch on her days off, was living with the head bartender at the same tavern. I like to think that today Labatt's would not be engaged in the beer business in four countries, as well as the fruit-juice, food, and grain businesses all over North America, if I had not been so successful in selling beer in the late forties and early fifties.

Hardy and I had some help, however, in the form of Hardy's longtime friend Tommy Holmes, whom Hardy brought with him to Labatt's when he joined the company in 1949. Previously both men had worked for Hardy's dad, who owned Hardy Cartage. Though Holmes had limited education — he had left school at the age of fourteen — he had a sharp mind and was extremely well read. Hardy and Holmes were an incredible duo who revolutionized the Ontario beer business in the late forties and the fifties. Labatt's chief competitor, Canadian Breweries, makers of Carling and O'Keefe beers, was controlled by Argus Corporation, a company controlled in turn by E.P. Taylor, Colonel Eric Phillips, Wallace McCutcheon, and George Black. At the time Canadian Breweries was by far the dominant force in the Ontario beer market, and our job was to cut it down to size. Hardy and Holmes decided to begin by capitalizing on their long-standing relationships with most of the public house owners in the Toronto area, several of whom were clients of my father. We succeeded to an amazing degree, and before long Labatt's had placed a group of its friends and supporters on the executive of the Ontario Hotel Association.

In the early fifties Canadian Breweries gave pub and hotel owners an added incentive to switch from Carling and O'Keefe to Labatt's when it applied to the Ontario Liquor Control Board for a price increase of twenty-five cents on a case of twenty-four, a modest enough demand. Labatt's opposed the increase and let this be known to the Hotel Association. The hoteliers were enraged by the increase; the association boycotted Canadian Breweries, and for almost two weeks nothing but Labatt's and a few kegs of Molson's beer were sold in the hotels and public houses of Ontario. It was an important breakthrough for Labatt's, which gained several market points even after the boycott ended.

The Ontario Hotel Association's annual convention was a major event in the brewing industry, and brewing executives turned out in force to entertain the hotelmen. Labatt's had a great edge at the convention, because it made certain that Hugh Labatt, the president, and Hugh Mackenzie, the general director, were always present and that they socialized with the hoteliers. In the many times that I attended hotel conventions with Labatt's I never saw any of the owners of Canadian Breweries. Labatt's entertainment bills were enough to meet the national debt. At one convention, at the King Edward Hotel, we held a large party on the last night for newly elected hotel executives in the suite of association president Micky Wilson. When the bill arrived it ran to several thousand dollars, a huge sum in the fifties. The brewery of course was expected to sign the tab. Shortreed, the self-proclaimed host of the evening, suddenly got writer's cramp. Hardy grabbed the check, said, "Let me take care of this," and signed it. Next morning when Shortreed was checking out and going over his account, he let out a howl of anguish. Hardy had signed the night's tab "W.L. Shortreed."

In the early sixties, J.H. (Jake) Moore, originally a partner at Clarkson Gordon, became president of Labatt's. Hardy continued up the corporate ladder and moved to London, and I became a director of the company, in 1966. Under Moore's direction, Labatt's ceased being a regional brewery and spread across the country. As well, Moore launched the company into a diversification program, acquiring the Montreal-based Ogilvie Mills Limited, a long-established flour and food company that owned Catelli's, which specialized in pasta.

When Hardy became president he decided that an association with professional hockey would be beneficial to the growth of the brewery, and I was retained as counsel for the venture. The Oakland Seals of the National Hockey League were controlled by Barry van Gerbig, a wealthy American. Van Gerbig and his partners, who included Bing Crosby, were growing tired of losing big money in operating the Seals. At the same time the people of Vancouver were growing tired of waiting for the further NHL expansion that would allow them to apply for a franchise; and Labatt's was growing tired of Molson's stranglehold on hockey television rights in Canada. (Molson's TV monopoly had made them the front runner in B.C. beer sales.) In 1968 Labatt's entered into an agreement to purchase the Seals' franchise and the team, conditional upon receiving NHL approval for moving the team to Vancouver.

In Vancouver, Labatt's put together a group of gold ribbon,

gold pocket-book community leaders and sports enthusiasts, among them John Davidson, who was in insurance, football, and soccer; Coley Hall, owner of a few hotels and former owner of the Vancouver Canucks' minor-league hockey team; L.G. Bentley of Canadian Forest Products and some shipping companies; his son, Peter, who owned everything his father didn't; Max Bell, chairman of F.P. Publications; Foster Hewitt, the hockey newscaster; and a host of others.

The National Hockey League governors were unimpressed by this élite array. They were not going to allow the Seals to move because in due time they wanted to charge an inordinate amount of money for the franchise when the league was expanded. Toronto and Montreal were opposed because they did not want to share television rights and revenues. I flew all over the United States and Canada with Hardy trying to drum up support, but to no avail. When I finally appeared in front of the NHL board of governors in New York, I was clobbered. After it was clear that we had lost, Toronto and Montreal voted for our application. Labatt's failed to get the franchise but benefited nonetheless when their efforts boosted their B.C. sales over Molson's.

The 1969 failure did not deter Hardy from trying again. In May 1971, he was approached by Doug Smith, a sports broadcaster with extensive international experience, particularly in European hockey. Smith had formed an association with Dan Dooner, a Montreal tavern owner and a valued customer of Labatt's, and the two had devised a plan to form an international hockey league with European teams in Russia, Czechoslovakia, and Sweden, and three teams in North America. The latter would include two in the United States and one in Canada. Long Island, New Jersey, Atlanta, Dallas, Hamilton, Quebec, Winnipeg, and London were on their list of franchise possibilities. Smith had strong contacts in the three European countries. He also was a friend of the czar of international hockey, J.F. (Bunny) Ahearne, president of the International Ice Hockey Federation. Ahearne was the one person who could persuade the European national teams to enter the league.

I drew up a contract between a newly incorporated subsidiary of Labatt's and Smith and Dooner, and in August Allan Johnson of Labatt's, Smith, Hardy, and I were off to Geneva to meet Ahearne and the representatives of the European hockey teams. After three or four days of encouraging negotiations, the Europeans left to get instructions from their federations and we returned home.

The arrangement called for Smith and Dooner to get one American franchise and Labatt's the Canadian franchise. Word came back from Europe that the Russians and Swedes were in but the Czechs were dragging their heels. Hardy and I flew to England to meet with Ahearne to discuss how we would work on the recalcitrant Czechs. Ahearne was confident that he could bring them in and we flew back to finalize the North American arrangements.

Then the bubble burst. In 1971 the World Hockey Association announced its formation and our plan was in the ashcan. The subsequent collapse of the World Hockey Association in 1979 and the success of Alan Eagleson's Canada Cup were to prove that we had been on the right track.

After broadening the scope of Labatt's activities and enlarging the areas of its expansion, Hardy, who became vice-chairman of the Labatt's board in 1973, made early arrangements for his succession, pole-vaulting young Peter Widdrington into the presidency. A sophisticated manager, with a hands-on style, Widdrington has not only accelerated Labatt's expansion in Canada, but has made amazing inroads into various food businesses in the United States.

His responsibilities have not prevented Widdrington from chasing adventure. Seven or eight years ago I planned a trip to Nepal with Bernie Ghert, Jerry Sheff, Tom Kierans, Mike Prentiss, and Peter Widdrington. We were going to make the famed Annapurna trek. Widdrington begged me to say nothing of the trip to his wife, Betty Ann, promising that he would tell her "at the appropriate time." Six months passed. Two weeks before our departure, Peter and Betty Ann, who lived in London, were in Toronto, staying at the Park Plaza. I was in the hotel for a breakfast meeting when I ran into Betty Ann. I said, "Hi, Betty Ann. Is Peter in town with you?"

"Yes, he's upstairs."

"Is he getting excited about our trip?"

"What trip?" she queried.

"Our trekking trip to Nepal," I replied innocently.

"Nepal!" she exclaimed. "He hasn't told me about that. When?"

By now my slow mind had grasped that the "appropriate time" to tell Betty Ann of our trip had not yet arrived. I was in bad odour with Widdrington for weeks, but not as bad as he was with his wife.

Today Peter Hardy is better known in the world as the chief executive officer of the Toronto Blue Jays baseball team, which is partly owned by Labatt's. Hardy is recognized across the continent as the man who set the policy that allowed Pat Gillick and Paul Beeston to build up a successful baseball organization in Toronto in only a few years. Widdrington is on the Jays' board and my partners Herb Solway and Gordie Kirke are the team's lawyers and self-appointed advisers to Hardy Gillick and Beeston, the team's management. They do not accept any assessment as to who is responsible for the Blue Jays' success that does not include them.

In 1979 Peter and Edward Bronfman, through their holding company, Edper, acquired control of Brascan (which had effective control of Labatt's) after a much-publicized fight with management led by Jake Moore. Labatt's, concerned about the effect of the change on its future fortunes, formed a board committee with no Brascan ties, of which I was the chairman. The committee's role was to consider ways of ensuring that Labatt's did not become a casualty of the struggle. We considered a reverse takeover of Brascan by Labatt's, but decided that we should sit the fight out. In the end, I played a role in the peaceful transfer of power from Moore to Edper. Trevor Eyton, Brascan's president, and Jack Cockwell, its executive vice-president, then proceeded to build on Brascan's strong liquid base until today it is one of the strongest forces in Canada in resources, finance, and consumer goods. In 1985 I accepted an invitation from Peter Bronfman and Trevor Eyton to go on the Brascan board.

In October 1953, there occurred a fortunate circumstance that was to have a more significant effect on the growth of my law firm than any other single event. Its genesis was in 1950, when my father gave me the job of acting on a simple landlord-and-tenant application. Our clients were two middle-aged Jewish gentlemen who had rented out a tiny chicken slaughterhouse at the rear of a house on Baldwin Street in downtown Toronto for a modest rent of a few dollars a month. When the tenant decided not to pay any rent, they not unreasonably wanted the slaughterhouse back, and that was the purpose of my application. Since neither of my clients spoke English well, preferring to speak Yiddish, of which I know only a few words, they brought along as interpreter one of their sons, Joe Berman. I won the case and received a $200 fee.

Berman and I became friendly, and he retained me in several other matters. In the late summer of 1953, Berman called to ask if I would have dinner with Jack Kamin, a successful entrepreneur, a wartime navy friend of Berman's named Eph Diamond, and himself. They were going into the development business together. Diamond was a superintendent of building with Principal Investments Limited, a leading early development company owned by the Bennett family whose members have contributed both to the business and cultural life of the country.

We had dinner at the Town Tavern and discussed the partnership. The three men agreed to put in $100,000 altogether, with Kamin and Diamond each investing 40 per cent and Berman 20 per cent. Diamond was borrowing his $40,000 from the bank on the strength of his reputation, backed by Kamin's guarantee. He possessed nothing at all but a house with a fair-sized mortgage. When the talk turned to what to call the new company, Kamin, who owned a Cadillac, said, "I want to name the company Cadillac Developments." I replied, "We will never get that name past the government, but I'll try." To my surprise the provincial secretary approved it and the enterprise was on its way.

When the company started to expand, Gerald Shear, a bright chartered accountant, became a partner, followed by Jack

Daniels, an entrepreneurial architect who replaced Jack Kamin. Although I had no financial interest in the company, I sat on its management committee throughout.

The last half of the fifties and the sixties saw a revolution in housing in Metropolitan Toronto. The need for shelter at reasonable prices resulted in strong pressure for multiple-family housing of ever-growing densities. Cadillac — at one time the largest landlord in Ontario — was in the forefront in providing that housing. But it was soon followed by many other developers: Greenwin Development, Meridian Developments, Belmont Construction, the Glen Group, Erin Mills, East Woodbridge, Camrost Development Corporation, Metrus Management and the Cogan Corporation whose owner Eddie Cogan spent his time finding deals for the other developers. I spent a good part of my professional life travelling across the province trying to obtain the rezoning by-laws, official plan amendments, and development agreements that enabled many such companies to build the houses, apartment buildings, and commercial developments needed to meet the demand.

While apartments were particularly at a premium in Metropolitan Toronto, many owners of single-family dwellings in the vicinity of the proposed developments routinely opposed them. They would turn out by the hundreds to fight the applications for rezoning before development committees, councils, and the Ontario Municipal Board. The object of their venom was usually the developer's lawyer — and far too often that was me. They tripped me, spat on me, jostled me, and called into question my veracity and my motives. Developers are not the most popular members of society. Quite unfairly, the importance of their role in supplying housing stock for people to live in and providing a favourable environment for business and industry is rarely recognized. Landlords have often been denigrated and despised; yet real estate is one of the great entrepreneurial arenas in which many fortunes have been built.

When Cadillac Fairview was in the process of converting streets in the High Park area into a high-rise sector, they were vigorously opposed by the local ratepayer group, led by a sensible woman called Pat Adams, and supported by city alderman and anti-development activist John Sewell. Just before the annual meeting of Cadillac Fairview, many of the ratepayers bought one to ten shares of the company in order to attend the meeting. They brought the media out in force.

While the TV cameras whirred, the meeting progressed. Diamond was gracious and informative. The new shareholders stated their position, which was that the company should not try to make a profit by building apartments but should give them to the tenants when the mortgage was paid off. They nominated several individuals from their organization for positions on the board. When the proxies were voted for the management slate, I got the most votes. Pat Adams had kindly voted for me alone of management's nominees. I said to Diamond, "You're through. I got the most votes. I should be chairman of the board."

While I rarely raised money in any municipal political campaign, I did extract about $1,200 from three or four developers in support of Phil Givens' mayoralty bid. Givens, a Liberal, had been an articling student in our firm. Eph Diamond, ever naïve, frankly admitted to Ron Haggart of the *Toronto Star* that at my request he had become one of Givens' contributors. I was immediately named next day as Givens' "bagman" in a feature story on the front page of the *Star*. Givens, who was well ahead of his opponent, former Mayor Allan Lamport, went into a funk, but I was unperturbed. I knew Givens would win. I sent him a wire saying, "Don't worry, Phil, it's in the bag." He may not have shared my sense of humour, but I was right and Givens won the mayoralty.

The administrative law section of my firm soon required more and better than I. Herb Solway, not being suited for real estate or interested in commercial work, joined me. He was a fine counsel, but even together we needed help and we found it in Allan Leibel, one of our students, whom we recruited at lunch in United Bakers, a dairy restaurant on Spadina Avenue. Today Leibel is a leading counsel in the profession, ably supported by his colleagues Kathy Robinson, Julia Ryan, Roslyn Houser, Steve D'Agostino, Mark Noskiewicz and half a dozen town planners.

At University of Toronto undergraduate law school, I had become friendly with Charles Dubin, a bright student in the year behind me. Dubin studied with another of my friends, Irv Gould, using my illegible notes from the previous year. The two of them were not doing well together, but fortunately for Dubin, Gould and I went into the services and from then on he won the gold medal every year. He subsequently married Anne Levine, also a medallist. After graduation, Dubin and Jack Kimber formed a law firm, which Anne joined on graduation. (Kimber was later to become chairman of the Ontario Securities Commission and president of the Toronto Stock Exchange. He and I had first become friendly after we had engaged in serious fisticuffs in the middle of an intramural football game — an escapade that nearly got us barred from interfaculty sports for life.)

Dubin quickly established himself as one of the ablest young counsels on the Ontario scene. My dad and I often engaged Charles as counsel. In the mid-fifties both firms needed space, so we decided to share offices, which we found in the same building that my father had occupied since the early twenties.

Anne and I did the little administration that was done around the office. One day she quite properly told me that we were not getting sufficient service from the nice lady in charge of the switchboard and that we would have to dismiss her. I insisted that Dubin accompany me on this unpleasant mission. When we began to talk to her, the switchboard operator immediately started to bemoan the problems she was having in bringing up her daughter, saying that she really couldn't do it satisfactorily on her present salary. When we left the office Anne asked, "Well, how did you do?"

I mumbled sheepishly, "We gave her a $10 a week raise." Charles tried to argue that because she had wanted a $20 raise, he thought she would quit if we only gave her $10. That explains why he was a more successful counsel than I was.

It is my belief — a belief that is shared by members of the bench and the bar across the country — that Charles Dubin, one of the most creative and lucid jurists the country has ever had, should have been elevated to the Supreme Court of Canada. A series of unfortunate circumstances, among them Ontario's loss of one of its appointments to the Supreme Court, has prevented him from joining the nation's highest bench. Some years ago when there was a vacancy, after much hesitation, I wrote a lengthy letter to Pierre Trudeau setting forth the reasons why Dubin merited the appointment. Also at that time, I found out later, a chief justice of one of the western provinces had told Minister of Justice Mark MacGuigan that Dubin would be an adornment to the Supreme Court. MacGuigan had replied, "How can we appoint Dubin? He is a Tory and a great friend of Eddie Goodman's. As a matter of fact, not only is he a friend of Goodman, but his wife is a very close friend of Goodman's." The story was related to Dubin by the western chief justice, who wanted to know just how close a friend of Dubin's wife I was. The story ends happily, however, with Dubin's recent appointment as associate chief justice of Ontario, an appointment he much prefers to the bench in Ottawa.

In 1972 Cadillac Development merged with Fairview Development, the real estate arm of Cemp Investments, a series of trusts of which the beneficiaries were the family of Samuel Bronfman, the founder of Seagram's. Cemp was then run by Leo Kolber out of Montreal. Fairview's major holdings were in commercial real estate and shopping centres, and the advent of residential rent control made the merger a good one for Cadillac, which would gain the benefit of Fairview's portfolio of commercial properties. Eph Diamond was made chairman and chief executive officer of the merged company. Under his leadership, Cadillac Fairview grew significantly across Canada and in the United States. Diamond put the absolute lie to the public image of developers. He never went back on his word, he was always concerned about his tenants, and he became the most respected man in his industry. In 1988 he was inducted into the Business Hall of Fame. I have repaid his friendship by persuading him to go into the harness horse business with me. He now enjoys the privilege of losing tens of thousands of dollars, something not even the magic of Jack Kopas, our trainer, can prevent.

Shortly after the Cadillac Fairview merger, Neil Wood, the company's president and chief operating officer, retained me to work on the arrangements with the City of Toronto for the proposed Eaton Centre development, a massive shopping mall and office complex on Yonge Street, Toronto's main drag. While the development faced a myriad of obstacles, Herb Solway put together a development agreement that was finally approved by council. Toronto is now the richer for the Eaton Centre, today the city's number-one tourist attraction.

Time and pressure took their toll and Diamond retired as chairman and chief executive officer to be followed by Jack Daniels, who later decided he liked being on his own and left the company to develop land. The eighties saw Cadillac Fairview continue to prosper under Leo Kolber, chairman of the board, and subsequently under Bernie Ghert as president. Kolber's and Ghert's task was to make certain that the overexpansion of the company that had occurred in the preceding few years was brought under control. Kolber and Ghert effected the change, disposed of the land and housing division and the fringe assets, and radically cut the company's debt.

In 1986 the Bronfman family decided to liquidate their holdings and JMB, an experienced American real estate company, bought all the company's shares, for 2.5 billion dollars. Jim Bullock, who had shown great talent in developing the firm's shopping centre business both in Canada and in the United States, took over as president and chief executive officer of the new company. The old board resigned, and my thirty-four-year love affair with Cadillac Fairview was over, although we continue to perform many of its legal services.

The Law Society of Ontario is the self-governing body for the lawyers of Ontario. It is run by a group of benchers, formerly thirty now forty, elected by the profession, and a small number of government-appointed benchers. In 1966, I decided that it was my professional obligation to stand for election and give some of my time to the Law Society rather than all of it to the Conservative Party. The profession was not quite as enthusiastic as I was about my altruism; I was elected by a two-vote margin and was the thirtieth chosen out of the ninety candidates, the last elected seat. At the next election, however, I moved up to third place for the Toronto benchers, and today I am a life bencher.

While I was concerning myself with the various aspects of administrative law, my partners were engaged in many other fields, strengthening the firm with a broad variety of clients, many of whom became very successful. One such client is Co-Steel International. This company, which started as an idea in Gerry Heffernan's mind, developed from a small specialty plant in Whitby to what is today the most productive specialty steel company in North America, with large plants in Canada, the United States, and Great Britain. Nothing can have been more satisfying to Lionel Schipper, who served on the board and acted for Heffernan from the outset, than to see Co-Steel's growth and success.

The internationalization of the financial business has resulted in the breakdown of many of the distinctions between various types of financial institutions and has allowed substantial cross holdings. Many countries have also lowered their barriers against foreign financial institutions. These changes have affected the professions and businesses — including Goodman & Goodman — that provide services for financial institutions.

Our securities section consequently became much busier and, of necessity, larger. Originally, Lionel Schipper had been the head of this section and Arnie Cader had been his right hand. When they left the firm for careers in business, Lorie Waisberg took over. In the past half decade, Bill Rosenfeld, Steve Halperin, Jon Johnson, and Earl Rotman have become partners in the section with a host of associates, such as Jonathan Lampe and Dale Lastman, who are on their way to partnership. There has also been a sizeable increase in other sections, particularly the tax section under Neil Harris who succeeded Sheldon Silver, and the corporate and commercial law sections, which look after banking loans and other commercial work under Charles Schwartz who succeeded Phil Schwartz and the real property section, with Don Pierce, Gerry Ross, and Ken Karp. Goodman & Goodman recently became part of an international law firm in association with Phillips and Vineberg of Montreal. Goodman, Phillips &

Vineberg now has offices in Hong Kong, New York, and Europe. At one time Sheila Forbes took six lawyers to London.

These world financial changes led to the growth of Canadian financial institutions. I became a director of Central Trust, a Nova Scotia-based trust company controlled by Reuben Cohen of Moncton and Leonard Ellen of Montreal, with both of whom I was destined to form a warm friendship.

Born in Moncton, Reuben Cohen started professional life as a lawyer and built up a sizeable real estate and commercial practice. Montreal-born Leonard Ellen was in the family lumber business until he formed a Damon and Pythias partnership with Cohen. Members of the Maritime financial establishment were not too receptive to a Jewish intrusion into their small-minded world and bitterly resisted the growth of Central Trust and its allied companies. The careers of Cohen and Ellen merit recording by a more skilled chronicler than I. Suffice it to say that their decency and intelligence enabled them to prevail over their opposition and Central grew, qualities that made our personal and professional relationship very rewarding.

Central moved into Ontario in the wake of the Leonard Rosenberg scandal, a scandal that put three trust companies (including Crown Trust, one of Ontario's most respected trust companies) into receivership at the behest of the Ontario government and the federal government's deposit insurance agency, CDIC. The Ontario government and the CDIC chose Central to manage Crown Trust.

Cohen and Ellen were eager to obtain the services of Peter Cole, a senior executive with the Canadian Imperial Bank of Commerce, to head a restructured organization of their disparate interests. My task was to help Ellen negotiate with Cole, then to help Cole restructure their various financial interests. I knew Cole both professionally and because of help he had given me at the Royal Ontario Museum. Tall and good-looking with greying hair and an enigmatic smile, Cole was also one of the most creative and best-connected men in financial circles. In the conservative world of banking he was known as a maverick who liked a good time. During the negotiations Cole insisted on bringing Tom Hodgson of Canada Permanent Trust in with him.

Hodgson hid a mind like a vast computer memorybank behind an inscrutable smile. Cole talked as though they were a two-for-one sale — and it wasn't a one-cent sale.

Ellen was more active in these negotiations than Cohen, who was occupied elsewhere. Time and time again he and I said to each other, "What the hell are those two Siamese twins going to do when we finally hire them?"

On a quiet Friday in June 1987, we received the answer to our question. With the help of Bob Graham, the entrepreneurial president of Inter-City Gas, a company related to Central Capital Corporation, under the noses of two much larger, but more bureaucratic institutions, Central signed a letter of agreement to acquire the interest of the McCutcheon family in Canadian General Securities Limited. This company controlled the Traders Group, which consisted of Guaranty Trust, three insurance companies, and a personal finance company. On Monday, we closed the purchase and Central Capital's holdings made them the fourth largest trust business in Canada. That transaction has been only the first in a long line of Central's acquisitions, which have become too numerous to list. All in less than two years.

Central then turned to the task of building a strong management team. Struan Robertson of Halifax remained Chairman of Central Capital. Alan Lenczner, McCarthy and McCarthy's star counsel, was seduced to become president of Central Capital Management. David Rattee, then president of Lloyd's Bank, took over MICC Investments, and Lewis Dunn became head of its insurance group. Henry Knowles, former chairman of the Ontario Securities Commission, became CEO of United Financial Management, and Earl Bederman became president of BGH Central, the money management subsidiary in which Central acquired a half interest. Then in May of 1988, the Honourable Mr. Justice Estey left the Supreme Court of Canada and subsequently became chairman of Central Guaranty Trustco.

All this activity has changed my role in the law firm drastically. In the early years of practice, in addition to handling litigation I was doing almost every type of transaction, usually alone. Today, my partners won't let me act alone, only as part of a team. When

Goodman & Goodman was retained by Leo Kolber and Bernie Ghert in the sale of Cadillac Fairview Corporation, the completion of the sale required a team of eight or ten lawyers headed by Lorie Waisberg, together with Sheldon Silver, Cliff Lax, Ken Karp, Gerry Ross, Carla Salzman, and me. For the past three years, I have spent countless hours working with Chuck Schwartz, Arthur Jacques, Gord Kirke, Cliff Lax, and Jay Carfagnini — each of whom thinks he is heading the team — to advise Garth MacGirr, Bill Grace, and other partners of Price Waterhouse. Price Waterhouse are the liquidators of the insolvent Canadian Commercial Bank, the first Canadian bank to fail in almost eighty years. Today the complexity even of administrative hearings usually requires the skills of two lawyers and an expert adviser.

None of these big shooters in the corporate world of high finance could compare with the person I have given the title of my most memorable client, James Mathieu of Atikokan in northern Ontario. Mathieu was sent to me at the age of 91 by Alex McKenzie in the mid-fifties. He was involved in a serious tax dispute with the Ministry of National Revenue. He had discovered an iron deposit in northwest Ontario and the ministry would not allow him the prospector's deductions. They alleged that no one at the age of ninety is out in the wilds prospecting. They didn't know Jim Mathieu.

He walked into my office on the first occasion having flown in from Atikokan wearing his vicuna coat and wide-brimmed stetson, plunked down a bottle of Robertson BEB scotch and said, "McKenzie says you're smart. Tell those damn fool revenue collectors I caught pneumonia while sleeping out in the open prospecting. I would have lived to a hundred if I hadn't made that trip." (He died at 97.)

Entirely apart from his prospecting, Mathieu had made and lost several fortunes in lumber since the time he had been a member of the provincial legislature, along with my dad's former boss, E.W.J. Owens, in the late teens about forty years earlier. I won the tax case by the simple expedient of flying Mathieu down to Ottawa where the appeals office soon surrendered in amazement at his vitality at 91. His next step was to go back into the lumber business where, at 94, he personally supervised the building of a mill which he then gave to his grandson, an act he very much regretted as he felt he could run it better himself!

In lieu of fees he kept sending me Robertson's BEB scotch through the mail which usually arrived in smithereens, but he never bought me the vicuna coat that he had promised me. We need more Jim Mathieus.

Fortunately, my practice has not been confined to large corporations but has offered a wide variety of experience. Late in 1982, I received a visit from Louis "Smokey" Bruyère, the president of the Native Council of Canada, and Gene Rheaume, who was in the employ of the council. They retained me to assist them in the approaching constitutional conference on the rights of Native people. I accepted with alacrity. My partner Kathy Robinson and associate Joseph de Pencier also worked on the brief.

After a series of pre-conference meetings with the public servants and responsible ministers, Kathy Robinson said to me, "Something strange is going on at these meetings. Smokey and the chiefs will not attend because the prime minister of Canada does not attend personally. Jim Sinclair, the vice-president from Saskatchewan, represents the Native Council and takes a position contrary to my instructions from the executive. He is playing a different game."

I called Bruyère and said, "Smokey, Kathy tells me that Jim Sinclair is not following the positions that your executive have laid down. You had better start attending these meetings."

Bruyère, a down-to-earth fellow, with whom I had occasionally had a Blue, said to me, "There is no way that I go to a meeting that the prime minister does not attend. Indian protocol is firm about this."

"Smokey, I have warned you; you had better start attending these meetings."

A week before the conference was to begin, de Pencier and Robinson came to my office. "The Saskatchewan Council, with the support of Alberta, wants to break away; it has applied for a separate seat at the conference and separate funding. The

Government of Canada is going to take away one of our seats and give it to them."

I grabbed the phone and called Mark MacGuigan, then attorney-general. "Mark, you can't support the splintering of the Métis people and the weakening of the Native Council of Canada." There followed about five minutes of argument, after which he said he would look into the matter.

The next day I received a call from the deputy attorney-general, who said, "I have discussed this matter with the prime minister. He is most anxious that we do not in any way weaken your delegation and agrees that we should try to keep the Native Council intact."

I replied, "Good for the prime minister. Is that what's going to happen?" He replied, "I certainly hope so."

Unfortunately, when the matter went to John Munro, then minister of Indian affairs and northern development, and back again to Mark MacGuigan, we lost. The government agreed to a separate seat at the conference for the western Métis, although the Native Council did not, after all, lose a seat on that account.

March 15, the day of the conference arrived. Pierre Trudeau rose to make the opening address when a chant was heard in the distance. A group of the treaty Indians danced into the room intoning Indian prayers. Just as he was about to begin anew, the chiefs appeared to smoke the pipes of peace. The television cameras were rolling and the flashbulbs were popping as the Prime Minister and the treaty Indian chiefs prepared to perform this historic ceremony. At the crucial moment the inimitable René Lévesque, sitting beside Trudeau, took out a cigarette, flicked a match on his fingernail in the style that he made famous, and lit up. It was the funniest scene stealing I have ever seen.

The representatives of the various delegations then presented their views about what aboriginal rights they believed should be embodied in the constitution. The western provincial govern-ments would not make significant concessions to my client's claim for land and rights of self-government in the north. The briefs of the various groups contained a wide variety of conflicting views, and the conference was a long way from any consensus on the priorities or scope of aboriginal rights.

One of our client's important demands was equality for Native women, who, unlike their men, lost their treaty rights when they married a non-Indian. Although this was vigorously opposed by the treaty Indian males, Premier Richard Hatfield strongly supported our position, and the principle of equality for Native women was agreed upon. The conference adjourned for an evening working session to draft the technical provisions, a session from which lawyers were excluded, since so many of the clients wanted to be present.

That night I asked what had transpired and was told that the original resolution on Native women's rights had been adopted. At the formal meeting next morning a formal resolution was approved by the various governments and the conference adjourned. When I arrived home, however, my clients informed me that after the night session the original resolution had been greatly altered unilaterally by the federal government's lawyers. The equality of Indian women we had fought for and thought we had won was ephemeral, as was the overall quest for enhanced aboriginal rights.

This chapter skips lightly over forty years of my professional life, which still actively continues. For the unavoidable puffery I apologize. In addition to trying to instil in my younger associates a love of the law, I have tried by example to convince my colleagues that their obligation is to contribute to the community as well as the firm. I have been reasonably successful. This year I obviously carried things too far when my partner Kathy Robinson was elected president of the Liberal Party of Ontario. Clearly David Peterson had to turn to Goodman & Goodman for help.

CHAPTER TEN

ME AND THE MEDIA

My career in law and my interest in politics have brought me into contact with a wide spectrum of media personalities. As my practice broadened my clients included communications and publishing companies as well as many leading personalities in the media. There is no segment of a democratic society for which the paraphrasing of an epigram by Winston Churchill is more apt. Churchill said, "Democracy is the worst form of government except all those other forms that have been tried from time to time." I feel the same way about a free press, whatever its flaws. When all is said and done there is no more important protector of our democratic freedoms than a totally free press.

Unfortunately freedom has too often become licence and freedom of the press has been distorted to mean that individual reporters and columnists, too many of whom are irresponsible and undereducated, have the right to be free from control by editors and publishers. In Canada this development started with a desirable reform. During the period immediately after the war, it was a rare publisher who would allow a columnist to dissent from the editorial position of a newspaper on a public matter. The first Canadian daily newspaper publisher to allow it as a matter of policy was John Bassett in the Toronto *Telegram*. The columnist was that courageous and literate Canadian journalist Judith Robinson, whose father, Blackjack Robinson, had been one of the earlier editors of the *Telegram*. From this embracing of meaningful dissent has grown the practice of filling the daily press with a scarcity of facts and a surfeit of ill-informed opinion. There is almost as much editorializing on the front page of most newspapers as there is upon the editorial page.

My first personal experience with how newspapers can twist the news occurred when I was a freshman at university. I had high hopes of following up my high school success with a Varsity football career. It became clear when I became an early cut that I would be relegated to interfaculty football, so I joined *The Varsity* newspaper sports staff instead. There I rose to the magnificent heights of assistant sports editor and sports columnist. My closest friend was Art Fremes, a medical student who played hockey with the Varsity Blues. I immediately designated myself to travel with the Blues and report many of their out-of-town games. No matter how good a game anyone else played, Fremes was reported in *The Varsity* as the star of the team. Finally, Muchy McIlquham and Mac Craig, the other two members of Fremes' line, came to him one day to complain: "Listen, Art, how about telling your friend Goodman that we are also out there on the ice skating our guts out." The result was more balanced sports reporting for the rest of the season.

In 1958, the new Diefenbaker government announced that it would be issuing a series of additional private television station licences in eight major cities across Canada. On the recommendation of Charles Dubin, who was the *Telegram*'s counsel and who knew of my previous experience acting for broadcasters, John Bassett retained me to act on his application for the licence for the Toronto region.

Our shared experiences both in the army, where Bassett had served in the Seaforth Highlanders with distinction, and in politics, where he had been a Conservative candidate in Sherbrooke in 1945, formed a strong bond between us. Bassett is one of the warmest, brightest, and most articulate of men, but highly volatile. To say that he does not suffer fools gladly is an understatement — he does not suffer them at all. My brother-in-law, Mark Gross, a diamond merchant, says that even the most beautiful diamonds usually possess several flaws. To me that describes John Bassett. A man of great loyalties, he is quick to love but also quick to anger. His good mind is sometimes premature in judgement and he needs people around him who are prepared to tell him when they think he is wrong. That was not always easy to do. His closest friend, Charles Dubin, and

I—since we were both totally independent of him—usually performed that role.

When the *Telegram* was put up for sale, Bassett, with the financial backing of John David Eaton, became the successful bidder, whereupon Bassett put the Sherbrooke *Record*, which he also owned, into a joint Eaton-Bassett trust. The trust provided that the Eaton infant children owned 70 per cent of the equity and the three Bassett boys born at that time owned 30 per cent. Bassett had no beneficial interest himself but was given total control over the management of the publishing business. John Bassett was not an accumulator of wealth. He never tired of saying that he did not want to die a millionaire as long as he could live like a multimillionaire, which he did.

Immediately after the government announced the new TV licences, Bassett told Eaton that he intended to apply for the Toronto licence and proceeded to arrange for the necessary financing. His friend Roy Thomson had large holdings in newspapers and broadcasting interests in Canada and Great Britain, and the two agreed to apply together, with the *Telegram* group holding the controlling interest. Thomson immediately made available Rai Purdy, who had been the program director of the Scottish Television network, which Thomson owned, and his Canadian engineer, Don Williamson, to work with me on the application. The engineer spotted the best piece of land in the Metropolitan Toronto area for the transmitter tower at McCowan and Highway 401. This was purchased at once, giving the company enough property for both the tower and a large building to house studios and offices.

A few months after Bassett and Thomson joined forces, Thomson met with Andrew Stewart, chairman of the newly formed Board of Broadcast Governors, which was responsible for issuing licences. Thomson got the strong impression that his extensive existing holdings in broadcasting and newspapers would doom a Bassett-Thomson application from the start; in order not to jeopardize Bassett's chances of success, he told Bassett to proceed alone or with other partners. Bassett at first refused this offer, but Thomson was adamant and Bassett went looking for other partners in what was to become Baton

Broadcasting.

Shortly after Thomson was out, Bassett notified me that he had made a deal with Foster Hewitt to become part of the application, with a 10 per cent share. Hewitt, the dean of hockey broadcasters, was one of the most popular of Canadians. Bassett and Hewitt were friends from their association in Maple Leaf Gardens. Hewitt's thrift was the reverse image of Bassett's attitude toward money. He would take the bus to Florida, although he was worth millions of dollars.

Bassett dispatched me to meet with Wallace McCutcheon of the powerful Argus Corporation, which controlled Standard Broadcasting, the owners of CFRB Radio. CFRB at that time was the premier radio broadcaster in the Toronto area and a strong candidate for the TV station licence. I offered McCutcheon 35 per cent of a joint venture in which Bassett would have 45 per cent of the equity and would exercise control through a preferred voting share arrangement. McCutcheon's scornful refusal was immediate and total: "There is no way that we'd go into an application without control, and we don't need partners because we are undoubtedly going to win. You tell Bassett that. How could the Board of Broadcast Governors refuse a group like Argus?" He was soon to find out.

Paul Martin, an unsuccessful candidate for the leadership of the Liberal Party just a year before, then approached Bassett on behalf of Paul Nathanson of Sovereign Films Distributors. Bassett told me to put Nathanson in for a 10 per cent share, saying, "It won't hurt to have a big Grit supporting us. Besides, Nathanson knows the film business, which should help." This turned out not to be entirely the case. Nathanson was also to acquire an interest in my uncle's television station in Hamilton in the midst of the licence application hearings, a move that muddied the waters of our proposal somewhat.

The final party to the application—other than Dubin and I, who held 4 per cent jointly—was a company formed by Joel Aldred, owner of the most famous vocal chords in Canadian broadcasting, and young Ted Rogers, now head of Rogers Cable and a prominent media mogul. Rogers' father had invented the batteryless radio and had founded CFRB. I knew the son as head of the Young Progressive Conservatives of Canada. Rogers and Aldred had approached Bassett and showed more confidence and ambition than Planters had peanuts. Their enthusiasm impressed John, but I was worried that, with Bassett and Aldred to control, it was going to be a rocky road to the hearings. My other major concern was that the newly appointed Board of Broadcast Governors would be reluctant to grant the Toronto licence to a company owned by such high-profile Tories for fear of arousing charges of patronage.

The hearings for the licences in Vancouver and Winnipeg preceded the Toronto hearings, and I attended to see how the new board operated. I returned firmly convinced that, to succeed, Baton Broadcasting's application would have to leave the others in the dust so that the board could feel politically comfortable granting us the licence. We needed a detailed, knowledgeable presentation, but one that was also imaginative and exciting. The job of creating it fell to me, with the help of Del Perigoe, the financial man of the *Telegram*, and Rai Purdy.

About half way through our months of preparation, Purdy came up with the inspiration that probably ensured our success. "This is nuts," he said. "We are preparing everything on paper for an old-fashioned oral presentation. We should be doing a great deal of our presentation in the medium we claim to be knowledgeable about—television. We should have a closed-circuit television presentation as the main part of our proposal." It was so simple and so obvious. Bassett gave the okay and Purdy, Perigoe, and I went to work on a multi-faceted video presentation that covered Baton's business structure, its finances, its programming, and its production capabilities. As the application progressed, my law partners Herb Solway and Lionel Schipper joined the team.

When the hearings rolled around in March 1959, the board assigned a half day to each of the ten applicants, to be divided between the presentation and questions from the board. Ours was the fifth application to be heard and we appeared on St. Patrick's Day. As I started the presentation with an introduction of the players, the lights blew in the old Oak Room at Union Station, the site of the hearing. John Graham, the lawyer for

Aldred and Rogers, whispered, "St. Patrick's Day," and I quickly joked, "Mr. Chairman, if everybody would relax I am certain that the elves who come out every St. Patrick's Day will not harm a fellow Irishman like John Bassett, even if he is an Ulsterman. The lights will come back on." Sure enough, in about three minutes the lights were back on.

We had arranged it so that pairs of board members shared a television set on which to watch our presentation. Our *pièce de résistance* was a videotape showing the various types of programs we were proposing to produce. The news section contained an important announcement by Mayor Nathan Phillips, given from City Hall. At Bassett's suggestion, we'd had Phillips record the announcement in private the day before he made it officially for the press. When the *Telegram*, *Globe*, and *Star* came out later the following day with the announcement, they had already been scooped by our closed-circuit television tape.

The interest in the Toronto hearing was incredible. The board had appointed Graeme Haig, a Winnipeg counsel and an old Fort Garry Horseman, to act as their special counsel and to carry out questioning on this application. Knowing Haig's professional integrity, I was sure he would feel compelled to lean over backwards to give us the roughest time. Fortunately, Haig's thoroughness worked in our favour; because everyone in the presentation was so well prepared we looked very knowledgeable.

My main problem in getting our group of prima donnas working as a team was that Aldred thought that as soon as he stepped up to the mike and spoke in his mellifluous voice, the board members would be so enchanted they would rush over to hand him the licence. With help from Bassett, I managed to confine Aldred's speech to a reasonable length. I also had to contain Bassett's overconfidence that our group was a shoo-in for the licence, a view he was impolitic enough to express to the other applicants. In fact, the person the board was most interested in was Foster Hewitt.

While the other applicants contained many able, high-profile, and talented people, including veteran broadcaster Spence Caldwell, and Jack Kent Cooke, the owner of CKEY, they did not present the unified front that Baton did. The only applicant that gave me serious concern was Standard Broadcasting, owners of CFRB through Argus Corporation. The Argus group at the time consisted of E.P. Taylor, Wallace McCutcheon, Eric Phillips, and George Black, all of whom had reputations not only in business but as philanthropists. Phillips was at one time the chairman of the board of the University of Toronto, and McCutcheon had run highly successful capital campaigns for the university and for Toronto General Hospital. Counsel on their application was an Ontario lawyer, Joseph Sedgwick, who was very experienced in criminal and administrative law, especially broadcasting law.

After Standard's presentation, the board's lawyer, Graeme Haig, asked Wally McCutcheon, "Who controls CFRB, Mr. McCutcheon?"

"The board of directors," McCutcheon replied.

Haig smiled. "I know, Mr. McCutcheon, but who elects the board of directors?"

"The shareholders," answered McCutcheon tersely.

"Mr. McCutcheon, would you please tell me, who is the controlling shareholder?"

"The Argus Corporation."

"Mr. McCutcheon, would you please tell me who controls the Argus Corporation?"

McCutcheon turned to Andrew Stewart, the board's chairman, and asked, "Do I have to answer that question?"

Stewart replied angrily, "You certainly do."

McCutcheon cited Taylor, Phillips, Black, and himself. I whispered to Foster Hewitt, "We have just won ourselves a television station licence." CFRB had erred in being cagey about its owners, who came off looking like some sort of secret cabal of the wealthy.

Several years later, Edward Dunlop, who was on the board, told me that their decision in favour of Baton was hard fought, but that the minority who were opposed did so merely because of our strong Tory connections. They admitted that in its knowledge, presentation, and breadth of experience our group had merited the win.

CFTO, owned and operated by Baton Broadcasting, was

launched in January 1961 with a telethon for retarded children. It was to be a while before the station did anything more successful than the telethon. Joel Aldred, CFTO's president and chief executive officer, bought hundreds of thousands of dollars worth of modern television equipment, including what was required for colour broadcasting in the future. While he showed astute technical foresight, Aldred never looked at the top half of the profit and loss statement to see what revenues were coming in. The first seven or eight months were a disaster. The station was from its inception the largest private television station in North America, but it hadn't earned a dollar yet. As we headed towards bankruptcy, Bassett relieved Aldred of his duties and bought him out at a handsome profit, to take over the operation of the station himself. He received expert guidance from staff members Larry Nichols, Ted Delaney, and Murray Chercover.

When Spence Caldwell failed to get the Toronto station licence, he applied for a network licence for the major private stations across the country. The need for the CTV network was clearly there, but the venture was underfinanced and not thought through by Caldwell, the stations, and the Board of Broadcast Governors. It certainly was a case of the tail wagging the dog, because the scheduled stations all had strong obligations by way of Canadian content to meet and large capital investments to amortize. On a comparable basis, the network investment was small. In spite of the Trojan-like efforts of Caldwell and Gordon Keeble, the network venture was doomed from the start.

While Caldwell was getting the network started, Bassett outbid the CBC for the television rights of the Eastern Conference of the Canadian Football League. Football was one of his many loves, and the *Telegram* controlled the Argos. With a little help from me, Labatt's agreed to be the major sponsor, and the others came easily. The stations were no problem to find as they were hungry for large-audience Canadian content. I applied to the BBG for a temporary network licence, which was granted. Later CFTO transferred the football broadcasts to CTV when the new eastern stations agreed to join Caldwell's new network.

CTV as originally structured could not survive under the income-sharing arrangements forced on Caldwell by the new licensed stations. It was soon deeply in debt, and the affiliated stations agreed to purchase control to prevent total insolvency and the loss of the original shareholders' investment.

The problem was not making a deal with the network. It was broke and had no clout. The problem was working out a form of co-operative network agreement that would be acceptable to the nine affiliated stations. Stu Griffiths of CJOH in Ottawa and Larry Nichols of CFTO in Toronto worked with Lionel Schipper and me to try to achieve this minor miracle. A meeting of all the affiliated stations was held in Winnipeg. There the stations, with strong pressure from Griffiths, Nichols, and me, agreed that the financial burden of both capital and operating expenses would be shared on the basis of audience size and ability to pay. Control was simply one vote per station regardless of the size of the share. This together with the advantages of a joint program-buying and time-selling arrangement carried the day. Co-operation was encouraged by the spectre of a BBG-dictated agreement looking over the station owners' shoulders. When Bassett, Schipper, and I arrived at Malton airport to catch the plane for Winnipeg for the final station meeting, we learned that the flight was going to be delayed for a couple of hours. Bassett said, "I'm not going. You have my proxy for the meeting. Get the damn thing settled, Benbo," and he was gone. Schipper joked, "Well, that's 25 per cent of the problem solved." CFTO was to pay 25 per cent of the expenses under the formula.

Once the Winnipeg agreement was signed, all I had to do was win the approval of the BBG at the scheduled hearing. At this stage, my uncle Ken Soble appeared out of left field to oppose the application. He had a brand-new proposal to start a network, with CHCH in Hamilton as the flagship. I was not too concerned about my uncle's proposal. If the CTV stations could hang together, his network would founder. My mother, however, was appalled. "How can you be opposing your uncle?" she asked. "Mother," I replied, "he is opposing me. He is the villain." This simple reasoning failed to overcome her feelings of loyalty to kith and kin.

My strategy at the BBG meeting was to keep the owners out of the presentation and let the broadcast executives help me. For the lead role I chose Murray Chercover from CFTO, who was, along with Stu Griffiths, our most knowledgeable broadcaster. I pushed him front and centre, and he performed impressively. Larry Nichols provided me with all my financial data, and the application was approved. CTV was reborn with Chercover as its president. Unfortunately, my relationship with Chercover and the network did not last.

While events in the next decade established that Baton Broadcasting was the most important communications invest-ment made by the Bassetts and the Eatons, there could not be any doubt that John's true love was journalism. He revelled in being publisher of the *Telegram*, although by the mid-sixties television's fight both for audience and advertising revenue was making serious inroads into the daily newspaper business. The second newspapers in major cities were struggling to keep their bottom line black, and the *Telegram* was in a tough three-paper market against the *Toronto Daily Star* and the *Globe and Mail*.

The antediluvian attitude and editorial policy of management at the *Telegram* before John Bassett and John David Eaton had ignored the changing realities of Toronto. The city's Anglo-Saxon Protestant majority was shrinking with the influx of immigrants, and the Orange Order was no longer politically significant. The *Star* had realized this faster than the *Tely* and held the lead in circulation by 150,000 on weekdays and 200,000 on Saturdays.

In spite of new equipment, a new building, more exciting journalism, and the style and élan of its publisher, the *Telegram* was hard pressed to recover. The two or three years before 1971 had shown a deep red bottom line, and Bassett knew it was impossible to continue unless he received the co-operation of the unions. Bassett while generous was a bad labour negotiator because he didn't play his cards close enough to his vest. He would state his final position at the outset of the negotiations and leave very little, if any, room for compromise. He would hang tough with what he believed was a fair position come hell or high water. Unfortunately, hell usually came before high water, and the result was an occasional strike. In the 1971 negotiations, Bassett informed the unions at the outset what he needed to survive, including important wage and salary concessions. To obtain their confidence he opened his books to independent auditors approved by the union, but though the auditors corroborated Bassett's figures, the unions would not budge.

That September the Bassetts, the Peter Worthingtons, the Dubins, and the Goodmans continued their annual summer rites of going to the U.S. national tennis championships during the last few days of the tournaments at Forest Hills and Flushing Meadows. Journalists Peter Worthington and Yvonne Crittenden and Suzie and I had become friendly over the years, drawn together by our mutual interests in politics, journalism, and tennis. Worthington and I, both walkers, took time off from the spectators' benches to go walking through New York City. At the time the *Tely*'s union negotiations were just starting. We were standing at the corner of Fifth Avenue and 54th Street when Worthington suddenly said, "I don't think the *Telegram* will survive. The unions are too stupid to realize Bassett is not bluffing and cannot afford to carry on this way."

"To fold would be heart-rending for John," I said. "He's a journalist, not a broadcaster at heart. What will you do yourself if the paper closes?"

"A few of us would like to start a morning tabloid, racier than the existing papers, with lots of photos, centred on Toronto, an answer to the *Star*'s left-leaning tendencies. We think we could kill the *Globe* and eat into the *Star*. We would call it the *Toronto Sun*."

"Who are 'a few of us'?"

"It's Doug Creighton's idea. Senior editor Andy McFarlane, Don Hunt, the syndicate manager, and even Johnny Bassett are interested."

"Have you spoken to John?"

"Yes. He thinks it will never fly. He says the failure of the Sunday *Telegram* proved how conservative the city is."

"What do you think?"

"I think we could make a go of it," he said confidently.

"What's the price tag?"

"Three quarters of a million would get it started." Then out of the blue he said, "Could you raise it?"

Long pause, followed by a gulp. "I might be able to. How long would I have?"

"Not long," said Worthington. "We'd like to open the day after the *Telegram* closes."

As we discussed the financing in more detail I grew excited by the prospect and agreed to start making some quiet inquiries of potential trusted investors, provided John Bassett, Sr., didn't object.

By early October it was obvious that the unions were being obdurate and that Bassett was losing patience. He had an opportunity to recoup a fair amount of capital value of the *Telegram* by selling the building to the *Globe and Mail* and the subscription list to the *Star*. Still, he would have kept the *Telegram* alive if he had thought there was any possibility of the paper's breaking even over the next few years.

In the meantime, there were considerable second thoughts among the group of *Telegram* employees who were proposing to launch the new tabloid. Johnny Bassett would have been a great asset to the *Sun*, but he decided that he was going to pursue sports, his first love. MacFarland had an opportunity to become the head of the journalism department at the University of Western Ontario and opted for security. Fraser Kelly, who had considered joining, became faint of heart and opted for broadcasting with CFTO and CBC. Doug Creighton, the leader of the venture, was offered a top-echelon communications job with Air Canada. When I told him, however, that I was confident that we could get enough money for the paper, he stayed in, as did Peter Worthington and Don Hunt.

On September 16, 1971, the union voted on the management's final offer. The vote of the non-skilled members of the staff outnumbered that of the journalists and technicians, the offer was refused, and the *Telegram* was dead. On October 30 Bassett folded the love of his life and walked out of his office without looking back.

Earlier in the month, when it had become apparent that the *Telegram* was probably terminally ill, I realized I was going to have to produce on my promise to find the money for the *Sun's* start. Financing a venture of such a highly speculative nature was not my usual cup of tea. I told everyone I approached, a group consisting mostly of my clients and friends, that they should be prepared to write this one off, but that they would have a lot of fun losing their money. For my own part, I had three strong reasons for helping start a successor newspaper to the *Telegram*.

The first was that it was to be a Toronto newspaper reporting on the daily events of Metro and not posing as either a national or international newspaper. The second was that the three main founders, Creighton, Worthington, and Hunt, wanted to publish an independent newspaper that would not bend to every left-wing cause that came along, and that would be strongly pro-NATO and anti-Communist. The third reason was that, under Bassett at least, the *Telegram* had been a great friend and supporter of the State of Israel and its passing would leave a gap. While there was no suggestion that the *Sun* would fill that gap or that the editorial policy wouldn't allow journalists to criticize Israel, it was to be a newspaper that would recognize and support the concept of a national Jewish homeland and the need for a real democracy in the Middle East. Although Worthington was reputed to be sympathetic to the Arabs, I was confident that he possessed an admiration for the courage and democratic idealism of those who had forged the State of Israel.

The agreement reached by the *Sun's* founders was that Creighton was to be the publisher and that the investing shareholders of the newspaper would not interfere with his freedom to determine the editorial policy of the paper. With an opinionated and influential editor-in-chief like Worthington, that agreement was to prove hard to enforce. Don Hunt was to be the business manager.

Among my prospective investors, Jack Daniels of Cadillac Development was the first to express an interest and to agree to help raise the money. Between us we got a modest commitment from developers Rudy Bratty, who was ultimately to become an important factor in the *Sun's* progress, Eph Diamond, and Joe Berman. Phil Roth of Meridian also made a sizeable investment, as did Paul Hellyer, who was a friend of Worthington's. I tackled

Bill Kelly, the Conservative Party's finance man, who made an investment, but later asked to be bought out. I also successfully twisted the arm of Peter Widdrington, the president of Labatt's. Other early investors included the Mendelson family, Lionel Schipper, Herb Solway, and myself.

The formation of the Toronto Sun Publishing Corporation presented me with a small conflict problem. At that time the CRTC had a somewhat vague policy of keeping the broadcasting media and the print media separate where possible. I was both counsel to and on the board of Baton Broadcasting. I came to the conclusion that I should not go on the *Sun's* board.

Lionel Schipper suggested Edward Dunlop become the president of the company and work on the business end with Doug Creighton and Don Hunt. Dunlop was the bravest and most disciplined man that I have ever met. Our paths first crossed in England when we started joint operations training for the D-Day invasion. Dunlop was a platoon commander with The Queen's Own Rifles, a Toronto regiment in the Eighth Brigade of the Third Infantry Division. The Fort Garrys supported that brigade on the Normandy landing, and we got to know many of its officers and men. During training of the invasion, Dunlop was assigned some very raw recruits, compliments of Mackenzie King's despicable policy on conscription. One of them pulled the pin on a live grenade and dropped it into the slit trench where he (the recruit) was standing. Dunlop jumped into the trench, grabbed the grenade, and threw it, but it went off just as it was leaving his hand. His hand was blown off and he was permanently blinded by fragments of shrapnel. Dunlop was awarded the George Cross. He was sent to St. Dunstan's Hospital, where Dorothy Tupper, Sir Charles Tupper's lovely great-grandniece, was nursing; they fell in love and married. On returning home, Edward took charge of the Veterans Affairs Rehabilitation program, then became executive director of the Canadian Arthritis and Rheumatism Society and later an MLA and cabinet minister in the Davis government.

The *Sun* was located in the Eclipse Building on King Street, recently bought by architect Jack Diamond. At that time, the building was very much the worse for wear, as Diamond had not yet renovated, so the rent was right for a fledgling newspaper. The early morning of November 1, 1971, when the first edition of the *Sun* tabloids rolled off the leased printing presses to be carted off to the repainted *Tely* street boxes stationed along the subway routes was an unequalled occasion of triumph and hope for everyone involved.

Creighton, Worthington, and Hunt had assembled the brightest, bravest, and looniest of the *Telegram* staff. They were the most loyal, dedicated, and talented group of journalists ever to embark on the stormy sea of chance: George Gross, John Downing, Joan Sutton, Paul Rimstead, Doug Fisher, Ed Monteith, Trent Frayne, Lubor Zink, Eric Dowd, John Webb, John Belanger, Jim Coleman, Bob Blackburn, to name a few. These professionals were thrilled at the opportunity to exercise their craft with colleagues they respected in an atmosphere that was quite different from that of such institutionally run newspapers as the *Toronto Star* and the *Globe and Mail*.

From the outset the success or failure of the "Little Paper that Grew" depended on the leadership shown by Creighton, Worthington, and Hunt. The directors agreed that they should have a substantial share interest in the publishing company. This turned out to be an excellent arrangement, as it gave them a financial security that few working journalists enjoy, while also giving the *Sun* continuity. They earned every cent of the stock's appreciation and made large sums of money for those who had had the courage to invest in the *Sun*.

Some months after the first issue, reservations were expressed as to whether Doug Creighton was tough enough to be publisher. These doubts were voiced by some of the leading journalists and technical staff at the *Sun*, including Peter Worthington, columnist Joan Sutton, press manager John Webb and others. At most newspapers, the people in the editorial office and on the printing floors believe that the people in the executive offices know nothing about newspapers and do not work as hard as they do. In this case, however, I was surprised, because no one could doubt that Creighton's career in journalism, from police court reporting to managing editor, had given him a vast experience. Looking back, I see that the doubts were partly caused by Creighton's relaxed management style and, to a greater extent, by the fact that the paper was run on a shoestring, both financially and in terms of its human resources.

I met with the disaffected parties individually and found their concerns to be genuine and not self-motivated. I discussed the problem with Edward Dunlop and Lionel Schipper. Dunlop had formed a close relationship with Creighton and knew the paper's finance and administration much better than I did. Dunlop expressed his support of Creighton in the strongest terms, declaring him essential to the *Sun*'s success. Still, Worthington was the hero of the newsroom, and his opinion had to be listened to. Throughout the insurrection Creighton showed remarkable charity to all the participants, working alongside his detractors without the slightest show of animosity. In the end Dunlop's view prevailed and Creighton received a strong endorsement.

The essence of leadership is the capacity to work with and to attract people. Both Creighton and Worthington had this in a large measure. Strangely enough, though Worthington was brought up in a military family, lived in army camps for much of his youth, joined the navy at an early age, and was a highly disciplined journalist, he did not understand discipline in the executive suite. Creighton was the recipient of more resignations from Worthington than a mink farm has little minks. Eventually he did leave. Nevertheless, in a strange sort of way, the chemistry between the two worked in spite of the frequent flare-ups. Worthington, a knowledgeable, daring journalist, is undoubtedly the best foreign correspondent this country has produced. Creighton exercised his creativity and daring in the executive suite, and without him the *Toronto Sun* newspaper would never have reached its present influence and prosperity. Sun Publishing, which today is an independently run and partially owned subsidiary of Maclean-Hunter, now owns four daily papers.

The best example of Creighton's entrepreneurship was the launching of the *Sunday Sun* in 1973, recommended by Creighton and Hunt and opposed by Worthington and Goodman as premature. Our pessimism was nutured by the dismal earlier failure of the *Sunday Telegram*. The *Sun* was still a financial fledgling, and we felt the risk was too great, but Creighton and Hunt, with Schipper's backing, prevailed and the *Sunday Sun* today has a circulation of 459,952.

In 1978 Worthington, Creighton, and the *Sun* were charged under the Official Secrets Act in one of Canada's most publicized criminal trials. The charges resulted from a column that Worthington had written concerning Communist infiltration into Canada and the failure of the country's security system. The column clearly required the possession of classified information. Creighton, who was not in the country at the time the column appeared, was charged as publisher.

When the matter broke I was out of the city, but I received the news in a long-distance telephone call from David Stockwood, then head of my firm's litigation section. Goodman & Goodman did a great deal of work for the *Toronto Sun*, which kept our litigation section busy. I came home immediately. Everyone agreed that the case required separate representation for Creighton, Worthington, and the *Sun*. In consultation with Creighton, I retained John Robinette, "the dean of Canadian lawyers," to represent him. Worthington chose Julian Porter as his counsel, and Stockwood and I, along with Alan Shanoff, then a junior in my office, represented the *Sun*.

Charges under the Official Secrets Act are rare in Canada. Most of the jurisprudence is to be found in the British courts. While I had not done any criminal work since the late fifties, I threw myself into this case and enjoyed innumerable days searching the law for the theory that would entitle us to have the case thrown out at the preliminary hearing. I had little sympathy for Worthington, as he had known what he was doing when he wrote the column. Julian Porter and I had the feeling throughout the case that he would have liked to have been a martyr and gone to jail for a short but dramatic period. Creighton did not appear to have any such desire.

The day of the opening of the preliminary hearing, the steps of City Hall and the corridors outside the courtroom were crowded with reporters from across the country. You could not walk a step without having a microphone shoved in your teeth. The only major paper in southern Ontario that did not have a reporter in the courtroom was the *Toronto Sun*. During the morning break I asked Creighton, "Surely you fellows feel that this case is newsworthy?" Both nodded. "Then how come the only newspaper in Canada that isn't here to cover it is the *Toronto Sun?*" Whereupon they went scurrying off to find out who had screwed up in their newsroom.

As the case went on, the Crown argued strongly that the national security system of the country had been endangered by the Worthington revelations. I decided that the defence was entitled to read the background files of the various matters that had been referred to in the column. The judge granted an adjournment, and Julian Porter's colleague Wendy Wherry and I obtained security clearance from the RCMP to inspect the files. We journeyed down to Ottawa to spend two days in the bowels of the RCMP building going through the supposedly endangering files. A detailed examination of several dozen allegedly sensitive files showed that the charge was much ado about nothing. The most damning allegation of the Crown was that the column had placed at risk the security co-operation of the United States because it called into question the use of a Canadian businessman as an espionage operative. The files revealed that the Americans had complained about the operative long before the column had. The judge dismissed the case on the grounds that the Crown had not established a *prima facie* case to allow it to proceed to trial.

I have taken a lot of needles for my close relationship with the *Toronto Sun*, particularly from the Big Blue Machine, but I am very proud that I played a small part in its birth and its growth. It has been a strong force in furthering independent journalism in Canada in a manner that the person in the street can understand. Is it often intemperate? Certainly, but never for improper purposes. Has it made serious mistakes? Certainly, but it has always acknowledged them frankly. Has it ever seriously disappointed me? Certainly. Its inhumane position on homosexuality is scandalous. But no newspaper has tried to stay as close to its readers as the *Sun*, and no publisher, editor-in-chief, and business manager have cared as much for the welfare of the staff as Creighton, Worthington, and Hunt.

CHAPTER ELEVEN

THE GREATEST PRIME MINISTER CANADA NEVER HAD

Three straight days of constant television exposure during the 1967 leadership convention made me a better known Canadian face than my old roommate Lorne Greene, and certainly better known than Lester Pearson or Bob Stanfield. I could not walk down the street without being stopped by total strangers every hundred feet. It was a heady experience.

A month after the convention I was invited to the Dennis Coolicans for drinks. Their eighteen-year-old son (subsequently married to Mimi Stanfield) had been in charge of construction and a tower of strength on my convention committee. A woman came gushing over to me and said, "Mr. Goodman, I have been simply dying to meet you, I think you are wonderful!" I modestly protested. She would brook no denial and continued, "You have the most wonderful dress store in Toronto. I buy almost all my clothes there." I was now back to earth.

Stanfield following his victory stepped back to examine the party apparatus he had inherited. Dalton Camp and his supporters felt that the new leader should immediately clean house and whisk away any vestige of the Diefenbaker era, but the new leader looked upon himself as an instrument of reconciliation rather than revolution. Bob Stanfield firmly believed that confrontation was not the way to achieve results, either in dealing with the problems of the country or in his relations with people. This did not mean that he lacked courage. He proved his willingness to face difficult situations many times over, as his support of bilingualism and the Official Languages Bill showed. He just tried to avoid creating bitter divisions within the party and the country.

Indeed, Stanfield had not turned his back on any of his old friends. He asked me and Norm Atkins, Dalton's brother-in-law, quietly to investigate national headquarters and come up with some recommendations as to how it should be run. Subsequently, he appointed me national chairman of organization. While I certainly was never part of Dalton's so-called Mafia, I had played a fairly instrumental part in the change of leaders. My appointment was not a repudiation of what Dalton believed in. Certainly John Diefenbaker would not have thought so.

Stanfield asked Gene Rheaume to act as temporary national executive director while he slowly put the pieces of the party back together and we reorganized national headquarters. There remained unreasonable bitterness within the caucus, particularly among those closest to Diefenbaker. After Stanfield won his by-election in Halifax he was to be introduced to the House of Commons. He very much wanted John Diefenbaker to present him to the Speaker, and Gordon Churchill promised to make the necessary arrangements. Knowing there was no way Diefenbaker would co-operate, I joked to Stanfield, "You must be smoking grass." Sure enough, Diefenbaker stayed away from the sitting, and Mike Starr and Théo Ricard ushered Stanfield into the House.

Voter preferences in the polls during the period from the summer of 1967 to early 1968 were extremely volatile. Just before they called the convention, the Conservatives were in third place behind the Liberals and the New Democrats, with only 25 per cent of the voters' preference; the Liberals were at 37 per cent, the NDP 28 per cent, and the Social Credit 10 per cent. In October, after Stanfield was elected, the Tories moved into first place, with 43 per cent; the Liberals had 34 per cent, the NDP 17 per cent, and the Social Credit 6 per cent. Even in January 1968, by which time much of the excitement and enthusiasm generated by the convention had subsided, the Tories were still in public favour with 38 per cent; the Liberals had sunk to 32 per cent, the NDP were at 18 per cent, and Social Credit was at 12 per cent.

I was concerned about the effect that Stanfield's style of leadership would have on public opinion; he had a tendency to examine every side of every public problem rather than to give a simple clear-cut answer. I remained confident, however, that he would be able to defeat Pearson in an election. Unfortunately, he was not going to have that opportunity. Recognizing that if he could not obtain a majority against Diefenbaker in 1965, he would certainly have a hard row to hoe with Stanfield in 1968, Pearson had announced his resignation in December 1967 and a Liberal leadership convention was called for April 1968.

Immediately after Pearson's resignation, there was a minor parliamentary crisis that revealed again Stanfield's basic decency and his willingness to put country before self. Pearson was holidaying in Jamaica when a government tax bill was defeated in the House. Because the defeat was on a money bill, immediately all three opposition parties, together with the national press, began calling for an election. With the Liberals leaderless and Stanfield ahead in the polls it would have been an excellent time for Stanfield and the Tories to force an election.

Pearson returned to Ottawa and persuaded Stanfield to meet with Louis Rasminsky, the governor of the Bank of Canada, and also to give Pearson a day before he met the House. Rasminsky told Stanfield that an election at that time, when the government was struggling to protect the Canadian dollar and the world was in the midst of a minor monetary crisis, would undermine international confidence in the Canadian economy. Having used what was supposed to be the most independent of public servants in this political manner, Pearson then took the day of grace given to him by Stanfield and went on television to persuade the country that his defeat on a minor tax bill did not require him to resign.

In the meantime, the Liberals went to work on the Social Credit members to ensure that they did not vote against a motion of confidence that the government was introducing to the House. The answer to that strategy was clearly a filibuster on the vote, which might have brought the government down, but Stanfield refused to follow this measure, although it was supported by most of the caucus. Pearson received his reprieve. Stanfield's political generosity cost him dearly. It set back his efforts to unite the caucus and obtain the support of the Diefenbaker diehards, who were not used to a leader who put the country's welfare before winning.

Stanfield telephoned me during the excitement. "I will probably hurt myself in caucus by not staging the filibuster, but I believe that what I am doing is right," he said. "What do you think?" My answer was that in the long run he would probably be stronger for following his conscience. In hindsight I was probably wrong and should have urged him to try and force an election, which he would undoubtedly have won.

Stanfield did make one tactical error that the Liberals were later to use to advantage. In February 1968 a disagreement between the government of Canada and the government of Quebec caught the attention of both public and press. Quebec wanted the right to send a representative to a conference of French-speaking nations that was to take place at Gabon in Africa. The federal government, ever jealous of what it viewed as any encroachment on its foreign affairs' jurisdiction, strongly opposed Quebec's sending an independent delegation.

After my appointment as chairman of organization, I decided that it would be helpful for Stanfield to have an off-the-record dinner party for the Toronto press at the Albany Club, the home of many Tory gatherings. The purpose was to allow the press to meet Stanfield on a more personal level and give them the opportunity to obtain his views on a variety of matters. The dinner was attended by about forty or fifty of the local media. It had been made clear to all the guests, both with the invitation and at the dinner, that this was to be an informal meeting, strictly off the record. Stanfield made a short speech after dinner and fielded questions. In response to a question about the Gabon conference, he said that he saw nothing that endangered Canada's unity if, in addition to the federal representation, Quebec sent its own representative to discuss matters that fell within the province's jurisdiction. The next morning, the *Globe and Mail*, with its usual disregard for promises of confidentiality, and without having spoken to us at the meeting, published a story about Stanfield's Gabon position. Stories then appeared across the country suggesting that Stanfield would give foreign affairs jurisdiction to Quebec. Nothing could have been farther from the truth, but the opportunity was now available for Pierre Trudeau, soon to become the Liberal leader, to give credibility to his self-portrait as the preserver of a united Canada. Today, in light of the Meech Lake Accord, which enshrines Quebec as a "distinct society" within Confederation, the Montmorency discussions and the Gabon remarks appear very mild indeed.

There was never any doubt in my mind following Pearson's resignation that the one person we could not beat, Pierre Elliott Trudeau, would be chosen to lead the Grits. The only two candidates who had an outside chance of defeating him were Paul Hellyer and Bob Winters. Hellyer had been Pearson's defence minister, and Winters, a former minister of trade and commerce, had previously been chief executive officer of Brazilian Traction, Light and Power, until Mike Pearson persuaded him to return to politics by promising to make him minister of finance (he then reneged on the promise). Hellyer blew his chances of winning by making a very poor speech. When the last ballot was counted between Trudeau and Winters, Trudeau won handily.

While Trudeau had, during the course of his campaign, clearly stated that he would not call an election if made leader, only a saint or a fool would have turned down the opportunity shown by a more than twenty-point lead over Stanfield in the polls. Trudeau was neither: three days after the convention he dissolved Parliament and called the election.

Stanfield asked me to be chairman of the election campaign and I accepted, knowing, however, that I was going to end up an object of hatred, ridicule, and contempt within the party. Whatever laurels I had won for running the convention would be down the drain after the election. Trudeau had risen like a rocket, and his unconventional style dazzled everybody but senior business, who nevertheless supported the Liberals because they knew they were going to win. Despite my misgivings, my admiration for Stanfield as a solid leader with a depth of intellect and a strong sense of decency made it impossible to refuse his request. I knew I could rely on the able assistance of two of his staffers, Lowell Murray and young Joe Clark, the former president of the Progressive Conservative Students Federation.

There was little permanent staff at national headquarters as we had just hired our executive director, Malcolm Wickson, who had barely put his rear end into a chair. I had to recruit a national campaign committee for which I drew mostly on young people and students. Flora MacDonald was teaching at Queen's and, while I was tempted to bring her back to national headquarters, from which she had been dismissed in 1966 by Diefenbaker loyalists, I decided that it would be a mistake to relive the past. Stanfield's staff, including Lowell, were all of the same opinion. We decided instead to use her out in the field with Stanfield and on special assignments. She was not happy about my decision, but I was convinced it was the correct one.

Even before Pierre Trudeau became leader the contentious issue of the *deux nations* policy, raised at the Montmorency Falls conference, ensured that our campaign would be an uphill fight. Stanfield viewed the whole controversy as a meaningless semantic argument that divided rather than united Canada. His simple position was that we should endeavour to understand French Canada and encourage French-speaking Canadians to maintain and strengthen their language and culture, a view not too different from Pearson's when he set up the Royal Commission on Bilingualism and Biculturalism.

We started the election campaign under financial constraint. Bev Matthews, the party treasurer, initially made a very conservative commitment of funds. Although towards the end of the campaign he was able to give me more than he had undertaken, by then the damage had been done. We decided that we were not going to be able to match the slickness of Trudeau's style and campaign. Our cost-saving strategy was to rent a more modest airplane that could go to the airports in smaller towns and cities across the country where a DC9 would not be able to land. We thought this would give our campaign a homespun appearance, in keeping with a homespun leader. We hired an inexpensive DC7, which the press dubbed the "Flying Banana," a reference to our leader's alleged love of bananas. We turned over the management of this part of the campaign to a loyal Tory who had a small airline in British Columbia, on the assumption that he knew something about arranging schedules and handling these matters. It was a disaster: he never seemed to understand the two-hour time requirement to warm up the old engines and we were always late.

Just prior to the campaign's start, Stanfield, Dalton Camp, and I met at the Constellation Hotel near the Toronto airport to discuss policy. The three of us agreed that the country would be much better off with a social program based upon a guaranteed minimum income for everybody instead of the hodge-podge of social programs that existed then and exist today. When we announced the proposal it was unpopular within the party and badly explained to the public. Neither Stanfield, Camp, nor I had thought it through, nor did we have the resources or the time to do so. Two years later at the Niagara Falls policy conference we fleshed it out and it received a much better reception. Unfortunately, social programs once embarked on are difficult to change or modify, and no government yet has had the courage to implement a minimum income policy, although it has won favour with some respected conservative economists. I like to think that we were just well ahead of our time.

In accordance with my usual format, the opening meeting of the campaign was to be a show of strength and to reinforce our strongest geographical position. We started the campaign in Winnipeg, partly because I wanted to get Duff Roblin, now a federal candidate, some high-profile coverage. For the opening meeting I had lined up John Robarts, the prime minister of Ontario, Ike Smith, the premier of Nova Scotia, Walter Weir, who succeeded Duff Roblin as premier of Manitoba, and Marcel Faribault, our most prominent candidate in Quebec. The preparations were well in hand and 4,000 people poured into the auditorium to a meeting that ended as a total disaster. The original speakers, notwithstanding my strict instructions, all went considerably over the time, especially Faribault, and by the time Stanfield was to speak we had missed almost all of national television. I was so infuriated that I nearly ripped the microphone out of several speakers' hands.

The next day we flew to Yorkton, Saskatchewan, to visit some grain farms and grain elevators. While Stanfield was being shown one of the more important grain farms, I sat on a rail fence watching a young lad ride a palomino horse bareback with only a halter. I have ridden all my life, so I asked him if I could take a turn. I then jumped on and took a canter around the field a couple of times. Unfortunately, the Canadian Press photographer saw me, and the front page of most of the western papers the following day carried a picture of me riding the palomino bareback, but none of Stanfield visiting the grain elevator. I received an invitation from Lowell Murray to return to Ottawa to run the campaign, with a not-too-polite reminder that my job was to get Stanfield's picture in the paper, not my own.

One aspect of the campaign, however, was running smoothly: we were attracting good candidates, particularly in Quebec. Stanfield had made it clear to me at the outset that one of his major objectives was to establish a beachhead in that province. He was spending a great deal of time learning to speak French and would not hesitate to embarrass himself by trying to keep a conversation going in that language, winning the respect and admiration of many francophones.

I was getting advice on the Quebec Tory scene from a young Quebec student of Irish-French origin by the name of Brian Mulroney. I found him bright and quick and able to fill the gap while I negotiated with Quebec premier Daniel Johnson. When I look back at how badly the campaign screwed up in 1968, I console myself by saying, "I had two future prime ministers of Canada, Clark and Mulroney, advising me, so maybe it wasn't meant to be." Johnson was very supportive of Stanfield and produced Jean Bruneau to run our campaign in Quebec and several fine candidates, including Marcel Faribault, president of Trust Général.

Finally, things on a local riding level began to improve, aided by the support of the organization I was putting together. It included such people as Julian Porter, Bruce Le Dain, Peter McKerracher, and Doug Bassett. Porter, a Toronto lawyer, later ran as a provincial candidate in 1985; McKerracher and Le Dain, who worked on my ads and pamphlets, were both from Montreal. Le Dain is today one of Canada's premier artists. Doug Bassett, John's middle son, now runs Baton Broadcasting.

As the campaign progressed, Trudeaumania was sweeping the

country and crowds of historical proportions were turning out to see the Liberal messiah. One day in the middle of the afternoon I received a frantic telephone call from my wife, who informed me that she was standing in my office, which in those days overlooked Toronto's City Hall. "I am looking out your tenth-storey window watching Trudeau. There are over 100,000 people in the audience. You've got to do something." I rather curtly told her to call me back when she had some good news and hung up.

Like any other mania, Trudeaumania is not easy to explain. The definition of mania is "mental derangement marked by excitement," and I am quite willing to accept that explanation for the unbelievable crowds that thronged shopping malls and public squares across the nation to cheer Trudeau. The future prime minister was not a great orator, or a warm human being, but his personal flair, sophistication, and irreverence offered a novel appeal to the voters. With many he scored points for appearing to be a French Canadian willing to tell other French Canadians that they were not entitled to special treatment. On examination, his policy in this area differed little in substance from Stanfield's except that Stanfield was prepared to discuss the issues with the nationalists, while Trudeau preferred confrontation. The fact that much of the press also succumbed to Trudeau's glamorous image, especially the obsequious *Toronto Daily Star*, made my job all the harder. The truth of the matter was that there was no way to reverse the flow. We simply had to fight the campaign riding by riding, while stressing the honesty and intellect of our leader.

It was a tough challenge to make the public appreciate Bob Stanfield's depth of character and leadership qualities. Unfortunately, changing the public image of a leader that has been formed before an election is well-nigh impossible during the campaign, particularly when the leader is far more impressive in small groups than before large audiences. Stanfield's performance in the House after he assumed the leadership had been lacklustre and had added to his reputation as a plodder who was no match for the mercurial Trudeau.

I decided that I would use some of my extra funds to have a

movie based on Stanfield's life produced and run it during prime-time television. The director I chose had the reputation of being sensitive, progressive, and a bit off-beat. He and his film crew were to travel with Stanfield wherever he went, and we expected nothing less than a masterpiece of cinematic propaganda. Julian Porter and I carefully chose what we believed to be the most advantageous time during the campaign to air the film, booked it, then started our publicity program to build up the audience. We made our ads provocative enough to attract Canadians who don't usually look at political television and waited patiently for the completion of the production. The great day arrived and Canada gathered around its television sets to have the sensitive, intellectual, witty Stanfield unveiled.

Unfortunately, our advertising campaign had been overly optimistic. Instead of a dynamic, compelling portrait of a man poised to grasp the reins of power, we watched clichéd shots of Canada's forests, lakes, streams, cities, and villages, plus some thoughtful philosophical views from the leader of the Progressive Conservative Party. We got scathing reviews for what was nevertheless a sensitive portrayal of our leader.

About halfway through the campaign, headquarters received a series of requests from the Jewish newspapers and periodicals for Stanfield's position on the Middle East. I got in touch with Lowell Murray and Joe Clark and asked them to send me at least a draft that I could use. Time went by and the newspaper deadlines were on top of us, yet nothing had arrived. I kept bugging Murray, who said that he had not been able to get anything out of Stanfield. I realized then that if our Middle Eastern policy was going to be made public it would have to be written by me. I wrote out for the press what I thought were the soundest reasons yet to be voiced by the western world for supporting Israel as the only democracy in the Middle East. Stanfield's lack of strong sympathy for the valid aspirations of the Jewish homeland always concerned me.

The polls, while they had shown some considerable improvement, still showed us running far behind the Liberals. We decided that we would publish our own poll based upon some rather superficial inquiries that Gene Rheaume would make across the country in the most optimistic areas. It would be published by Confederation Publishing, which was a wholly Tory Party-owned company. The Rheaume-Goodman poll showed the Tories with a comfortable lead out west, a small lead in the Maritimes, within striking distance in Ontario, and doing better than usual in Quebec. This added up to the Tories making considerable gains since the last published Gallup poll. I subsequently published the poll as a front-page splash in the party newspaper, which was made available to all the candidates to distribute in their ridings in the last week of the campaign.

Through a coincidence in the schedules of Stanfield and Trudeau, all the parliamentary press were in Ottawa, so I called a press conference. It was attended by more than sixty reporters from the major media outlets. I told them that I had two very important announcements to make. The first was totally confidential, and if anybody didn't feel that they could receive it in confidence, they should please let me know and I would ask them to leave. The second was available for publication.

I informed the breathless press gallery that I had it on absolutely impeccable authority that Pierre Trudeau was a lousy lay and that Bob Stanfield went home every day for a nooner. The gallery took that in the good-natured way that it was meant and waited for the momentous announcement. I then distributed the poll to gasps of disbelief and, in some cases, open derision. After a barrage of skeptical questions, I thanked them for attending and left.

No one had expected the poll to be believed. I had not tried to camouflage the fact that it was taken totally under the auspices of the Conservatives. I countered that criticism by saying we knew more about polls at headquarters than any pollsters did, which was probably true. The main purpose of the exercise, apart from giving Rheaume and me a few laughs, was to slow down the media's reporting of polls and perhaps make them question their accuracy. When I sent out the newspaper with the poll, about 25 per cent of my Conservative candidates also didn't believe a word of it and refused to distribute the newspaper.

Around this time I received a visit from Murray Chercover and Charles Templeton, the president and executive vice-president respectively of the CTV Television network. They wanted to broadcast a debate between Stanfield and Trudeau. Up to then, there had never been a TV debate during a federal election. I told them that I would think about it and let them know our decision within forty-eight hours. It was clear from our meeting with the network that the Liberals, although they had not definitely declined, were not eager to debate. Privately, I didn't blame them; they were already winning and had little to gain.

I spoke to the leader and to Lowell Murray, as well as to the inner campaign committee, including Flora. I also telephoned Dalton for his views. Together we decided that we should go for broke. I immediately told first the network and then the world that the leader of the Progressive Conservative Party was both willing and eager to debate with the prime minister. When the Liberals didn't respond to the challenge, I followed up with a barrage claiming that Trudeau was afraid to debate because the Liberals had no policies — which was true. Finally the Liberals replied to the network that they would debate, but they insisted that the NDP should be included.

I wasn't too happy with that condition because Tommy Douglas had a great deal more parliamentary experience than either Trudeau or Bob Stanfield. I figured, however, that perhaps the Grits had made a mistake, because Tommy could help Bob make Trudeau look bad, so I accepted. The Liberals, who had expected a Tory refusal, started to back-pedal. Now they would only debate if Créditiste leader Réal Caouette was included. This was getting to be more than I could stomach. The Créditistes had no seats outside Quebec. Our intention had been to pit Stanfield against Trudeau; the others were an unwelcome distraction. I consulted the campaign committee, and we agreed to allow Caouette to come on air for the last part of the debate. This was to be another serious blunder on my part.

When the night of the great debate arrived I plunked myself down in front of the television to watch what I thought might be my last opportunity for salvaging the campaign. True to my fondest hopes Trudeau made a poor showing. Stanfield was nervous at the outset, then gathered strength. Tommy Douglas was predictable. The hero of the evening was Réal Caouette, who came on late and made the most outlandish and ridiculous economic statements with great humour. His star performance was to have disastrous consequences for our campaign in Quebec.

CTV had a reception after the debate. On the way up to the CTV suite, I met Keith Davey and Trudeau, who went into the room ahead of me. At that time the only two people in the room were Flora MacDonald and Mary Stanfield. Trudeau turned on his heel angrily and started to leave, when Barbara Chercover arrived to welcome him. This made it impossible for him to escape. I walked across the room and introduced myself to the prime minister, whom I had never met. He snarled, "So you're the sonofabitch that started all this," and walked to the other side of the room. That encounter was the greatest satisfaction I had in the entire campaign.

Stanfield campaigned in 1968 with courage, integrity, and humour despite the many frustrations he faced. He and I spent the Saturday before the Monday vote helicoptering across Ontario from west to east, landing in London, Stratford, Oshawa, Port Hope, Peterborough, and Lindsay, all areas where we felt our chances were good but where the vote would be close. The only bitterness Stanfield ever displayed occurred when once, after a few drinks, he vented his rage to me privately at the dishonesty of the Prime Minister, the Liberals, the *Globe and Mail*, and many of the English metropolitan papers who, using the Gabon remark as evidence, were suggesting that he was less dedicated to a united Canada than Trudeau. Indeed, some of the local Liberal campaigns were so viciously distorted that even Trudeau had to apologize on one occasion.

One small example of Stanfield's personal courage occurred towards the end of the campaign when he was touring Nova Scotia in a small single-engine airplane with Julian Porter. A thunderstorm started and the pilot had to bring the plane down somewhere. The only place available was a nearby highway. While Porter sat white-knuckled, Stanfield showed no more fear than if he had been getting on his bicycle to go to the corner store for some milk. He sat back, quite relaxed, and let out a series of quips while Porter listened to his own knees knocking together.

When he returned to Ottawa, Julian begged me, "If I ever want to go out again with him, *please* stop me."

After the last swing through Ontario, Stanfield returned to his native province for the Sunday and Trudeau went to Montreal to review the annual St. Jean Baptiste Day parade with Daniel Johnson. Thousands of separatists joined the procession to express their views, inadvertently giving Trudeau his biggest boost of the campaign. They started to chant in derision at Trudeau and pop bottles were sailing everywhere. One of them landed on the reviewing stand near the prime minister. Police wanted to shield him, but Trudeau would have none of that and howled his defiance at the separatists. It was wonderful television. Although election campaign material was not allowed on television that day, news was. Canadians across the country witnessed Trudeau's courage. It was worth several hundred thousand votes in English Canada — Dalton Camp said forty thousand votes in Toronto alone — and, I am certain, cost us at least half a dozen close seats. As I watched the television set that night I mouthed every obscenity that I knew.

On the last day of the campaign, when we were flying together in a helicopter, Stanfield asked, "How many seats do you think we'll win?"

Over the whirling props, I said, "Between eighty and eighty-five."

"That wouldn't be too bad if we got a few in Quebec. Are you certain it won't be fifty?"

"Don't be ridiculous," I replied.

In fact, we won 72 seats, 25 less than the previous election. The Liberals took 115 seats. We had only 4 seats in Quebec, where the anti-Trudeau vote went to the Créditistes, who won 14 seats. The four Atlantic provinces remained loyal and we won 25 of 32 seats, 7 better than in 1965. It was Ontario, however, where we were shellacked, winning only 17 of the 88 seats. We also lost heavily in Manitoba and had no seats in British Columbia.

As the disastrous results started to flow in from Ontario and Quebec, Gene Rheaume came over to my desk and said, "How about a a drink, master."

"Bring me a cup of hemlock," I replied.

Stanfield called me the next day and asked me to fly out to his home in Halifax. When I arrived, Flora, Lowell, and Finlay were there. Stanfield and I spent an hour together alone. He said to me, "My brother Frank has told me that I absolutely must resign. What are your views?"

I disagreed strenuously. "You would be letting down the country, the party, but above all yourself. The Grits have come straight from a convention with a leader whom the country has fallen in love with but knows nothing about. We all know what happens to leaders, such as Diefenbaker, who fail to fulfil expectations. Only you can test Trudeau and prevent the party from falling into the hands of the rednecks."

He finally agreed to stay on for a couple of years, knowing that there would likely not be an election before 1972. It was now my turn to resign. "I made a whole series of mistakes during this campaign for which only I can be blamed," I pointed out. "If I go it will ease the pressure on you." He urged me to stay, saying that we had raised our popular vote during the campaign by 6 per cent, not bad for a tough campaign. Ever gracious, he said, "The election was lost in the fall and winter when I assumed the leadership of the party." Stanfield was a class act then and has remained a class act to this day. The greatest prime minister the country never had.

On June 26, 1968, the day after the election, the happiest man in Canada was not Pierre Elliott Trudeau, but John George Diefenbaker. His successor, an intrinsically sincere Nova Scotian who had given up a position of comfort to serve his fellow Canadians, had suffered a devastating defeat. The icing on the cake was that moderate, intelligent candidates representing, in many cases, those who had supported the party's effort to replace the leader had been defeated, while the rednecks, for the most part but certainly not totally from the west, had held on to their seats. It mattered not to him that Stanfield, in every election, and particularly in 1965, just three years earlier, had supported Diefenbaker with greater vigour and energy than any other provincial leader or premier. It mattered not that at every revolt prior to 1966 Stanfield had stood by the leader and endeavoured to put out the fires his own friends and supporters were igniting.

It mattered not that the party that had brought Diefenbaker to the highest office in the land and given him his place in history was in danger of being destroyed. All that mattered to Diefenbaker was that in his own mind his leadership was vindicated. Nothing, of course, was further from the truth. If Diefenbaker had been the leader in the 1968 election, we would have been routed in the Maritimes also, as we were in Ontario, Quebec, and British Columbia, and many of the members who did survive would not have done so.

Notwithstanding his general unpopularity, Diefenbaker still enjoyed a large reservoir of affection, especially among older people. There were many places, particularly in the west, where he could have helped Stanfield during the campaign. He refused to do so. All the requests and invitations he received from members, from his great friend Bill McAdam, whom I sent down to Prince Albert to convince him, and finally from Stanfield himself, fell on deaf ears. Diefenbaker would not speak even on behalf of a selected few of his loyal friends. I believe he made only one, unpublicized address during the whole campaign. At the time I was too busy to think about why, but in retrospect it was clear that he wanted to be able to say he had had nothing to do with the campaign, a boast he later made on several occasions. He lied blatantly, complaining that he was never asked to participate when I knew he had been asked at least a dozen times. In a perverse sort of way, after the election I was pleased that he had acted in this manner, because it confirmed everything I thought about him in the later years. He was every bit as petty, vindictive, and paranoid as I had known he could be.

Looking back at the three and a half years that followed the 1968 election, I am amazed that Bob Stanfield had the courage, the dedication, and the understanding of the country's needs to stay on as leader of the opposition. It was not fun to head what was certainly, at the outset, the most divided, disruptive group of members that the Conservative Party had ever had the misfortune to call its own. Even more trying was that while many of them were intelligent, few were contemporary in their outlook. Stay he did, however, and slowly and doggedly, with the help of a loyal and able staff, moulded that caucus, certainly not in his image, but at least into a responsible body that adopted policies that genuinely were in the best interests of the country. He revealed weaknesses in the Prime Minister who, on too many occasions, appeared intellectually arrogant and — even more unforgivable — intellectually lazy. No man deserves to be prime minister if he is not prepared to devote the time and care that it takes to understand the economic problems, both domestic and global, that face the country. Trudeau never did that. He never had a consistent economic policy during all the years he was prime minister.

Throughout this period, I thought of Stanfield as a great conciliator. He had the necessary determination and discipline to achieve his ends over what at times appeared absolutely incredible odds. He worked with every group in caucus and consulted friend and foe alike, including Diefenbaker. He made up his mind as to how far he could bring his caucus to his point of view without serious disruption and went about that task. He was ably assisted by Graham Scott, now a Toronto lawyer, Bill Grogan from Winnipeg, a wonderful wit, and Tom Sloan, a journalist and the group's social conscience, all of whom carried various burdens with loyalty and ability.

In the spring of 1969, Stanfield faced his first major policy crisis when the Official Languages Bill came in front of the House. Ever since winning the leadership, Stanfield had made clear the importance he placed on maintaining French not only as an official language but as a working language for as many Canadians as possible. His conciliatory views on French cultural aspirations had been distorted by the Liberals throughout the 1968 election and had not only cost him seats in English-speaking Canada, but had brought down upon him the wrath of many of his own members. Jack Horner, Robert Thompson, Bob Simpson, Stan Schumacher, and Robert Coates were his strongest critics on this issue. John Diefenbaker, the great exponent of loyalty to the leader, threw in his lot with the rebels. The polls showed that 44 per cent of Canadians overall and more than two-thirds of people in the West were opposed to the bill, but Stanfield was unmoved. From the outset he worked on his caucus member by member, and when the vote was taken in the

House on the second reading it was 191 in favour with 17 defectors, one of whom was Diefenbaker.

On superficial inspection one would not have believed the vote a great triumph for the leader, but in my opinion it was a considerable feat, given the level of public opposition. Rational arguments are always used to cover latent bigotry, and, of course, they were all trotted out during the debate. (The act that made Stanfield furious was that the opponents of the bill forced an individually recorded vote on the second reading.) Geoffrey Stevens, in his book on Stanfield, quotes Lowell Murray as saying that in the caucus that followed Stanfield made a "sulphurous speech. It was really sizzling," in which he said of the rebels that "their stupidity was exceeded only by their malice. There are some things one does not do to one's colleagues." Those who pushed Stanfield too far were likely to witness the firm mettle that lay under his amiable exterior.

Stanfield was always searching for policy ideas at an understandable level. Whether it was sending Heward Grafftey on a cross-country tour to get people's views on housing or suggesting to me, when I was invited to sit on the original Committee for an Independent Canada, that he was most interested in obtaining some deeper objective views on foreign investment, or commissioning Eric Ford of Clarkson Gordon to study capital gains, he always wanted to know more.

A Conservative policy conference in Niagara Falls, organized for October 1969, was to be a sounding board for members, leading party workers, and academics. I was concerned that it would be a total disaster, but with considerable help from Flora MacDonald and Stanfield's staff, it turned into a reasonable showcase for some of the more progressive ideas within the party. We generated a more detailed outline of a guaranteed annual income plan, the policy that had been such an albatross during the election campaign, and came up with some policies for tax reform, including a capital gains tax.

One August summer morning in 1970 I woke up to read the morning paper and find out that there had been some sort of half-assed western members' conference called by Jack Horner in Saskatchewan at which a group of right-wing members had assembled. By pure chance the press had discovered it and immediately called it a revolt against Stanfield's leadership. Jack Horner, who ran for the leadership in 1976, denied this vigorously, saying that the conference was called to make recommendations for a better party organization and to reduce my influence in the scheme of things. Never having had any overt disagreements with Horner or with any of the western members of the caucus, I picked up the telephone and suggested to Jack that perhaps, in view of what I had read in the papers, he and I should meet. I offered to fly down to Ottawa to lunch with him. The following week, we had a quiet lunch at the airport. I asked Jack directly, "What is your beef and what should I be doing that I haven't and what have I done that I shouldn't?"

Horner's reply was straightforward. "I have absolutely no beef against you whatsoever, but when we got caught having our quiet caucus, I had to have somebody that we were complaining about other than Stanfield and so I chose you." I thanked him very much for having lunch and told him that if he ever had any ideas, wanted me to do anything to motivate the provincial organizations in Saskatchewan and Alberta, please to let me know. Thus subsided the only open revolt against Stanfield's leadership. By September Stanfield was in control of the party and edging up in public esteem.

In Quebec there had been for several years some scattered acts of terrorism, including several bombings attributed to Front de Libération du Québec. Then in the fall of 1970, in two separate, unrelated incidents, James Cross, the British trade commissioner, and Pierre Laporte, the Quebec minister of labour, were kidnapped. On October 16 Trudeau declared that Canada was facing an "apprehended insurrection" and invoked the War Measures Act and, later, the Public Order Act, putting the country under martial law with none of the traditional protections of habeas corpus, freedom from arrest, right of assembly — in short a total revocation of all civil liberties. Furthermore, he refused to reveal to the public or to Parliament the basis for this draconian step. The action was one of the most shameful breaches of civil liberties in Canadian history, ranking with our treatment of Japanese and Italian Canadians in the

1940s. It has recently been revealed in the diaries of the late Don Jamieson, Trudeau's minister for external affairs, that the cabinet had no evidence of an apprehended insurrection when the act was invoked.

In his excellent essay entitled "Some Implications on Terror in Quebec," James Littleton points out that "terrorism is distinctly different from insurrection. Insurrection is the act of rising in open-armed rebellion against civilian authorities . . . . Terrorism is the instrument of a weak minority. It can succeed only because of the ineptitude or mistakes of its adversary."

No one could ever accuse Trudeau of lacking courage, so I am not prepared to give him the excuse that he panicked. The invocation of the War Measures Act was a clear, unadulterated political act. Trudeau was prepared to revoke all Canadians' liberties in order to build public opinion against the separatists. It would have been inexcusable even if it had achieved its desired effect, but I believe that, on the contrary, the handling of the terrorists in 1970 led to the acceleration of the separatist movement in Quebec, and resulted in the 1976 election of the Parti Québécois. The saddest part of the whole incident and the most damning indictment of Canadians' commitment to civil liberties was the reaction of the country. Polls reported that 87 per cent of Canadians supported Trudeau's actions.

Stanfield's own inclination was to oppose the bringing in of the act until the House had the opportunity to be told what was the basis of the apprehended insurrection, but very few in the caucus supported him. Indeed, there was only one member out of the total House of Commons who voted against the bill in all three readings, David Macdonald, a courageous Prince Edward Islander with a social conscience as large as a rhinoceros. Stanfield's final position was that he would support the bill temporarily, but that the government must bring in new legislation immediately to handle the situation and then restore individual rights. It left him with the worst of all possible worlds, neither a civil libertarian nor a tough-minded supporter of law and order. The NDP quite properly opposed the bill on the first two readings but chickened out in the final reading. I telephoned Stanfield to discuss the position that he had taken on the bill. He said, with his usual self-deprecating wit, "Which position?"

By the late spring of 1971, I knew I did not have the stomach, nor could I take the necessary time from my practice, to continue as national chairman of organization. I told Stanfield that I would like to resign at the annual meeting that was to take place in the fall. I advised him that I thought it essential for him to find someone who could devote himself full time to the position yet be independent of it at the same time. He was deeply appreciative of the time that I had spent. I left at the end of October and was succeeded by Finlay MacDonald. At the time I firmly believed that the country was reposing more and more confidence in Bob Stanfield and that he would become prime minister. Since the 1968 election the Liberals had fallen from 46 per cent in popularity to 38 per cent in October 1971, and the Tories were only six points behind. The election of 1972 was to prove how close I was to being right.

CHAPTER TWELVE

WALTZING WITH THE REDHEAD

The thing I enjoyed most about the federal political scene in the seventies after my resignation as Stanfield's chairman of organization in 1971 was my absence from it. Other than being a party to the seduction of Claude Wagner in 1972 and to a vain, but noble effort to make Flora MacDonald the national leader in 1976, I spent the decade immersed in my practice and my role as adviser to Bill Davis.

On September 1, 1972, Pierre Elliott Trudeau, totally confident of victory and giving the impression that an election was little more than an ancient tribal custom that His Imperial Highness was required to go through every four years or so, issued the writs of election for an October 30 vote. The statement with which he made the announcement left the country totally perplexed as to what he viewed the issues to be. He described the reason for the calling of the election as "to ensure that Canadians continue to exhibit the self-confidence and the assurance that will permit Canada to pursue its own policies and demonstrate the advantage of its value system." His national organizer, Torrance Wylie, said to the press, "I spend no time thinking about the opposition parties because I don't believe in elections as competitions." This disdain for the electoral process was shown by Trudeau throughout the campaign.

On the other side of the street, however, they were not sauntering through the election. The Conservatives fielded a formidable team, which included Finlay MacDonald, the Halifax broadcaster who had succeeded me as chairman, Liam O'Brian from Ontario, and Malcolm Wickson from Vancouver, both of whom had worked at national headquarters as national directors during my chairmanship, together with the ubiquitous brothers-in-law Norman Atkins and Dalton Camp. This group of professionals proceeded to make the best of their difficult position, and their best turned out to be very very good. When I had left a year earlier, the government was six percentage points ahead in the polls. The same differentiation still existed. Clearly the task was not hopeless.

In early summer of 1972, just prior to the election call, I received a phone call from Finlay MacDonald, saying that Stanfield would like me to take on a "little task" for the party. Wary of accepting "little" tasks through bitter experience, I asked what the leader had in mind. Finlay answered, "We have been courting Claude Wagner for months, and Brian Mulroney, in particular, has been working on him to get him to run for us in the next election. We seem to have got him to the brink of accepting, but we just can't get a firm commitment from him. Stanfield suggested that we ask you to intervene."

"My French is miserable, why me?"

"Wagner is particularly interested in knowing how he would be received in the party outside Quebec, and you are one of the persons he said he was interested in meeting."

Finlay then went on to tell me that they had done a poll several months earlier in Quebec that showed Wagner to be even more popular in that province than Trudeau was. Wagner had previously been minister of justice in the Lesage government and had developed a reputation as being strong on law and order. He had run for the leadership of the Liberal Party in 1970 against Bourassa, and the Liberal establishment in Quebec had crucified him. Jean Lesage, the retiring leader and former premier, used his authority to have delegates appointed who were pledged to Bourassa. Wagner was bitter about his treatment and hated Lesage. He subsequently said to me, "That man was a liar and not to be trusted." Wagner had done well with the constituency delegates, but not well enough to overcome the imbalance caused by the delegates at large who were pledged to his opponent. He was also bitter about the role played by Jean Marchand, then Trudeau's Quebec political lieutenant, in his defeat. After the election, Bourassa appointed Wagner as a provincial court judge.

I asked MacDonald, "What arrangements have been made up to now?"

"We have agreed on the riding, Théo Ricard's old riding, St. Hyacinthe. Brian will give you all the details. There doesn't seem to be anything that is holding it up, but he just won't give his final OK. Give Mulroney a call."

Before I hung up, I asked Finlay to send me the poll showing Wagner to be Superman. When it arrived I understood everybody's anxiety to persuade Wagner to run. He clearly was the most respected political figure in Quebec. I called Mulroney, who corroborated everything Finlay had said and gave me the details of his discussion with Wagner to date.

A few days later I flew to Montreal and was met at the airport by Brian, with whom I had worked closely in several elections and of whom I was very fond. "It's not a question of arrangements. We have agreed on everything," he advised. He had arranged for us to meet with Wagner in a downtown hotel. We spent about two hours with Wagner discussing his candidacy. There was no doubt that Mulroney and MacDonald were right. Wagner was anxious about how his conversion from Liberal to Tory would be received by the Conservative Party outside Quebec. I could see that there was no doubt in his own mind that he would bring a great deal of support to the party in Quebec, but he was looking down the road to what sort of future he would have. Brian was persuasive in painting a picture of him as Stanfield's Quebec lieutenant, a role that could eventually lead to his being the first French Canadian leader of the party since Cartier.

I said to Wagner, "Since 1965 and up until a year ago, I was the chairman of organization of the whole party. I know this party right across the country. They'll be excited and delighted by your candidacy. Tell me who you want to speak to and I will have them telephone you." We terminated the first meeting with the understanding that Wagner was to give the proposal some further thought and I was to sound out party feeling outside Quebec to be certain I was right.

During the next two weeks in Toronto I had a series of telephone discussions with John Robarts, Bill Davis, Finlay

MacDonald, and Brian Mulroney. I arranged for Robarts and Davis to telephone Wagner to relay their support and had Mulroney set up another meeting. When I arrived in Montreal Mulroney told me that Wagner would like to meet us, with his wife, at his house.

In the course of the meeting Brian continued to paint a glorious picture of Wagner's future, while I tried another tack. I told Wagner that if he was happy on the bench and content to stay with the law for the rest of his life he should not accept our blandishments. If, on the other hand, he was not content with a lifetime career as a lower court judge, he would never again have such a good opportunity to make a contribution to public life as the one now being offered. I supported Mulroney's view that if he performed well he had an excellent chance of becoming the next leader of the party. Shortly afterward Wagner agreed to run in the 1972 election in St. Hyacinthe riding.

The evening of polling day was one of great drama. Suzie and I watched the election returns with John and Isabel Bassett at their house in Rosedale. Would the massive Quebec Liberal vote balance the huge losses Trudeau was suffering in the other provinces? At the end of the evening, the whole election boiled down to who would win three undecided constituencies. The next morning showed the Tories with 108, the Liberals with 107. In the final recount in the riding of Ontario, just east of Toronto, Frank McGee, who had been in the last Diefenbaker cabinet, was defeated by four votes. The Liberals then held 109 seats to the Conservatives' 107. The balance of power was held by the New Democrats.

The election of 1972 wiped all the gilt and glitter off Pierre Trudeau. Stanfield handily defeated him in every province other than Quebec, where the Liberals took fifty-six seats to the Tories' two, and in New Brunswick, where the parties tied at five each. The Tory party leadership had been too optimistic about the ability of any one individual to reverse the situation in a province in which, since the war, the Tories had fared well electorally only in Diefenbaker's 1958 sweep. We won only two Quebec seats; Wagner squeaked through in St. Hyacinthe and Heward Grafftey was re-elected in Brôme-Missisquoi. Wagner's popularity could not overcome the traditional distrust of the Tories in Quebec.

As the extent of the Liberal setback became clear, I said to John, "I wonder who the Tories will get to speak to Dave Lewis. I hope they get to him fast and ask for his support. If they don't, the Liberals certainly will, and Trudeau, notwithstanding the voters' loss of confidence, will hang onto office."

Down in Ottawa, however, the thrill of the astounding Liberal rout seemed to have caused the party and campaign leadership to take leave of their senses. They were absolutely confident that the government was going to fall into their laps, either within the next few days or shortly after the House met. They did nothing to persuade the New Democrats to reinforce Stanfield's legitimate claim to become prime minister. All that would have been required for Stanfield to obtain the support of the NDP was mutual agreement on one or two pieces of progressive legislation that had been in Stanfield's campaign platform and the assurance that no election would be called within two years. Three days later the country was subjected to the unedifying sight of a government and a prime minister who had lost in nine out of ten provinces clinging to power through a deal with the New Democratic Party to support them remaining as the government.

Bill Davis had exerted every effort to assist the federal leader during the election. Not since 1957, when Frost played a large role, had any federal leader received as much co-operation as Stanfield did from the Ontario Tories. Davis was at the height of his influence in his early premiership, having just won a resounding victory in his first election in October 1971. Many people who had contributed to the provincial campaign came over holus-bolus to work in the federal campaign. The Tories increased their support in Ontario from seventeen to forty seats, while the Liberals dropped from sixty-four to thirty-six seats.

The black cloud that followed Al Capp's cartoon character Joe Btfsplk seems to attach itself to Tory leaders ensconced in Ottawa. It certainly followed Bob Stanfield after his near miss in 1972. He appointed Jim Gillies, the newly elected member for Don Valley and a former dean of York University's Faculty of Administrative Studies, as his financial critic. On Gillies's recommendation and after much discussion, the party and Stanfield adopted a policy of wage and price controls as the best method of fighting the rising inflation that was threatening the country. Unfortunately, they failed to sell the policy to the people, and it came under especially vigorous opposition from the trade unions.

On May 8, 1974, the Conservatives and New Democrats combined to defeat John Turner's budget, the government resigned, and an election was called for July 8. This was to be the only federal campaign since the war that I did not participate in. According to all the polls, the country believed that the Liberal government was handling the number one issue of inflation poorly. The Tories should easily have increased their popular vote and number of seats and taken over the government. Unfortunately, they had made the classic political mistake of believing that it is essential for the opposition to outline alternative policy instead of attacking the government's mishandling of the economy. While Stanfield should have been lambasting Trudeau's unpopular government, Trudeau was scoring points attacking Stanfield's unpopular solution.

The reason for the Liberal victory is simple. Having learned the perils of running a half-assed campaign in 1972, Trudeau simply out-campaigned Robert Stanfield. Taking a page out of John Diefenbaker's book, he simplified Stanfield's position on freezing wages and prices to three words: "Zap. You're frozen." With the vocal support of the trade unions, the Liberals regained their majority, with a nineteen-seat increase in Ontario. The Tory share of the popular vote remained the same and the Liberals gained just under 5 per cent from the NDP and the Social Credit. The combination of wage and price controls and a picture of Stanfield fumbling a football that appeared in every newspaper in the country had done him in. It tells you something about the press that the fumble occurred after Stanfield had successfully caught that football twelve times. No professional wide end does that well.

Fifteen months after regaining his majority, Trudeau swallowed his word and announced in October 1975 that an Anti-Inflation Board was being formed and that wage and price controls were being implemented. While the trade union movement under Dennis McDermott, head of the Canadian Labour Congress, bleated loud and long in opposition, the public, frightened by double-digit inflation, accepted the controls with equanimity. During the election campaign, Trudeau had promised to "wrestle inflation to the ground," and he now used Bob Stanfield's headlock to achieve his ends.

In the summer of 1975 Bob Stanfield announced his retirement and a leadership convention was set for February 1976 in Ottawa. About ten days after the announcement Flora MacDonald telephoned me. Without any preliminaries, she asked, "I am going to run for the leadership. Will you help me?"

I was a little taken aback, as I had not thought of her as a potential candidate. "What do you want me to do?" I asked, trying to cover my surprise.

"Take over the responsibility of raising the money for the campaign."

I gulped and said, "How much is that?"

"I will come to Toronto and we can talk."

A few days later we had dinner at the Albany Club. Flora, erect and clear-eyed, with her flaming hair, was a striking figure. Her animation and her agile mind made her one of the most interesting and entertaining of my friends.

After we sat down I asked, "What kind of campaign do you intend to run?"

She replied, "You would be amazed at the people who have responded to my announcement. The campaign will be managed and run by young people. Young people from Kingston and young people from all over the country. I am just thrilled at the response I've had."

Every politician, when he or she is aspiring to office, talks of the overwhelming support that he or she is drawing, but in Flora's case I knew it was true. While I did not think she would win the leadership, although she was the most popular of the candidates, I believed she would win the country if elected.

I pressed Flora to find out how much she thought the campaign would cost. She said the budget indicated that they could do the job for about $125,000. This sum would allow them to run a respectable national campaign, although it would certainly be the cheapest campaign of any of the serious candidates. I said, "Are you certain you can hold it at that figure?"

"Positive."

"It is certainly do-able if we can get a little help from outside Toronto." As always, the love of a good fight was enticing me.

She told me she had heard from Doug McCutcheon, the youngest of the McCutcheon brothers, and that he was prepared to help me. "What rules are we going to lay down about donations?" I asked.

"No one can give more than five hundred dollars. That should be the limit."

"We can raise that to a thousand. No one will think that you can be bought for a thousand dollars."

Flora grinned and agreed. "I want to make it clear that at the end of the campaign we are prepared to have anyone see the list of donors of over one hundred dollars."

I joked, "That will be the kiss of death. No respectable corporation will want to admit that they are supporting a Red Tory like you." Her peal of laughter rang throughout the Albany Club.

"There is one postscript, Flora. If Darcy McKeough decides to run, I'd continue to work for you, but I would also feel obligated to raise some money for him."

Ever gracious, Flora responded, "I have absolutely no problem with that. It would be a good thing if Darcy does run."

We talked until no one else was left in the oak-panelled dining-room. I was intrigued by the idea of using a large number of small gifts to help popularize the Conservative Party by appealing to a broader segment of the community. Apart from about two thousand dollars in fund-raising expenses that I absorbed personally, we lived up to the ceiling. What was even more remarkable, in the middle of her tour, when Flora appealed to the public to send in one- and two-dollar bills, we received

$17,000 in contributions from the public. None of these contributions was for more than ten dollars. I have never seen such an outpouring of grass-roots financial support in all my years of politics as the one Flora received in that leadership race.

With my usual exuberance, I was carried along by the amazing groundswell of support across the country for Flora's candidacy. This was the first time a woman had been a serious candidate for the national leadership of a political party in Canada, and there was a fair amount of "a woman hasn't got a chance of becoming the leader" to combat. With the fresh example of Margaret Thatcher I had hoped for better. It was infuriating to see usually intelligent people taking this cynical position instead of saying, "I hope that her sex won't prevent her from being chosen as the leader." The concern about a woman leader was not by any means limited to men. There were many older women who said the party was not ready for a woman. On the other hand, there were many of both sexes who had known and admired Flora for years and who worked vigorously for her election.

The second obstacle in the campaign was Flora's reputation as a "Red Tory," a reputation that was exploited by the other candidates to an amazing extreme. While Flora has always been progressive in her outlook, she is a fiscally responsible politician. There was no justification for the way those opposed to her candidacy tried to portray her as practically sitting at the feet of Lenin and Mao Tse-tung. At one of our planning meetings she said to me, "What these people forget is that anyone brought up in a thrifty Scottish household in Nova Scotia is going to be careful with expenditures, whether they be the government's or their own." Her record, first as secretary of state for external affairs in the Clark government and then subsequently as minister of employment and immigration and minister of communications in the Mulroney government has borne this out.

The spirit of Flora's campaign committee was as effervescent as a meadow brook in spring. There was an energetic mixture of young people from the universities across the country, seasoned women party workers, and young businessmen from Ontario

and the Maritimes. The campaign was considerably strength-
ened by the strong, open, and loyal support of Premier Richard
Hatfield of New Brunswick and federal member John Crosbie of
Newfoundland.

For the first time in history the two leading Conservative
candidates were from Quebec. Claude Wagner had built up a
strong Quebec organization together with some excellent
support in Ontario helped by the efforts of Hugh Segal and
others. The other front runner was Brian Mulroney who, from a
candidacy that had originally started almost as a lark, managed,
with well-financed business support, to build up a strong
backing from Quebec, Ontario, and the West. Mulroney,
articulate, quick-thinking, and attractive, built upon the
ever-present appeal that a new face has in politics. There lurks
within many voters a distrust of those who are already in public
life, so that subconsciously they search for a messiah to give the
country clear, simple, and honest answers. Properly handled, an
articulate young man like Brian Mulroney can exploit this
yearning.

The support Mulroney promised to Wagner in 1972 proved to
be ephemeral when Mulroney decided to run himself. There was
now a deep bitterness between the Mulroney and Wagner
camps. I felt that Wagner's failure to make a strong impression
on the country or in the House meant that Mulroney should not
in any way be inhibited from running because of our earlier
blandishments to Wagner, but I was infuriated by the attempt of
some of Mulroney's supporters to harm Wagner with unjustified
innuendoes. In particular, Peter White, who had been a leading
Wagner supporter and campaign organizer, switched camps with
a vengeance. White gave an interview to the press saying he
knew for a fact that in 1972, during the campaign, someone had
picked up a briefcase of bills of large denominations destined for
Claude Wagner from Eddie Goodman. Since White himself had
been the one who picked up the briefcase from me, his certainty
was hardly surprising. The briefcase contained only $15,000 in
one hundred-dollar and fifty-dollar bills. This sum had been
promised to Wagner by the central organization to help run
Wagner's campaign. The story from White's lips, given, he

claimed, "reluctantly," led one to imagine that huge sums of money were involved, but $15,000 toward campaign costs is a modest amount. This was no different from the sum received by most of the promising candidates in Quebec. While I was prepared to exonerate Mulroney of responsibility for his supporters' questionable tactics, I felt I had an obligation to Wagner to see that he was not hurt by these innuendoes.

My opportunity came when I was invited to appear on the CBC program "the fifth estate", just before the convention opened. I spoke glowingly of Flora's capacity to campaign effectively on a small budget and attacked the lavishness of "other" campaigns and the amount of money that they were receiving from business to finance them. I defended the propriety of Wagner's arrangements and ended by saying, "Nobody can buy the leadership of the Conservative Party." This performance was quickly brought to the attention of Mulroney and his major financial supporters. I started to get messages carried by friends who were not necessarily supporting Mulroney, such as John Robarts, of the anger toward me in the Mulroney camp. From Mulroney I got the total chill. On several occasions, both at the convention and for several years afterwards, he resolutely refused to speak to me. I was totally unperturbed by his hostility but then I did not expect him to become Prime Minister. (The breach was not fully healed until 1983 when, during the campaign leading to the convention, Senator Leo Kolber of Montreal, the head of the Cadillac Fairview Corporation, whose friendship Mulroney and I shared, had us both in to his Toronto office for lunch. There I told Mulroney that while I would be voting for Joe Clark at the coming convention, he had my assurance that I had no intention of impugning his candidacy or his integrity. Our relationship since that time has remained cordial, and I believe I was of some help in his 1984 election.)

Tim Kotcheff of the CBC had asked me out to lunch about six weeks before the 1976 convention. Even before we got our Perriers, Ted asked, "How would you like to be a participant in the CBC programming of the convention?"

"But I am a director and general counsel to CFTO," I answered in astonishment. Then the appeal of the idea grew on me. "Still it would be great fun to be a commentator for this convention. I know the players so intimately. But I can't be totally objective about Flora's candidacy although I will do the best I can."

He readily agreed. When he asked where he could find another interesting Tory to join the panel, I suggested John Bassett. He was dumbfounded at the suggestion. "How are you going to get Bassett to go on when he is on the board of directors of the other network and chief executive officer of their anchor station?"

"Leave it to me. Will you accept him?"

"I'm dying to have him."

That night I called John. "John, I am going on the CBC commentators' panel for the convention. They would love to have you do the same. What about it? We'll have a ball."

He thought for a moment. "Well, seeing that our own network has never had an idea like that and has never asked me to participate, why shouldn't I?"

And that is how the two of us, both closely connected to CTV and CFTO, spent three days working for the competition. I think we gave the audience some insights they might not otherwise have had. I found anchorman Lloyd Robertson, then at CBC, easy and knowledgeable to work with. We certainly confounded our own network and probably made them spruce up their coverage. A lot of the CTV station owners were not amused.

Once I arrived in Ottawa every minute I was not on the air I spent working for Flora. I set about speaking to my friends and former colleagues in various parts of the country to convince them that the party needed to come into the mainstream and that the best way to attract the non-partisan population of the country was to elect Flora MacDonald as leader. I received a sympathetic response, although scores of people said, "I can't make up my mind between Flora and Joe Clark, but if you assure me Flora is as responsible as you claim then I will go with her." If all of them had followed through, the results would have been different.

For me, sharing the enthusiasm, vigour, and ideas of Flora's campaign was like drinking from the fountain of youth. Our communication system was not highly electronic and costly but it worked. The parties we ran for the delegates were inexpensive but well attended. As Flora went from policy meeting to policy meeting and from provincial caucus to provincial caucus, the Tories whom she had served for decades in the national headquarters flocked to encourage her. I began to believe that the impossible dream might come true.

It was one of the rare conventions where the addresses of the candidates would have a bearing on the outcome. After the speeches, the general consensus was that Wagner's, which had been finely crafted by Hugh Segal, was the best and the most moving. Flora's speech, written by Hugh Hanson, was a first-class effort and next best. Brian Mulroney's speech was good, but not the barn burner his supporters had hoped for. Joe Clark's speech left him marking time. It was, however, the most ill-conceived of the speeches, Paul Hellyer's, that had the most effect on the convention results.

Hellyer had been in the Pearson cabinet and was a leading contender for the leadership when Pearson left. He was the favourite at the beginning of the 1968 convention. When the convention got under way he was running neck and neck with Pierre Trudeau and had the support of the Liberal establishment across the country, including that of "Rainmaker" Keith Davey and most of the Toronto Liberals. Paul Hellyer was a sincere, well-motivated, devoted Christian who modelled his own life upon the principles he believed in. Unfortunately he possessed a stubbornness not exceeded by even the king of mules and his beliefs were too right of centre to be accepted by the majority of Canadians. In May 1971 he had left the Liberal Party to start his own party, Action Canada, and had met with some moderate success at the outset. But messianic zeal cannot replace the organization and loyalties of the old-line parties, and he eventually ended up in the ranks of the Conservatives. Hellyer's strong conviction that he knew better than anyone else what was in the country's best interests had caused him to make a poor speech at the 1968 Liberal convention, where he dropped out after three ballots. The same qualities resulted in his making a disastrous speech at the Conservative convention in 1976, just when he was building up a cohesive body of right-wing support. The climax was a spirited attack on the Red Tories and the harm they were doing the country and the party. This was primarily aimed at Flora and Joe Clark, but also at others like Dalton Camp and me. Even Bob Stanfield joked, "I guess Paul has just read me out of the party."

The reaction of the audience to this attack on people who had served the party well was highly antagonistic. Hellyer had destroyed his own chances; and, unfortunately for Flora, his speech had rekindled the concerns of the people I had spent hours reassuring about her alleged left-wing proclivities.

Hellyer's speech resulted in the shift of a host of people from Flora to Joe Clark. When the first ballot was held we had scrutineers at every polling booth to check on the number of Flora buttons that were worn into the booth. More people were wearing Flora buttons than were wearing the buttons of any other candidate, a total of 283. Unfortunately, when the vote was held Flora finished sixth with only 214 votes. The surprise finish was Joe Clark who, with 277 votes, was positioned behind Wagner and Mulroney, with 531 and 357 respectively.

On the first ballot, the Nova Scotia delegates chose Pat Nowlan as their native son instead of Flora, with a view to switching on the second ballot, and that, combined with the attack by Paul Hellyer, ruined Flora's hopes of getting the important third place. Brian Mulroney had done well in garnering first-ballot votes, but the next ballot proved he had shot his bolt, having little second-ballot support among the delegates. With the speed of lightning, Sinc Stevens, who had waged a vigorous right-wing campaign and placed seventh on the first ballot, suddenly became a Red Tory and led the march to Joe Clark.

Immediately after the first-ballot vote was announced and I had made my commentary on television, I sped down to sit beside Flora, who had decided to stay for one more ballot before moving over to Joe Clark. Political defeat is always a tearful matter. Flora had commanded so much loyalty that her supporters' tears could have irrigated the Sinai Desert. She withdrew after the second ballot, when her support rose by only 25 votes to 239. I marched at her side to Clark. The final ballot was between Wagner and Clark, with Clark the winner at 1,187 votes to Wagner's 1,122.

During the convention, the Bassetts and the Goodmans had been sharing a two-bedroom suite at the Inn of the Provinces. John and I got up the next morning to turn on the post-mortems. Fraser Kelly of John's TV station, CFTO, was interviewing Jack Horner, who had been fourth on the first ballot. He asked Horner why he had not done better. Horner replied, "There were many reasons, but the main reason was the attacks on me by the press, particularly by that prince of the media John Bassett. When I say prince I spell it p-r-i-c-k." I was looking at Bassett while Horner went through this spelling exercise and exploded with laughter. Bassett didn't share my amusement and threatened to sue "them" for slander.

Trying valiantly but vainly to suppress my chuckles, I asked, "In view of the fact that Fraser works for CFTO and this interview is being broadcast by your station as well, are you going to sue yourself at the same time?" The look on Bassett's face was so incredulous that I laughed for an hour. I later wrote a letter to CTV on Bassett's behalf and received the appropriate apology.

Joe Clark was elected leader in 1976 because the delegates felt he was the perfect compromise. In his three years as leader of the opposition, he failed to inspire either the party or the country, but public disillusionment with Trudeau outweighed Clark's lacklustre performance and in the spring of 1979 he became prime minister of Canada.

When Joe Clark ascended to power in 1979 he was confident of remaining a minority prime minister for a good period of time. He was intelligent and gutsy and in the centre of the ideological spectrum. He had a potentially strong cabinet and politically astute advisers such as Lowell Murray. Unfortunately, he lacked the chemistry necessary to attract voters, and his cabinet had no one with experience in government. Notwithstanding my strong representations he refused to put George Hees, Alvin Hamilton, or Marcel Lambert into the cabinet. The feeling grew that the people around Clark were too young and too cocky.

In the course of the 1979 campaign, Lowell Murray telephoned me from Ottawa to ask, "What do you think of Joe's promising to move the Canadian Embassy in Israel from Tel Aviv to Jerusalem? Ron Atkey, our St. Paul's candidate and later minister of immigration, and Bob Jarvis, our Willowdale candidate, think it would be of great help to them in the election if we say we're planning to make this move."

I took twenty-four hours to think about it and called back to advise strongly against the move. While it would be dear to the heart of many Canadian Jews, including me, the proposal struck me as being too crass for the middle of an election campaign and as having a tinder-box potential after the election. Clark, however, made the commitment.

When Clark later indicated that his government intended to implement this campaign commitment, the repercussions around the world were thunderous. He finally had to send Bob Stanfield on a fact-finding mission to get him out of his self-made predicament. I knew that the embassy proposal was dead as soon as he approved Bob's appointment. It was an unfortunate beginning to Clark's prime ministership. From a Canadian point of view, the embassy in Israel was of little consequence to anyone other than the Jewish community, but the issue succeeded in reinforcing the impression of ineptness that had been the hallmark of his public image.

One day about three or four months after Clark had become prime minister, I was sitting in Bill Davis's office when he said to me, "The Prime Minister has asked me to find out if you would accept an appointment as Canadian ambassador to the United States. Peter Towe's term expires in about a year and we both feel that you would be an ideal replacement."

After I recovered from my shock, I responded, "Tell the Prime Minister that, while I am flattered by the idea, when he is in a position to make a firm offer of the appointment to me, I will decide whether or not I should accept. It's the only public appointment I would be interested in, but I think Suzie would hate it and I do not think it would be well received by the public, which would impair my effectiveness." The seriousness of Clark's intention was later confirmed for me by Jean Pigott, who kept the appointment lists for Clark.

In July 1979, the government of Ontario realized that the Clark government was going to make significant changes in the price of energy to the benefit of the energy-producing provinces and to the detriment of the consuming provinces, mainly Ontario. When the meeting of the provincial first ministers took place in early August, energy was high on its agenda. The government of Ontario had decided to prepare an energy position paper. I strongly urged that the paper be released prior to the first ministers' conference. This would make public Ontario's position before the federal position was known and before Clark or Lougheed could cut a deal based on the Alberta premier's demand that his province receive the world price for oil. The fact that the world price was then an international cartel-rigged price seemed of no consequence to either Clark or Lougheed.

Davis recognized that some oil price increases were inevitable and justified. Ontario's paper called for modest continuing increases, the setting up of a national oil fund to ease the impact on consumers, and the retention of Petro-Canada, which Clark wanted to jettison. While Lougheed was not going to get his world price, Clark clearly favoured immediate sizeable increases without significant counterbalancing help for the Ontario consumer. On the contrary, there was a proposal for a gasoline tax of twenty-three cents a gallon. Meetings between Davis and Clark and Lougheed and Clark achieved little for Ontario. On December 11, 1979, the federal budget was brought in with a tax of eighteen cents a gallon on gasoline and a large increase in the price of oil. The Ontario consumer would be financing the increased amounts for the federal and western provincial coffers. The government was defeated on the budget vote. This gasoline tax sounded the death knell of the federal Conservative government, which lost the support of Ontario voters even though Davis campaigned for Clark.

When the 1980 election was over, Trudeau was once again ensconced at 24 Sussex Drive, and the vote was 147 seats for the Liberals to 103 for the Tories. During the campaign I had made only one trip to Ottawa to ask Lowell Murray what Davis and the Ontario machine could do to help the Prime Minister. I was met with a degree of over-confidence that left me open-mouthed. How they expected the public attitude to change in so short a time I could not imagine.

While Davis was irked by his treatment during the Clark

regime, he recognized Joe's predicament and remained loyal through the election, the annual meeting, and the leadership convention in 1983. The Prime Minister's Office seemed to accept Davis's loyalty and help as justly due by virtue of the divine right of kings. They should have realized that that doctrine fell along with King Charles' head.

CHAPTER THIRTEEN

A COG IN THE BIG BLUE MACHINE

In November 1974 I received a call from Hugh Macaulay asking to see me right away. I was delighted to make time for Hugh, who had always fitted into my private category of "great Canadians." He was forthright and bright like all the Macaulay family; not as bright or creative as his brother, Bob, who bordered on genius, but more stable and far more predictable; loyal to his friends and all institutions he believed were good for Canada, which certainly included the Tory Party.

Macaulay came into my office, slumped into a chair, his wavy blond hair perfect as ever, and without more ado said, "I want you to take over my job and become Bill Davis's organizer and adviser."

My response was astonishment. "What the hell are you talking about? That is absolutely ridiculous. I haven't heard from you fellows for three years, since I retired from the federal scene. I know nothing about what's going on at Queen's Park except what I read in the paper, which means I know nothing. These days I'm only a simple lawyer."

Macaulay disregarded my remarks and continued. "I have done everything I can for Davis and it isn't working. We are dropping in the public's confidence like a shot goose. You are the only one I can think of who has the experience and the energy to turn things around."

The Davis government had just gone through an unpleasant series of allegations of scandal together with a run of five by-election losses culminating in a recent unexpected double defeat in Ottawa and Cornwall. The polls accurately portrayed the public's declining confidence in the Davis government. Looking back today from the perspective of the high esteem Bill enjoyed at the time of his retirement ten years later, it is difficult to appreciate the extent of his problems in 1974.

While Macaulay and I talked, my mind went back to when Davis succeeded Robarts as premier. In December 1970 I had received a telephone call from John Robarts asking me to come up to his legislative office. When I arrived, Ernie Jackson was already there. Robarts got quickly to the point. "I intend to resign within the next couple of weeks and I would like to have the convention to choose my successor reasonably soon. I do not want a lot of my colleagues criss-crossing the province for months taking shots at each other. I would like Ernie and you to take charge of the arrangements, get everything set in advance, and then we can have an early convention."

"I'm genuinely sorry to see you go, John," I said, "but I think it is a wise decision. You are still young enough to have a career in law or anyplace else you want. Everyone should quit politics while they are ahead." He later told me that he had made tentative arrangements with Stikeman Elliott, a Montreal law firm, to join a proposed Toronto office.

Jackson and I set about making the convention arrangements. We reserved Maple Leaf Gardens for February 10-12, made hotel reservations, and started to plan who would be on our committee. As I predicted, the provincial executive were furious that Robarts had appointed Jackson and me to arrange the convention. However, party president Alan Eagleson was no fool: where else was he going to find experienced help that made his job easy? He calmed the executive down once he established that he would be in the chair during the convention.

Once again I was on the horns of a dilemma. Should I support Bill Davis or Darcy McKeough? Both had many admirable attributes. I decided to go with Davis, whose philosophical approach was more in tune with mine and to whom I was indebted for stepping into the breach at Montmorency. I went to Darcy at once and told him. The other candidates were Allan Lawrence, Bert Lawrence, and Bob Welch, all of whom were in the cabinet.

Bob Macaulay and Charles MacNaughton, the provincial treasurer, helped persuade the great majority of the cabinet and

members to support Davis, who quickly became the establishment candidate. The knowledge he had gained in his long stint as
education minister and his willingness to help the members had
built this strong legislative support. MacNaughton and I brought
with us Hugh Latimer, and I had a great number of federal
connections and IOUs to call upon. Dalton Camp had indicated
his willingness to support Davis, but when his brother-in-law,
Norm Atkins, took over Al Lawrence's campaign and when a
few of the Ontario friends of Diefenbaker announced their
support of Davis, Dalton went on holiday. Al Lawrence ran a
strong campaign, but lost to Davis on the fourth ballot by
forty-four votes. I knew I had done a good job for Davis when I
learned that the Al Lawrence committee room contained a large
picture of me from the cover of the *Globe and Mail* magazine that
was being used as a dartboard.

On assuming the office of premier in March 1971, Davis
retained Robarts' deputy minister, Keith Reynolds, for almost a
year, then installed Jim Fleck as his deputy minister and secretary
to the cabinet. This appointment was made on the urging of John
Cronyn of London. Cronyn, a Labatt's senior executive, had been
the successful head of a task force appointed by Robarts to
modernize the government. Fleck had done a good job as
secretary of the task force. Unfortunately, as associate dean of
the Faculty of Administrative Studies at York University, Fleck
was far better at understanding business than at understanding
the need for flexibility, compromise, and the free flow of
information and discussion required in politics. The person who
is running the premier's office must be in touch with all the
ministers and their deputies to know what's happening at all
levels of government. Fleck, who was not a product of the public
service, did not have the vital network of friends in the
civil service to keep him informed. The result was that Davis was
seeing all the wrong people. It became as difficult for the
members of the Legislature and his cabinet to see Davis as it is for
the thirty-second vice-president of General Motors to see the
president.

A series of embarrassing incidents had bedevilled the
government in 1972 and 1973, enabling the opposition to suggest

that political contributions had obtained beneficial treatment for friends of the party and that inside information had been used for personal profit by people close to the government. None of these allegations alone was of consequence, but their cumulative effect, aggravated by the indecision with which the premier's office handled them, started to erode the public's trust.

In March 1973, Bob Nixon, the Liberal leader, alleged that developer Gerhard Moog, who bragged of being a "close, personal friend of Davis," had been receiving untendered contracts to build government buildings. The allegation centred on the present head office for Ontario Hydro. Don Smith, president of Ellis Don, a large construction company in London, and until recently president of the Ontario Liberal Party and still its major fundraiser, complained to the press, when Moog's proposal was accepted in preference to his, that there had been political interference in the process. Davis made one of his few political misjudgements when he resisted the opposition's request for a royal commission to inquire into the matter and instead appointed a special select committee of the Legislature to probe the Hydro deal, under the chairmanship of Tory member John MacBeth.

MacBeth could not control the committee, and its counsel ran the inquiry. The result was long weeks of hearings during which unproven innuendoes by the opposition members of the committee filled the press and broadcast media. In the end the Davis government was totally cleared of any impropriety. The selection process had been open for proposals by other developers and time was to prove that the arrangement that Ontario Hydro entered into with Moog was highly beneficial to Hydro and to the province. If every government building had been built under the same arrangement, the province would be hundreds of millions of dollars better off today.

After Macaulay and I had discussed these events, I said, "It's impossible for anyone to come in cold from outside and take charge in the manner that is required to get us out of this mess. While I know most of the players, plopping me down in charge will raise antagonisms and jealousies that would make the job impossible." I paused before adding, "I am quite prepared, however, to join the group and work as an assistant to you. Then, we will see if the retirement you want with the transition to me or anyone else is possible." Macaulay agreed and invited me to join his committee.

I then received probably the best advice I've ever had from anyone when Macaulay said, "Listen, one thing you must remember with Bill Davis is that you don't sit back and wait to be consulted or telephoned for advice or invited to a meeting. You simply push your way into his office at any available break in his appointments. The only formal meeting we have is a Tuesday breakfast meeting once a week. The group consists of Dalton Camp, Bill Kelly [Davis's finance chairman], Norm Atkins, party president Al Eagleson, and Ross deGeer, the party executive director. Now that Ed Stewart has been appointed to replace Jim Fleck as deputy minister in the premier's office, he is there. So is Clare Westcott, the executive director of the premier's office."

The news that Ed Stewart had replaced Fleck as deputy came as a surprise, indicating how far removed I was from the events of the day. The new arrangement also contained the acorn from which the huge oak tree of Davis's strength was to grow. Stewart, whom I barely knew, would provide sound management not only of the ministers and their deputies, but also of the unruly group of volunteer advisers to the premier. Loyalty, affection, and admiration for Bill Davis were the motivating factors in the group that helped the premier. The day-to-day handling of that group and the obtaining of the best of their capacity were the accomplishments of Ed Stewart.

Stewart came from Windsor and was as devoted to that city as Davis was to Brampton, although he had had the good sense to leave it. He had a working-class background and his father was an active unionist in the UAW. Stewart had been an elementary school teacher, and had lectured at teachers' college until he was chosen to work in the Ministry of Education. He rose rapidly in that ministry and ended up as the deputy minister not only of the Ministry of Education but also of the Ministry of Colleges and Universities when that department was formed.

Stewart, like Davis, was a man of great personal loyalty. He was loyal to his family, to his friends, to his Scottish heritage, and to his ideals. If he thought that something was wrong, either because it was improper or because it was not in the best interests of the government or the people of Ontario, you could stand on your head and do cartwheels and he would not budge an inch. This is not to suggest that he wasn't open to persuasion; he just was not open to the slightest impropriety. During the almost eleven years that I viewed his service to Davis from a close vantage point, he never once forgot who was the premier and who was the deputy, nor did he hesitate to speak his mind even when he knew the advice was not going to be welcomed by the premier.

Stewart and I got along well. I recognized from the outset that neither the policy of the Davis government nor its day-to-day direction should be set by part-time outside volunteers. Our job was merely to assist the public servants and the ministers. It was my belief that the best way for me to help Bill Davis was to assist Ed Stewart in performing his duties. Furthermore, rarely a day passed when there was not a legal aspect to a discussion, which allowed me to make contributions not just of practical advice but of professional assistance as well.

At the first Tuesday breakfast meeting I attended I was surprised to see that there were no members of the cabinet present. This was clearly an unsatisfactory state of affairs that would lead inevitably to friction. The main agenda for this meeting was to decide how to respond to a new allegation of impropriety made by Jonathan Manthorpe of the *Globe and Mail*. The allegation was that Ross Shouldice, a known Tory from northern Ontario, had had knowledge of the purchase of certain government land and that he had bought some of this land himself and profited.

There was no truth to the allegations, and we decided that Davis must go clearly on the offensive, issuing a strong statement that the opposition was prepared to take any idle rumour and try to turn it into a scandal. It was in this statement that Dalton Camp coined the phrase "a crock of sheer nonsense." This seemed to do the trick, because the allegations went no further.

I became a regular attendant at the Tuesday morning

meetings, and, as Macaulay had advised, I started to drop in on Davis and Stewart to discuss day-to-day governmental problems. It was my belief that the big dip in the government's popularity was serious, but that it was not insurmountable. If we could stay out of trouble long enough to re-establish our credibility we could survive the next election. I met with the Premier on several occasions and told him, in the strongest terms possible, that we must not try to legislate ourselves back into favour with ill-conceived programs or, for that matter, with well-conceived programs. We should simply try and stay out of trouble and let time heal the wounds. What the public wanted was a government that could manage the affairs of the province with integrity and efficiency, not a raft of innovative, costly legislation cynically contrived to win votes.

The next five or six months went by without the government getting into further problems. It was now more than four years since Davis had been elected in 1971, and we were approaching the time when we were required to call an election. There could be no doubt that after thirty-two years of Tory power, time appeared to be running out for the Davis government. They were behind the Liberals both in the Gallup and their own polls, and there was growing discontent inside and outside the party. The Liberals under Bob Nixon felt that victory for the first time in many years was tantalizingly within reach.

Fortunately, there were a mounting number of recent achievements to counteract the public concern about the scandals. The premier, some months earlier, had appointed a commission consisting of Doug Fisher, Dalton Camp, and Farquhar Oliver, the former Liberal leader, to inquire into election expenses. The result was a bill putting stringent restrictions on the amount of donations by individuals, corporations, and unions to any one party and providing for legislative budgets for research and for public assistance to bona fide candidates. This bill also set up an all-party commission on election contributions and expenses to oversee the application of the bill to registered political parties and to make public the annual audit statements of the individual candidates. I knew of no more stringent legislation in any North American democratic jurisdiction. It was to have far-reaching effects, in that it made it necessary for the parties to broaden their bases and make private individuals instead of corporations the main source of support for their political activities. It also bolstered public confidence in politics generally.

In the spring session before the election in 1975, the government brought in a series of programs to assist the building and purchasing of homes, particularly for first-time buyers, who received grants of $1,500. A limited plan for free prescription drugs for senior citizens was instituted. The two programs cost less than $100 million, but both were badly needed reforms that had a great deal of political appeal.

Two non-legislative steps were taken during the same period. The first was the appointment of a royal commission to inquire into violence in the media to be headed by former federal Liberal cabinet minister, Judy LaMarsh. The other two commissioners were Judge Lucien Beaulieu and journalist Scott Young. The decision was purely Davis's own and raised a great deal of controversy. The opposition to the inquiry centred on the fact that Judy LaMarsh was being paid $250 a day, which worked out to about $60,000 a year, not a great deal of money for someone of her standing and ability. Fortunately, the inquiry was strongly supported by many parents who were becoming increasingly concerned about the effect of television upon their family life. Throughout the opposition attacks, Davis just smiled and said, "The proof of the pudding will be in the eating." A decade later, there can be no doubt that it was a most worthwhile step and pointed a direction for future studies across the North American continent as well as abroad.

The government's second inquiry led to what may have been one of the Davis government's greatest contributions to public life in Ontario. Darcy McKeough, by now the provincial treasurer, appointed the former auditor-general of Canada, Maxwell Henderson, a person of great standing in the field of controlling governmental spending, broadcaster Betty Kennedy, and Robert Hurlburt, president of General Foods, to "review all future spending by the provincial government." During the next decade, McKeough, aided by Davis, was to keep control of the provincial expenditures in a manner that was to give leadership to the whole country and to maintain Ontario's position as the most fiscally responsible of all Canadian jurisdictions.

All during this period there was great pressure on the government both from elements of the public and from the right wing within the party to bring in anti-strike legislation against public employees, especially elementary and secondary school teachers. There had been a number of municipalities where teachers had gone out on strike, and the polls showed that the public was strongly against teachers' strikes. In various school boards the parents were pressuring trustees and administrators to support the no-strike legislation. I was very much opposed to taking the right to strike away from the teachers. It had always been my belief that the modern Labour Relations Act was merely a procedural structure for an inalienable right of workers. The collective bargaining system had worked well in Ontario to the benefit of the province as a whole. To single out the teachers, who had been tough but not irresponsible bargainers, would have been unfair and any political gains would be short-lived. I went first to Tom Wells, the minister of education, and urged, "It would be a great mistake to have your proposed legislation take away the right to strike from the teachers. It's wrong in principle and it is wrong politically because, while there is a lot of public support for it now by parents and in the press, that will change as soon as the union movement gets behind the teachers."

Wells agreed, but cited caucus and cabinet pressure for a no-strike clause. I suggested that a better solution would be to strengthen the conciliation process. I then went to Davis and said, "Surely, you better than anybody realize that the teachers in this province have done nothing which would justify taking away from them the right to strike."

"It would be a lot easier," he replied, "if some of those fellows at the Ontario Secondary School Teachers' Federation would be a little more responsible in their remarks. I object to being threatened."

"I agree, but this is an issue that in the long run we cannot win. We don't believe in taking away the right to strike and we don't want to run an election on an anti-labour issue."

While the great majority of labour leaders were supporters of the New Democratic Party, and the unions officially supported that party, the members of the unions voted in a manner they thought was in their best interest and that of the province. In most elections, the Tories got a good percentage of the labour vote. In this country the first Trade Union Act was brought in by Sir John A. Macdonald. There has been a long history of support for the trade unions in the Tory Party.

As discussions carried on from meeting to meeting, it became clear that Davis, with his knowledge of the operations of the provincial educational system, and Stewart, with his similar experience, were not going to let the right wing lead us down that perilous path. The new legislation that was brought in improved the negotiating procedure and conciliation processes, but allowed the unions the right to strike.

In July, Attorney-General Roy McMurtry achieved one of his cherished governmental reforms by having passed a bill creating the office of Ombudsman as a focus for citizens' complaints throughout the province. Arthur Maloney, the criminal lawyer who in 1966 had run against Dalton Camp for the presidency of the federal party, was appointed Ontario's first ombudsman.

The NDP's Stephen Lewis felt that he had hold of a good minor issue when the price of oil was raised by the federal government. He claimed that it would be a giant killing for the large oil companies at the expense of the consumer. I strongly urged Davis to put a clamp on the oil that was already in the pipes. He did better. He put a ninety-day freeze on the price. As Lewis commented ruefully to me, "How can you beat a Tory premier who is prepared to take a crack at the large oil companies?"

In August, Davis called the election and went on to the hustings. While Conservative support had increased and Liberal support had lessened over the last eight months, we were still running 6 or 7 per cent behind the Grits. If the election was going to be won by the Tories, the Liberals would have to screw up during the campaign, or we must get some help from Stephen Lewis and the NDP.

The opposition had three solid issues to campaign on. The first was a feeling around the province, particularly in Toronto, that the government was not as squeaky clean as it should have been. The second, outside Toronto, was the strong antipathy to regional government, a much-needed reform that had been brought in originally by Frost, first in Metropolitan Toronto, then by Robarts and Davis in several other areas of the province. The public felt that they were being over-governed and that the cost of government was becoming exorbitant. The constant squabbles between the area municipalities and the regional government and the delays in the complex planning process further diminished public confidence. While regional government provided better and more equitable distribution of services, such as sewage and water systems, roads, and parks, it was not popular.

The third and most emotional issue of the election was the question of rent control. Several months earlier Stephen Lewis had begun to attack the government on their failure to act on this issue. Davis had asked me to think about the possibility of bringing in some type of controls. He also asked me to discuss with Cadillac Fairview president Eph Diamond what the effect would be upon the supply of rental housing. Diamond and I met several times and reached the conclusion that rents, historically 25 to 30 per cent of earnings, had not moved with the cost of living over the past decade and were then around 18 to 20 per cent. During the past few months, however, fear of rent controls had caused landlords to raise individual rents too rapidly, and in some cases there had been unseemly increases. We decided to recommend a system of controls, a commendable indication of the integrity and objectivity of Eph Diamond, the largest landlord in Toronto. On receiving my recommendation, Davis mentioned that there was some strong opposition among his colleagues from Toronto to rent controls. He asked me to discuss the issue with Dennis Timbrell, who led the opposition against controls.

Diamond and I, aware of the disastrous consequences to the housing stock in other jurisdictions when controls were introduced, were prepared to be talked out of our position and I so reported to Davis. Though I would have been much more comfortable politically going into an election with a carefully thought-out plan on rent controls, if the Toronto members were prepared to go ahead without them, who was I to throw my body in front of the train? The proper course would have been for the government to further support increasing the housing stock; in two or three years at the most, the market would have looked after the problem.

Macaulay was the campaign chairman, Norman Atkins the campaign manager, and Ross deGeer, the executive director of the party, the operational head. We had a small group of about eight, which included Dalton and me as the campaign strategy, tactics, and policy group. We met three or four times a week, although I was at headquarters every day. The last election campaign I had run was Stanfield's in 1968. I was amazed at how much more sophisticated Atkins' and deGeer's arrangements were.

The Liberal's campaign centred on the government's corruption and their mishandling of the finances of the province. The NDP's campaign focused on rent control, where it was strongly supported by the *Toronto Star*. As this issue heated up, Davis became concerned. He asked me to remind him of some of my "more modest" proposals. I replied that modest rent control was like being a little bit pregnant, but that I firmly believed that he must do something. I outlined some possibilities. Davis mused, "It appears pretty certain that Ottawa is going to introduce some sort of wage and price controls, even though Trudeau fought Stanfield on the issue during the election last year. We would have to impose them then, so we might as well act now and slow down Stephen's campaign." He instructed me to check with Stewart and the housing officials to see that we were not making any serious gaffes. Within a few days, rent controls were born. Lewis could claim a victory for the tenants, and the Tories stopped bleeding. The following month, as predicted, Trudeau imposed wage and price controls.

That took care of the fight on the left flank. Now we could turn our attention to the Liberals. Here, we got some strong assistance from the people at Liberal campaign headquarters, who managed almost to destroy Bob Nixon with two damaging gaffes. The parties had agreed to a series of round-robin debates on CFTO. Nixon and Lewis were the first round. CFTO would not allow the print reporters into the room where the two leaders were debating, but had arranged a studio where they could see the debate taking place live. Stephen Lewis decided to grab some cheap chalk-up points with the print press and refused to debate under those rules; Nixon went in on his own to answer questions from Fraser Kelly, CFTO's political editor. Kelly asked Nixon whether he was questioning Davis's personal integrity and not just that of the government. Nixon replied, "The premier and the government." At that very moment, I knew that we had received a new lease on life. I was confident the public would object to this personal attack and that Davis would fight back vigorously. Nixon's answer had been thrashed out by the Liberals in advance. On the advice of their communications guru, Jerry Grafstein, they had decided to go after Davis personally.

The second wound was inflicted on Nixon by his research staff. They gave the leader figures based upon the federal deficit instead of the provincial deficit and had also made some serious errors when pricing their own school board reorganization scheme. The headquarters' miscalculations were so bad that the Oakville Liberal candidate took out an ad in the local paper disowning the party's claim.

Notwithstanding the Liberals' gaffes, we were still four points behind the Grits coming up to the debate between Nixon and Davis. While Davis and Lewis enjoyed a warm relationship, and the Premier was later to lend his support to Brian Mulroney's appointment of Lewis as Ambassador to the United Nations, Davis and Nixon were not too fond of each other. I did not share Davis's assessment of Nixon, thinking him to be intelligent and well motivated. His main flaw was his strong temper.

Before the debate, Dalton and I closeted ourselves with Davis at the Park Plaza Hotel to prep him for his performance. We went over every possible area of policy both for attack and defence. We urged him to throw away his reserved, rather diffident style of debate and to attack Nixon like a tiger. We reminded him that to lose would be to reinforce Nixon's allegations that he was personally corrupt. We psyched him up as he had never been psyched before and it worked. When the bell rang, he tore out of his corner like the Manassa Mauler and never stopped throwing punches. At first Nixon did not appear to believe what he was hearing and seeing. After a while, he started to fight back gamely but, to my unobjective eye, we had already scored a win.

The charge down the home stretch had a favourable result. Although the Tories lost their majority, they were ahead both in the popular vote and the number of members elected. The Tory share of seats went from the 78 following the previous election, in the 117 seat legislature, to 51 out of 125. The Liberals increased from 20 seats to 36, but the NDP soared from 19 to 38, which suddenly pushed them into the position of official opposition.

CHAPTER FOURTEEN

A SENSE OF HISTORY

When Bob Nixon, after being clearly in the lead for most of the election campaign, slipped so badly in the last two weeks that he ended up in third place, he felt honour-bound to resign. He was succeeded by Stuart Smith, a Montreal-born psychiatrist who was not too formidable as a leader. The threat to the Tory dynasty came from Stephen Lewis on the left. Fortunately for the government the NDP gains were due more to electoral quirks than to public support.

Roy McMurtry called me a few days after the election inviting me to have breakfast with him at the Westbury Hotel. Roy's dad, Roy, Sr., was a lawyer, and the family had lived for many years next door to my family on Glenayr Road in lower Forest Hill Village. The four McMurtry brothers have excelled in teaching, medicine, and law. My mother was most patient and long-suffering with the McMurtry boys, who in their younger days were a lively group. She alleged that they lived on our garage roof, and she uncomplainingly paid the local glazier to fix the constantly broken windows. When I was living with my first wife at my parents' home, my stepson, Ian, had found the McMurtry front door open one rainy spring day and proceeded to make a great number of mud cakes and put them inside the house. Mrs. McMurtry was quite properly incensed and let my mother know it. My mother only murmured her regrets and smiled. When I came home she exulted, "Revenge at last!"

Roy began by saying, "Bill Davis wants you to take over as head of the advisory group. Hugh Macaulay feels that five years of service is all that should be required of even the closest of friends. He wants out now that the election is over."

"It could be fun," I responded. "But I have to warn you that I cannot devote as much time to the job as Macaulay because I still have to practise law and earn a living. Bill might be better off with someone else." Roy shook his head.

Seeing that I wasn't going to get off that easily, I tried another tack. "I have two conditions before I accept. One is that I want to know from Davis himself that he wants me to do the job. I have seen him almost three times a week now for months and he has never even murmured the suggestion to me. I know that he doesn't like to deliver bad news, but he is so reserved that he hates to ask for the slightest help. The main condition, however, is that we must change the composition and the structure of the Tuesday morning advisory group. I think it is a huge mistake that those meetings are attended only by non-elected advisers and that, except for Stewart, we have neither cabinet ministers nor civil servants at them. It creates real rifts between the government members and the advisory group. It makes people think we are a non-elected kitchen cabinet that has far more influence than it should or does have. It alienates the public servants.

"There should be some permanent cabinet members and perhaps backbenchers. More important, we must never discuss a problem unless the responsible cabinet minister and responsible deputy minister are present when we discuss it. Then we will know what the hell we are talking about."

McMurtry strongly agreed and asked me to talk to Davis. The next day, I dropped in on Helen Anderson, Bill Davis's magnificent secretary, who had also served John Robarts and Frost. Helen had come into the public service in the early thirties. She retired when Davis did, after more than fifty years of government service. She was replaced by her assistant, Laird Saunderson, who is Davis's executive assistant today. A measure of Bill Davis was the depth of affection felt for him by all who were on his staff, either officially or unofficially. While his shyness made it difficult for him to articulate his personal feelings, his staff knew that their affection was reciprocated.

I gave my usual salutation: "Is the great man alone?"

"There is a small delegation who will be finished in about five or ten minutes."

When I entered the Premier's office, I found him gazing out the large windows overlooking College Street. I said after the simplest of greetings, "Roy has been speaking to me about filling in for Macaulay. Do you really want me to do this job or am I being pressed upon you by others?"

"No," he replied quickly. "Hughie is anxious to get back to the private sector full-time, and I really would like it if you would take over. I think your enthusiasm and fresh outlook are needed under the new circumstances. Being in a minority position is going to make things a lot harder in the House and outside the House."

I explained to him that I had a busy practice to look after and would not be able to spend as much time as Hugh, but that I was pleased at the opportunity. I then embarked on the discussion I had had the previous day with Roy. "We must dispel the impression that any group is taking over the function of the cabinet. On Tuesdays we should discuss the important issues with the responsible minister and deputy present and work out the various alternatives. Then on Wednesday cabinet will have time to make the final decision. The direction of your government will be shaped to a considerable extent by the persons you choose from both the elected and non-elected group to advise you.

"Now that we are in a minority position, the house leader is very important. He must be patient and fair in order to get along with the opposition, which will be very cocky." (Eventually Davis appointed Bob Welch, a first-class choice who got along very well with the opposition parties. He was succeeded a few years later by Tom Wells, who did an equally competent conciliatory job.)

"It is damn important," I concluded, "that in the session ahead the government should be regarded as progressive and moderate and not as right wing or in any way reactionary. This will be difficult under the present financial restraint."

I was anxious that reform-minded persons like Roy McMurtry, Bob Welch, Tom Wells, Bob Elgie, and later Larry Grossman be part of the advisory group. But this plan would not work unless the strong ministers who were more conservative were also included. These were obviously Treasurer Darcy McKeough, Bette Stephenson, then minister of labour, and Frank Miller, then minister of health and later treasurer. Dennis Timbrell, whose outlook I had some problem slotting in my own mind, but who was a good minister in a series of cabinet positions, was also brought in.

Davis's response was heartening. "You meet with Ed Stewart and the two of you work this out," he said. "Ed and I will put it into motion."

I went to Stewart's office immediately, plumped myself down on the chesterfield, and quipped, "You are going to see a lot more of me, Stewart. For better or for worse, I've agreed to take over from Macaulay."

He offered me his condolences and joked, "What did you two fellows decide without me?"

"That the Tuesday morning meetings will have more elected Tories together with some public servants and will therefore have to be more policy oriented. We aren't going to depend solely on you guys for political advice. You'll have us in the soup like you have done this past four years."

We started to discuss various persons who might comprise the newly constituted group and found that we were pretty much in accord. Then Stewart asked, "Where does Dalton fit into all this?"

"I suppose that depends on what Dalton intends to do with his career and his life during the next few years," I replied. "This is something for Davis and Camp to decide. I have worked with Camp closely for almost twenty years and I think he is bright and helpful, though prickly and sensitive on occasions. However, those two guys have their own relationship; let them work it out." Stewart agreed totally with my assessment and I assume he discussed it with Davis. From that day on, for whatever reason, I never saw Dalton at a Davis meeting.

Dalton's brother-in-law, Norman Atkins, on the other hand, played an important role, especially during elections, and exhibited a good sense of the effect of government steps on the public. Though Norman remained something of an enigma to me throughout the Davis years, Davis was extremely fond of him and had a high regard for his common sense and operational experience. Norman, like Dalton, was touchy and quick to take offence. In a free and easy group like the Big Blue Machine this required careful handling.

I would often visit Stewart's office or meet with Davis, who might call in Hugh Segal, who joined the advisory group after the 1975 election, or a cabinet minister whose department was affected by the problem under consideration. These meetings were never secret, but Norman and some others began to feel that they were being slighted, that there was an "in" group and an "out" group. I had a dozen blue t-shirts printed with "Big Blue Machine" on the front and "A Team" or "B Team" on the back. Stewart and I kept the B Team shirts and gave Norman and some of the others the A Teams.

In his interesting but totally unobjective book on Bill Davis, Claire Hoy quotes me as saying: "I have a theory that the 1975 campaign was the turning point, when Davis got that minority. You know what it's like — it's like a boxer taking a hell of a punch on the jaw, shaking his head and realizing he has taken the very best the other guy had and he's still on his feet." That remains my view today. There was an amazing change in Davis after that election. He was far more relaxed, more in command. His speaking style loosened up and he allowed his natural sense of humour to take over. At his best Davis was one of the greatest stand-up comics in public life. While Hugh Macaulay, Dalton Camp, and Norman Atkins had supplied excellent advice and guidance during the first four years, they were all greater worriers than Stewart, myself, or Hugh Segal. We balanced Davis's natural caution and he started to enjoy the premiership.

The best non-elected recruit of that time was undoubtedly Segal. At that time Hugh was twenty-nine, overweight and undergroomed like me, his errant shirt-front constantly exposing his generous belly. He possessed a creative, innovative mind, a pungent sense of humour, and a warm laugh. He was irreverent, occasionally undisciplined, but always entertaining. If during a meeting, we were having trouble catching the essence of an idea,

Hugh and I would try to find the Yiddish equivalent with our limited vocabularies, leaving everyone else bewildered. He humanized the group and dispelled the mysterious aura that the press was endeavouring to spin about our meetings. After all, who could think evil about anyone as ingenuous and forthright as Segal?

I had first met Segal in 1971 when he was a newly elected national officer of the PC Youth Federation and had supported my economic nationalist stance at the annual meeting in Ottawa. He ran in the 1972 federal election, when he was nearly elected in a strong Liberal seat in Ottawa Centre. He was grateful to Davis for supporting him on that occasion. When he lost again in 1974, he moved over to work for Davis in the 1975 provincial election.

Another important recruit was Tom Kierans, president of McLeod Young Weir, the investment bankers and brokers. Tom also had a creative mind and broad experience in finance.

On the strength of my ten years of working with Bill Davis I am often asked, "What manner of man was he?" Despite his reputation as an enigma, Davis was not a hard man to understand. At any given time Stewart, Segal, or I could tell you what his response to a situation would be — even the words he would use. What is more difficult is to describe him to those who didn't know him. First and foremost he totally met my father's test of decency and mine of compassion — not only in behaviour, but in thought and action. Recently, a long-time friend of Davis's, Joe Dobbs, died. Davis was stricken, but agreed to do the eulogy at the funeral at Grace United Church in Brampton. As he delivered his address to the two hundred-odd friends and family, with tears running down his face, I said to myself, here is the essence of the man: a simple Christian with all the small-town virtues, yet who possesses more sophistication, intellect, and political acumen than he has ever revealed.

One night I was having dinner with my stock-broker friend Larry Brenzel at Il Posto in Yorkville when Davis joined us with Nick Lorito. The four of us held a lively discussion during which Lorito voiced most of the opinions. When Davis and Lorito left, Brenzel commented: "That fellow Lorito seems pretty clued-in.

Is he the president of Davis's riding association?" I replied "No, the riding association president is Ron Webb. Nick is Bill's driver."

My chief role with Bill Davis was to support and reinforce his basic views on government and to protect him from the forces of the right, which were eventually to cause the defeat of the Progressive Conservative Party upon his departure. Davis was a pragmatist who did not approach government with an inflexible philosophy of the right or the left. He believed that the balancing of opposing forces gave the equilibrium that a state needs, and that the obligation of his administration was to provide the province with careful, steady reform of its institutions.

Davis is rarely, if ever, described as tough-minded, but he could be. He believed strongly in the importance of the Ontario Institute for Studies in Education as an important force in raising the standards of education and resisted the attempts of his own backbenchers and the press to destroy it. He created TVOntario, the public educational television network, and opposed efforts to limit or interfere with its programming activities. He created a system of community colleges that played a key role in Ontario's having one of the best post-secondary educational systems on the continent.

Environmental assessments and restrictions on the use of many chemicals always meet strong opposition from the ministries they interfere with. Davis, who believed in protecting the environment in every aspect, asked me to assist in the passage of environmental legislation. He was an admirer of Donald Chant, the founder of Pollution Probe, and his government used Chant's services on several occasions. He was totally convinced that the work of such activist groups as the Canadian Environmental Law Association (CELA) and Pollution Probe brought great benefits to the community. When the Environmental Assessment Act was being considered by cabinet for presentation to the Legislature, the Ministry of the Environment, concerned that the act would not obtain cabinet approval if it contained too many teeth in the review process, was thinking of limiting the public access to the process. I arranged for Davis to meet with Tony Barrett, Gar Mahood, Cliff Lax, and other representatives of Pollution Probe and CELA. After the meeting, in face of strong objections by the cabinet, who did not want the interference or expense of environmental reviews of any of their projects, Davis and I personally drafted strengthening amendments. Despite the carping of the opposition, Ontario in the seventies and early eighties was a North American leader in environmental protection. On certain occasions Ontario intervened in the United States environmental review process on acid rain, to the chagrin of both federal governments. No one was better suited than Bill Davis to be appointed Mulroney's acid rain ambassador in Washington.

Hugh Segal was constantly reminding our planning groups of the demographics of the province, which projected large increases in the aged as a result of the baby boom that took place immediately after the war. The projections in the need for further services for the aged and the drain on the public purse were and are serious matters, which must be faced. There has always been a bitter struggle between the Ministry of Health and the Ministry of Community and Social Services (COMSOC) for both turf and dollars. The homes for the aged came under COMSOC, while the chronic care hospitals came under Health. The hospital system was based solely on public hospitals, while the rest of the care for the aged was bifurcated. On the one hand homes for the aged were run by municipal and charitable organizations, on the other nursing homes were operated by licensed private entrepreneurs.

The many medical advances of the past half century and, in particular, the advances that are being made in geriatric medicine and in understanding the psychiatric problems of the aged increased the pressure to help the ever-growing seniors community. The province has responded well to this ever-expanding need. At the same time the Ministry of Health annually consumes one-third of the provincial budget, and the existing general hospitals' burgeoning demands for beds and equipment have restricted the growth of chronic-care hospitals.

In 1976, when Frank Miller was minister of health, the Davis government attempted to rationalize the hospital system in various parts of the province by shutting down some hospitals and shifting the pattern of bed use. This program was anything but a success. The local municipalities and the local hospital boards rose in revolt, and the government beat a not too orderly retreat. It was only Miller's innate sense of humour that saved the day. After the failure of that initiative Miller and I discussed whether the controversy had done irreparable harm to his future political career. I assured him that on the contrary I felt his coolness under fire had helped him. Frank was thinking even then of succeeding Davis, although he changed his mind several times between 1976 and 1984.

Caring for the aged has long been one of my major interests, and the Baycrest geriatric centre has been the focus of my activities. The close relationship between Baycrest and the government of Ontario that commenced with George Drew continued through the reigns of Leslie Frost, John Robarts, and Bill Davis. In 1973 or 1974 the Jewish community realized that it was essential for a new, modern hospital to be built, and applied to the Government of Ontario to build a chronic-care hospital on the adjacent land, which already housed special apartments for the aged and sundry other services. The Ministry of Health was less than responsive. It had other priorities in its effort to meet the demands of the regular hospitals, as well as applications for chronic-care hospitals in other parts of the city and the province. For about ten years the ministry, through successive ministers, refused to agree to the usual government grant, even when Baycrest offered to raise substantial funds itself. As we neared the end of the seventies, on three occasions I importuned officials of the ministry and the minister, to no avail. I realized that I had to take my case to the Premier. The question was when.

In early January of 1981 we were into our fourth year of the electoral term. Davis's approval rating was high. No insurmountable problems seemed to loom on the immediate horizon. I could smell an election within the next six months.

Early one morning just after getting back from Christmas week in Florida, I walked into the Premier's office to find him tanned and rested after his own sojourn in Florida. I opened with, "Now that you've had a chance to relax, I have a matter that I would like to discuss with you."

Davis quipped, "That doesn't sound too good. Maybe I should have stayed a few more days in Fort Lauderdale. Are you sure it's me you want to see and not somebody else?"

"I have tried 'somebody else' for about seven years and have failed, so now I'm coming to the ultimate fountainhead, the well-spring of power."

He laughed resignedly, sat down and said, "OK, counsellor, go ahead."

I briefly reminded him of the leading position that Baycrest had on this continent in the field of geriatric centres. I pointed out that other chronic-care hospitals in Toronto had made application to build additions much later than Baycrest and had received approval. I stressed the tremendous pressure caused by lack of beds, and noted that the patients were no longer limited to the Jewish community. I reminded him that the hospital had agreed to raise $20 million, which would have made it the largest hospital campaign in the private health sector to that date. I also pointed out that North York and Metro had agreed to make a grant of $4 million. Finally, I reiterated that there was no point in my going back to the health minister, Dennis Timbrell, that I had worn a groove in the carpet to his office, but that he was in the grip of the public servants who, for reasons I could not comprehend, had been holding us up for years.

Davis listened patiently, but made no promises. A few weeks later at one of our meetings, he suddenly volunteered, "That hospital matter of which you were speaking to me will be all right. I have checked it and have satisfied myself that there really is a need and that the research that will be carried on at the hospital will benefit the whole field of geriatric health care. We will talk some time soon about how we announce the grant."

I was elated and rushed back to Goodman & Goodman to inform my partner Norm Schipper, who was president of Baycrest, that we would be getting the grant and would be able to start work very soon on building the hospital. I told him that he was not to say anything until I found out what the plans were for the announcement.

Two weeks later Norm Atkins was successful in persuading the Premier that we should call an election. I was slightly dubious, as I wanted to wait a little longer for the warm weather, but Atkins' view prevailed and an election was called for March 19.

In the discussions concerning the Premier's itinerary I saw to it that we arranged an early appearance at the Baycrest Centre, at which he would announce the grant for the new hospital. The necessary arrangements were made, and the board of directors was informed of the coming announcement. A few days later I was thunderstruck to hear that the management of the home had agreed to allow Eleanor Caplan, the local Liberal candidate, to bring in Liberal leader Stuart Smith prior to the Premier's visit. At the time of getting this information I was at Queen's Park. Within seconds I had Norm Schipper on the telephone. Why I bothered to get him on the phone I do not know; if I had just opened the window he could have heard me screaming at him from a mile away.

"Norman, I have just heard that Stuart Smith is coming to Baycrest a day or two before Davis's scheduled appearance."

"I just found out about that myself and I guess there is nothing I can do about it now," Schipper replied.

"I'm not asking you to do anything, Norman," I said, trying to restore the calm to my voice. "I'm just telling you that Davis won't be there at all during the campaign."

"What do you mean he won't be there? It's all laid on."

"Well, then, lay it off because we're not going to be a follow-up act to Stuart Smith."

"How do you intend to announce the grant?"

"We don't. I'll certainly go back and take up that matter again after the election is over, but that's the risk you're going to have to run, Norman. As you know Health are not happy about this whole matter, and unfortunately this will give them another couple of months to work against it, but you certainly can't expect Davis to go after Smith when I made arrangements quite some time ago for him to be there."

In the end, Stuart Smith did not visit Baycrest, although he was offered an opportunity to come following the Premier's appearance. I hated to bluff my oldest partner and close friend (Davis would never have gone back on his commitment), but I had put in thirty-four years of constant effort to obtain government support for this world-renowned institution and I was not going to have the crowning achievement stolen from my leader and from me by the Grits. Besides the hospital was in David Rotenberg's riding and he was a very able member who was in a tough fight with Eleanor Caplan.

Schipper had the last laugh. He inveigled Eph Diamond and me into being the co-chairmen of the campaign to raise the necessary private-sector money for Baycrest. This took a good portion of time for more than a year out of our lives. Diamond deserves the greatest measure of the credit that accrues because he devoted himself with great zeal to the campaign.

The main gift to the Baycrest fund-raising campaign and the one that sparked its success came from an elderly couple by the name of Ben and Hilda Katz. Ben Katz called Harry Gorman, a strong Jewish community worker, whom he knew slightly, and told him they wanted to give a gift to the new hospital. Gorman sent them to Sam Ruth, who for many years was the executive director of the centre and at that time had taken over the foundation that supported it. Ruth is one of the leading geriatric social workers on the continent. Katz had run a clothing store in the town of Chesley for many years and then had retired and moved to Toronto. He had made a small investment in land in the County of Peel and now said to Sam, "My wife and I do not have any children. We are going to make a very good profit in this land deal and we would like to donate a million dollars to the hospital."

Ruth picked himself up off the floor and accepted graciously. Before the year was over Katz returned to say, "My profit on the land deal is much more than I expected. I am raising our gift to $3 million." It is people like Ben and Hilda Katz who keep me at least a little humble.

If the Premier of Ontario had been a lesser man than Bill Davis,

Canada would never have patriated its constitution. Within a year after being sworn in as premier, Davis attended the three-day constitutional conference in Victoria called by Prime Minister Trudeau for June 1971. At that conference, Davis strove mightily to reconcile the conflicting interests of the various provinces and the federal government. When the participants left Victoria, they all believed that they had reached an agreement on patriation and the constitution. A few days later Quebec Premier Robert Bourassa changed his mind and refused to accept the constitutional changes on the flimsy pretext that not enough rights had been given to the Province of Quebec on social matters.

For the next decade Pierre Trudeau and Bill Davis continued to call for patriation of the constitution and the entrenchment of a bill of rights, but any attempts to reach agreement became embroiled with the federal-provincial struggle for control of the country's energy resources. In no matter were Bill Davis and I more in accord than in supporting the patriation of the constitution with an amending formula and an entrenched charter of rights.

Those who are blind to the realities of political life have accused Davis of changing his position on specific matters during the long struggle for patriation. There can be no doubt that he was prepared to make compromises throughout that decade in order to bring about the ultimate act of Canada's sovereignty and to protect its people from the excesses of government. But he never lost sight of his main objective to bring full constitutional powers to Canada without leaving the country in a state of disunity. To achieve this goal he was willing to risk his own political fortunes.

Shorty after he again became prime minister, Trudeau called a constitutional conference for June 1980. In preparation for this meeting, Davis set forth the principles of his approach to the renewed process. These included immediate patriation of the constitution, the protection of minority language rights, the entrenchment of a bill of rights, the elimination of internal trade barriers, senate reform, and certain concessions for Quebec. All these I supported. He also wanted provincial participation in appointing Supreme Court judges, which I believed then and believe now, after the Meech Lake Accord of 1987, is a mistake of the first magnitude.

It was clear even prior to the June conference not only that the road to constitutional reform would be strewn with mines, but also that its travellers would suffer severe strafing and bombing. As the conference revealed, Peter Lougheed of Alberta, Brian Peckford of Newfoundland, Sterling Lyon of Manitoba, Allan Blakeney of Saskatchewan, René Lévesque of Quebec, John Buchanan of Nova Scotia, and Angus MacLean of Prince Edward Island all had objections based on the entrenchment of a bill of rights and the amending formula and a desire for a wider jurisdiction. Unless Trudeau and Davis could forge a compromise in the months ahead the process would end in disaster. At the annual premiers' conference, which took place later in the year in Winnipeg, Davis and New Brunswick's Richard Hatfield, who also supported the federal position, were almost totally ostracized by the other premiers in an unequalled display of bitterness. Claire Hoy described Davis as being treated like a "leper."

The right wing of the Conservative Party lined up to fight the enshrinement of a charter of rights in the constitution. It was particularly ironic to me that Trudeau should be the champion of personal rights and liberty when he had been prepared to sacrifice them in such a cavalier manner during the FLQ crisis. For this reason, if for no other, Davis's support for the charter was essential to the process. He had the credibility that Trudeau lacked.

In politics it takes courage to hold an unpopular or a lonely position. It takes far more courage, however, to take positions on the same side as your traditional opponents who are looked upon by your regular supporters as enemies. Time and again through those months countless Tories would call me, write to me, or say to me, "How could you allow Bill Davis to be on the same side as that bastard Pierre Trudeau?"

The arguments of the right wing against the charter generally consisted of some vague, usually inaccurate references to the British common law system and parliamentary democracy.

Some of the opponents even went so far as to allege that a charter was a denial of the monarchy and would lead to a republican system of government. The opponents would reason that a constitution would turn too much power over to the courts, which would be its interpreters. My response was, "I don't see how you can say first that we don't need a constitution because the common law as enunciated by the courts has protected our rights through centuries, and then that you're afraid this system will give too much power to the courts." I never got a satisfactory answer.

The danger in relying on common law is that basic rights can be changed by a simple act of Parliament. Once rights are enshrined in the constitution they are protected and can be changed only by the amending formula, which in the Canadian Constitution Act is difficult to implement. It is highly unlikely, in the rights-demanding society we live in, that any amendment diminishing basic individual rights would be enacted. Before the charter was passed, federal and provincial legislatures were constantly impinging on individual freedoms that I believed urgently needed protection.

By the spring of 1981 the battle was being fought on four separate fronts. The provincial premiers who were opposed to what Trudeau — supported by Davis and Hatfield — was trying to achieve had formed what was known to the press and the country as the "Gang of Eight." In the House of Commons the Tories were attacking the propriety of Trudeau's view that the federal government had jurisdiction to enact the Constitution Act without the consent of the provinces. The opposition insisted that the federal jurisdiction should be resolved by a reference to the Supreme Court of Canada.

The third battlefield was in some of the provincial supreme courts. The supreme courts of Manitoba and Newfoundland, and the superior court of Quebec were asked to rule on whether Ottawa could act unilaterally to amend the constitution. Their decisions were divergent, and finally the federal government succumbed to the pressure of the opposition and referred the question of the Parliament's power to the Supreme Court of Canada.

The fourth front was the British Parliament at Westminster. The federal government believed that the British government could not under any circumstances refuse a formal petition from the Canadian government to pass the statute replacing the British North America Act with the new Constitution Act. The Conservative opposition and the opposing premiers, however, had gone to considerable effort to create public and parliamentary support for the requirement of provincial consent. They had been lobbying the British Parliament to refuse the legislation unless it had overwhelming provincial support. This made a favourable Supreme Court decision crucial.

Throughout all the partisan struggles, Bill Davis maintained his position. He refused to heed insult from the "Gang of Eight." He refused to become a sycophant and simply echo the Prime Minister's views when he differed with Trudeau. Pushing, shoving, heaving, and hoeing, he brought the sides closer and closer, all the while aware of the devious game Lévesque was playing and the manner in which the other seven premiers were being used to further the cause of separatism.

It was a frustrating period for me. While I spoke to Davis and Hugh Segal almost daily, there was no place for me in the process, nor was I present at any of the federal-provincial conferences. Finally, when Roy McMurtry was away in London courting the British government, I had an opportunity for a walk-on role. Under strong pressure from the police chiefs of the province, McMurtry had written to the House of Commons Committee that was considering the act and requested them to modify the sections detailing a citizen's rights on being arrested. Also Davis personally was concerned about the wording of Section 23(3), which deals with minority language educational rights. Ontario was prepared to provide minority (i.e., French) educational facilities, but wanted to be sure that the charter included a limitation requiring a reasonable number of students in the school area. I met in Toronto with Davis, Segal, Michael Kirby, Trudeau's right-hand man during the constitutional negotiations, and Jim Coutts, the Prime Minister's principal secretary. After an hour of debate during which we discussed the principles to be enunciated, Davis left and the four of us sat down to finalize the wording for both sections. We agreed to accept substantially as proposed the federal wording for the legal rights upon arrest. I then wrote out the new statutory wording for Section 23(3) dealing with the limiting condition for minority language instruction. That wording stands today.

There were many heroes in the constitutional negotiations, both self-appointed and press-appointed. The press has chosen to identify Roy McMurtry, Roy Romanow, and Jean Chrétien as the heroes of the compromise, an accolade that Chrétien was quick to accept in his book, *Straight from the Heart*. Their work was important, but the story is not quite that simple. The necessary consensus had to be reached between first ministers, not between their attorneys-general. In particular the western premiers and Newfoundland's Brian Peckford had to be brought on side. Davis provided the link between the federal government and the opposing premiers. He was greatly assisted by Hugh Segal, who shuttled among provincial capitals drumming up support and who also established a close relationship with Kirby.

There can be no doubt that, without Davis keeping the line open to Trudeau during all the stormy sessions, there would have been one of the most harmful breaks between the provinces and the federal government in the history of this country. It was also Davis's individual discussions with the various premiers that gradually allowed the final compromise to emerge. Realizing that their opposition was to some extent fuelled by the federal government's rigidity on energy pricing, Davis endeavoured to move Ottawa in this field. Regular infusions of intelligence from the network Hugh Segal had developed across the country sustained Davis's strategy. The discussions with Allan Blakeney, who was more open to compromise than Sterling Lyon, Peter Lougheed, or Brian Peckford, perhaps because the federal NDP supported Trudeau, were particularly helpful. I must admit, however, that I had expected more leadership from Blakeney than he showed. There could be no doubt that Lougheed was the leader of the western premiers.

The Supreme Court of Canada's decision on unilateral amendment was delivered on September 28, 1981. The court ruled that the Government of Canada had the jurisdiction at law to enact constitutional amendments and to request them to be enacted by the British Parliament, but that the force of "constitutional convention" that is, established custom, and called for the federal government to have substantial agreement from the provinces before requesting the Parliament at Westminster to pass the constitutional amendments. Trudeau had won, but not quite.

While it is difficult to imagine Margaret Thatcher's government meddling in Canadian affairs by listening to requests from anyone but the federal government, the provincial lobby was hard at work, and very successful. The need for some type of provincial consensus was now very important. The final First Ministers' Conference was called for Monday, November 12, 1981. On the Sunday night before the conference, Trudeau, Kirby, Davis, and Segal met at 24 Sussex Drive. Davis emerged from that meeting downcast. He sensed a fatalism in Trudeau's approach that could be harmful to compromise.

On the first day of the conference, although both Hatfield and Davis suggested certain compromises to the opposing premiers, the eight refused to budge. The next day Trudeau said in exasperation, "Perhaps we should all agree to repatriation and have a referendum on the charter and other substantial matters." Lévesque quickly agreed, thus enraging his colleagues in the opposition, who had taken a lot of heat for aligning themselves with the "separatists." Now, Lévesque seemed prepared to subject his cohorts to what they feared most — a nation divided and a losing referendum challenge on the charter. When the conference resumed, Ontario and New Brunswick, hoping to salvage something, reluctantly pledged to support the referendum. Quebec remained enthusiastic, although with certain caveats. No others would come on board.

Earlier that day Trudeau, in his most mischievous, joking mood, had said, "What we may have to do is what Ian Smith of Rhodesia did — unilaterally resign from the Commonwealth and declare ourselves a republic." Dick Hatfield replied, "Fine, Pierre. I'll handle Maggie if you'll hand in the resignation to Liz."

In the afternoon of the next day the conference seemed to be foundering. In frustration, Davis demanded a coffee break, and the Ontario delegation went on a war footing to keep the conference alive. Davis's message was clear. If this window closed, the opportunity might not return for generations. The discussion continued.

Trudeau's patience was now at the breaking point. With the intellectual arrogance and flippancy that often marred his otherwise superb mind, he said, "There is no agreement. I guess we should call in the cameras." At that point, Peter Lougheed, who has never received enough credit for this act of statesmanship, responded, "We can admit defeat any time, Mr. Prime Minister. Why not break for dinner — it's almost eight PM — and reconvene in the morning to see where it all sits." With that simple suggestion the door was opened to the compromise that needed to take place.

Over the previous few days officials in British Columbia, Ontario, Saskatchewan, and Nova Scotia had been circulating a law journal article by Paul Weiler on the *non abstantia* approach to a charter of rights inclusion. That approach would allow "opting out" from compliance with the fundamental freedoms and legal rights clauses when parliament or the provincial legislature has to bring in special legislation to promote Native rights, or seniors' rights, or special language rights that might be in breach of the charter. The elegance of the option was undeniable. It allowed there to be a charter, but it also enabled provincial premiers to protect their jurisdiction in matters of provincial civil rights. It established the constitutionalized moral force and legal reality of a charter without limiting the supremacy of provincial legislatures to act.

Davis spearheaded the efforts to bring the seven opposing premiers — Quebec was not included in the discussions — over to the *non abstantia* approach. As the premiers appeared to be making progress, it was decided that Davis would have to ensure that Trudeau did not scuttle this compromise, which was too flexible to appeal to the Prime Minister. Davis made his views known through Michael Kirby, who arranged for him to talk on the telephone with Trudeau late that night. Davis returned to the living-room after the private telephone conversation and simply said: "We have had our words of prayer."

Kirby and Segal returned later to Davis's suite. Trudeau would reluctantly agree. Peckford would propose the compromise. Quebec would stand aside. The rest is history.

Prior to the final meeting on November 5 and before the camera sesson, the entire Ontario delegation gathered. Tom Wells said with quiet eloquence, "We would not have this deal today and there would be no compromise and no new constitution without our premier. He simply never let Canada down." There was not a dry eye in the house. The applause went on for ten minutes. Davis could not speak, and tears were running down his cheeks.

There is little question in my mind that, in his fateful phone call with Trudeau, Davis had told the Prime Minister that Hatfield and he would move to the side of the seven if Trudeau did not accept a fair compromise. He had stood firm with Trudeau through many trials, but he also knew what he had to do when the chips were down. Davis pushed on until unity was achieved. Such are the actions that build nations.

The energy expended by Bill Davis on the repatriation of the constitution and the Charter of Rights took its toll. Shortly after the Queen came to Ottawa for the formal proclamation of the act, he confided, "Well, counsellor, I don't mind admitting that I'm tired. The others weren't always gentlemen."

Our relationship was such that we never flattered each other, but I felt that this occasion merited a tribute. "You have the satisfaction of knowing that you performed a great service for the whole nation. None of your predecessors in Ontario, including Robarts, could have accomplished this. He did not have the patience to negotiate and to make the compromises and accept the shots that you have during the past couple of years. I guess what I'm groping to say is that you had the necessary sense of history."

The final ironic footnote to Davis's heroic role in the constitutional negotiations occurred when the Queen came to Ottawa for the formal signing ceremony and celebrations. While the platform was crowded with dignitaries, many of whom had played no part in the negotiations, Davis and his wife, Kathy, stood, uncomplaining, in the rain.

CHAPTER FIFTEEN

DROPPING THE BATON

The general meeting of the federal Conservative Party had been set for January 28, 1983, in Winnipeg. All the polls taken leading up to the meeting had shown the Tory support in the country as high as it had been for fifteen years, just under 50 per cent. Joe Clark had worked hard and long since his defeat in 1980 to rebuild the party's strength and to prepare it for the next election. His leadership in the House during the constitutional debate had been sound and responsible. By all normal criteria he should have received a resounding vote of confidence at the annual meeting when the question was put as to whether or not a leadership convention should be called.

At the 1981 meeting, following the election defeat of 1980, 66 per cent of the delegates had voted against calling a leadership convention, and Clark had felt that the two-to-one vote in his favour entitled him to continue as the leader. Since that annual meeting public support had increased, but this had not been reflected by caucus support in Ottawa. There existed a large group of Tory malcontents eager to replace their leader. While Clark had served the party well and tried to enhance his image in Quebec, there was growing support for Quebec native son Brian Mulroney.

In the late winter of 1982, the delegates were being selected by their riding associations for the Winnipeg meeting. Under the federal constitution, Ontario was entitled to appoint twenty delegates at large for the annual meeting. This was done by the provincial executive in consultation with the premier and the executive director of the party, at that time Bob Harris, an effective and trustworthy organizer. Harris had played an important role in helping Norm Atkins regain a majority for Bill

Davis in 1981.

My intention in attending the Winnipeg convention was to help ward off attacks on Joe Clark. Bill Davis and I had discussed Clark's leadership on several occasions, and although we both had not been happy with the consideration that Ontario had received in the short period he had been prime minister, especially in his energy policy, we recognized his problems and felt that, given another opportunity, he could regain power and govern effectively. On January 20 Davis made a public statement of support for Clark, and he remained loyal to him throughout the convention.

On arriving in Winnipeg I wandered around, looking up a few old friends, sampling the general feeling of the meeting, and trying to dig up a few votes for Joe. Clark's supporters at the national headquarters had organized the meeting well, both from the point of view of logistics and of maximizing support and enthusiasm for the leader. The general feeling both in much of the press and the upper echelon of the party was that in order for Joe Clark to emerge from the meeting with control of the caucus and a clear endorsement for the next election, 70 per cent of the delegates would have to vote against the holding of a leadership convention.

There was considerable concern about Clark's leadership in Ontario, particularly in the Metropolitan Toronto area and in the youth organization, which had fallen into the hands of right-wing Young Conservatives. I was confident, however, that with his strong showing in the polls and Davis's support, Joe would do better than he had in 1981 and get his needed endorsement. My optimism was strengthened by a better-than-adequate speech by Joe and by my personal reading of the delegates.

Rarely have I been more wrong. When the votes were counted, there were 1,607 against and 795 in favour of calling a convention. Clark was 75 votes short of the necessary number for a 70 per cent endorsement. According to the pollsters, the main source of opposition to Clark, other than in Newfoundland, was in Ontario, where only 60 per cent had voted against a leadership convention. The Newfoundland figures reflected the hope that John Crosbie, who had built up a strong following across the country, might emerge as the leader at a new convention. The Ontario vote was a surprise to me, but I put it down to the growing influence of the right wing. Joe's reaction was immediate and courageous. He asked the party executive to call a convention and announced that he would be a candidate.

The convention was called for June 9, 10, and 11 in Ottawa. In a short time all the candidates, Joe Clark, Brian Mulroney, John Crosbie, Michael Wilson, David Crombie, Peter Pocklington, Neil Fraser, and John Gamble were in the field. Only one issue was unresolved: would Bill Davis stand for the leadership? Within a week of the Winnipeg convention the press was full of conjecture about Davis's candidacy. No one recognized better than I did Davis's lifelong interest in national politics. As early as 1967, when I had persuaded him to take over the chairmanship of the Montmorency conference and of the policy committee for the national convention, we had discussed his interest at length. In simple terms, Davis was a patriot and his country was Canada. His record showed that the people of Ontario felt he had a great deal to offer his country.

As the days went by I realized that stories about Davis's possible candidacy were being planted in the papers. A campaign of "Your party and your country need you" was being orchestrated to pressure Bill Davis into running for federal leadership. I decided to go directly to the premier for confirmation of my suspicions. One day in mid-February I strode unceremoniously into Davis's office and asked, "Are you seriously contemplating running for the federal leadership?"

His reply was more perplexing than enlightening. "No, not seriously. I think that would probably be a mistake for me at this stage. However, Norm Atkins is certainly urging me not to foreclose that option. He is very anxious that I should run."

"Screw Norman," was my immediate retort. "This is your life, not his, and I think it would be a mistake of huge proportions if you stood for the leadership. Your only obligations after twenty-five years are to your family and yourself. You would hate Ottawa and would not enjoy fulfilling the obligations of a federal leader of the opposition. While I believe that if you were to become the leader you could carry the country in an election,

I am not as certain that you could carry a convention."

Davis replied, "Don't worry about it. It is highly unlikely that I will run. If I do, you will be the first to know about it." This might have been the only time he ever lied to me.

It was clear that there still burned within Bill Davis the spark of his youthful ambition to become prime minister, a spark that Norm Atkins, Bill Kelly, and Hugh Segal were busily fanning.

As February passed into March, the stories and pressures on Davis continued to increase. The *Globe and Mail* did an editorial urging him to run. A newspaper story came out about an earlier meeting between Davis and Clark, in which Davis had announced that he had told Clark he had no definite plans to run, but had made no promises. I decided that I had better find out what was happening in the real world outside Queen's Park, so I took myself down to the provincial headquarters to see Bob Harris. Harris shared my view that Davis should stay on in Ontario, that he wouldn't find Ottawa congenial. He pointed out that Davis's hesitation waltz in declaring his candidacy could have disastrous consequences if he did decide to run, because the Ontario delegates were already starting to make their commitments to other candidates and Davis would soon miss out on their support.

Meanwhile Bill Davis went down to Fort Lauderdale for a week of quiet contemplation. While Davis was in Florida, Clark, worried about the effect that a Davis candidacy would have on his own chances, was indiscreet enough to say to the press that Davis was "a regional candidate." It was a serious blunder, infuriating those who were counselling Davis to run, while giving them ammunition in their efforts to persuade the premier. It also enraged those of us who were urging Davis not to run and who, if he did not, would become Clark supporters. Above all, the remark made Clark look foolish when Davis had just performed a great national service in the struggle for the patriation of the constitution and the charter of rights.

I called Finlay MacDonald, one of the leaders of the Clark campaign, and delivered a frank invective about his leader. Then I called Davis in Florida to see what his reaction had been. He laughed and said, "One or two more of those remarks could help me make up my mind."

I decided to consult Davis's principal secretary, John Tory. Along with Hugh Segal, John Tory was the most promising new face in the Big Blue Machine. Tory is a third-generation lawyer in his family's outstanding law firm, Tory, Tory, DesLauriers & Binnington. His grandfather, J.S.D. Tory, was of great help, both with advice and financial resources, to George Drew. When young John went to law school I had high hopes of persuading him to article with Goodman & Goodman, as Tory's had a no-nepotism rule, but when Trevor Eyton heard of the policy, he managed to get the rule cancelled and I lost John to the family firm. John Tory would be my choice as the next leader of the provincial party, although he is still in his thirties.

I walked into Tory's office, sat myself down, and said, "All right, what's new? And don't hold anything back."

He hedged, "What's new where?"

"Don't fence with me, John. What's new in the saga of the Premier's candidacy for the federal leadership campaign?"

"I think you're losing. Eventually they will persuade the Premier to run."

"Why?"

"Segal is telephoning and flying all across the country trying to line up important support and they are building up the pressure on the Premier."

"Support from whom?"

"The premiers of New Brunswick, Saskatchewan, and probably Nova Scotia, and of course they've got Kinsella and Wickson out in British Columbia, and Nate Nurgitz in Manitoba. And Marcel Masse in Quebec."

"They won't get Grant Devine, or Buchanan of Nova Scotia. Masse may be a big name, but that's not the way you organize in Quebec."

I went back to my office, telephoned a mutual friend of Peter Lougheed's and mine in Edmonton, and posed the question, "What would the reaction be in Alberta if Davis decided to run for the leadership?" The answer came back to me the following day. "You'd get some very real opposition out west." That response was rather ironic, considering Davis's offer of support to Lougheed prior to the 1976 convention.

I then called my own Nova Scotia network and learned, as I had suspected, that unless Buchanan strongly and openly went out to garner delegates for Davis, Clark would take the greatest number of the Nova Scotia delegates. There was no antipathy, in fact only admiration for Davis, but Nova Scotians don't go back on their commitments easily.

Segal and I were still enjoying a pleasant relationship in spite of our difference of opinion over Davis's candidacy. He kept telling me about the strong commitment of Marcel Masse. I had known Marcel since the mid-sixties, when he was a force in the Union Nationale, and I did not doubt that he could be an asset to a Davis campaign. It was my opinion, however, that the situation in Quebec was too far gone to permit any one individual to make a significant difference in the choosing of delegates. I said to Segal, "For you to get a sizeable number of delegates out of Quebec now, either Clark or Mulroney would have to drop dead. In Quebec there are few strong permanent constituency organizations. There are only guys at the top who manufacture Tories like sausages for purposes of conventions or annual meetings and whose loyalty is to an individual not the party." Since the Mulroney forces had failed to dislodge Clark in 1981 they had been organizing the province for the next opportunity. Clark and Marcel Danis had put together a group of organizers that were to provide Clark with at least as many delegates as Mulroney.

I berated Segal: "Do you think you can do in a month what Clark and Mulroney have done over a period of years? Even more important, do you think you have anybody of capacity who would get down in the mud like those who are working for Clark and Mulroney? You're all nuts, and you're leading Bill down a garden path that will end in a lily pond."

When the Legislature opened a new session on March 20, I met with Tory and Stewart in Stewart's office. "What do you think he's going to do?" I asked. Stewart replied, "I think you may be fighting a losing fight, counsellor." Tory added, "There is no doubt in my mind. They have convinced him first of all that it is his duty to the party and to the country and secondly that he will win."

"I won't let those bastards get away with this. First of all Bill Davis doesn't owe any duty to anybody. He has paid his dues and made more of a contribution to the whole country than any premier in my lifetime. Secondly, he is not cut out for Ottawa and would hate it even if he became prime minister. Finally, it is too late for him to get into the race now and he'll be hurt."

I turned to Tory. "You and I are going to get hold of Michael Adams and get him to take a delegate poll so that I can satisfy myself that I am right. I'll take it from there."

On April 27, Peter Blaikie, who had been a leadership candidate from Quebec, withdrew from the race. At Segal's urging, a group of his supporters came to Toronto to convince Davis to run. After the meeting, Tory told me that their enthusiasm had really made an impression on Davis. I asked, "How many were there?"

"There must have been twenty or more."

I pressed him further. "How many are delegates? The selection finishes in two days."

"That I don't know," he admitted.

"I do. At most eight. I wormed that out of Segal."

The next day I reminded Davis of his commitment to see me before he made any announcement. On the first of May I learned that plans were being made to have a press conference on the fourth, and I got Stewart to arrange a meeting of Segal, Atkins, Kelly, Stewart, Tory, and myself at the Davis home in Brampton. The meeting was called for three. That morning I got the poll and went to Brampton at two o'clock. It was clear from the poll that, while he had an outside chance of winning, it was highly unlikely that Davis could carry a convention.

"I came out here early," I explained, "because I must talk to you before the others arrive. Tell me frankly, do you have confidence in my political judgement?"

"I value no one's judgement more highly than yours."

With that encouragement, I forged ahead. "I have been at every convention, both federal and Ontario, since 1938, other than the federal convention in 1942 when I was overseas. I have been chairman of two federal elections and been prominent in Ontario in three others. I know those bastards in Ottawa and how they behave. I simply want to make these points: a) the federal caucus is uncontrollable and far more right wing than ours in Ontario and will cause you much grief; b) a person with your temperament and background will not enjoy the federal leadership, especially in opposition; c) Stewart is not going to be with you in Ottawa, although I think Tory might be persuaded to go. Still, you will not have anything like the rapport with your staff and advisers that you have today.

"I believe that if you win the convention you would have a good chance of winning the country and becoming prime minister, but that you would find that equally frustrating, because in Ottawa you can achieve so little in this regionally dominated country. Finally, I have had a special poll done, which I will keep to myself although I will show it to Norman. It is my opinion, having seen that poll, that it is highly unlikely that you could win the convention because this idea came up much too late for an effective organization to be built in the other provinces, particularly in Quebec. Even in Ontario you won't get as many delegates as the others are predicting."

My arguments were bolstered by an earlier call that day from Premier Grant Devine of Saskatchewan to Davis, expressing his regret that he could not stay with the position of "constructive neutrality" he had promised he would take when Segal had sought his support. This made it clear that Davis would face not just Peter Lougheed's single-minded opposition but an organized regional antipathy. Davis's opponents would not be content to support someone else. They were coalescing to try and stop Davis, whose candidacy now had the potential to tear the party asunder.

As we talked I could see that I had gone a long way toward persuading him that he was about to make a classic mistake. When the others arrived, I repeated my speech and said that I would like to speak to Atkins and Segal in another room before I left. I showed them the poll, saying, "I know that you two guys both love the Premier. How can you do this to him?"

My parting words to Stewart were: "Ed, he has decided not to run. Don't you let those bastards change his mind."

The following day Davis announced that he would not be a candidate, stressing that he had fought divisiveness all his life and would not promote it now. It was not until months later that I found out that the plan to make Davis the prime minister of Canada had been prepared well before the Winnipeg annual meeting by Kelly, Atkins, and Segal, unknown to Davis. Most of the delegates at large and many constituency ones had gone to Winnipeg in January 1983 prepared to vote for a leadership convention. That was why Clark's support in Ontario was only about 60 per cent. There had been only one piece missing to make the operation successful: Bill Davis's early consent to run.

A month later, Kelly hosted a dinner at the Albany Club for more than 150 Conservatives from right across Canada. I didn't go only because I wasn't invited. It was Davis's way of saying thanks to the MPs, senators, and party stalwarts from across the country who had held out, waiting for his decision.

Standing in front of a banner that read "Davis — Next Time," the premier gave an unscripted speech calling for moderation and compassion in national affairs, and unity in the Conservative Party and across Canada. He said simply, "I love this party, because I love this country. I make no apology for protecting Ontario or fighting for a charter of rights and patriation of our constitution. I will not divide!"

When I asked John Robarts in 1967 whether he was going to be a candidate for the federal leadership, he had simply said, "I am not up to it, Eddie. It will take all my energy to run the campaign later this year and stay for most of another term." Bill Davis had served much longer than Robarts in more difficult times and I asked myself if he had the strength to continue in politics much longer. When I urged him not to run for the federal leadership, I privately felt the time had come for him to leave politics. He was at the height of his popularity, and I believed that he should quit while he was way ahead. Twenty-five years in the Legislature, twenty-two years in the cabinet, and fourteen years as premier had taken their toll on Bill Davis. While he almost always appeared benign, unflappable, and relaxed, he could churn on the inside with the best of us. Although I had no intention of trying to influence his decision on retiring, I was determined that if he wanted to leave he should not be pressured to remain for another election against his will. We had had several discussions on the possibilities of a new career; many boards of interesting companies wished to obtain the benefit of his services as a director, and many law firms would be pleased to have him join them as a partner. He had said jocularly on several occasions, "If I decide to retire, I'll employ you as my agent at your usual fee."

Out of the blue one day Davis said to me, "Segal thinks that I should go through this last election and retire not too long afterwards." I replied, "I do not believe you can do that. The question will arise during the election campaign as to what your intentions are, and you are not constitutionally capable of dissembling on that one. You would have to serve for at least a further two years."

His response was direct. "I don't think I am capable of doing that." I knew then that if it were not for the pressures that were sure to be exerted upon him, he would retire. I also knew that my advice not to run federally had been right.

On the Thursday before Thanksgiving Davis told his cabinet of his plans to retire before the next election. He called me after the meeting, and I went to see him immediately. Davis was clearly in a turmoil. He said, "I cannot tell you what an emotional experience I have been through. When I told them that I was seriously considering retiring, they would not accept it. Bob Welch made an eloquent speech, as did Roy McMurtry. They were crying and I was crying. They really would feel that I had let them down if I were to leave before an election."

"I told you this decision has got to be yours alone," I reminded him. "You've got to consider yourself and your family first. You've already told me that you cannot go through an election and then quit. My suggestion is that you take the weekend to let the emotion subside, then make a reasoned decision."

On Thanksgiving Monday, Davis came back from his cottage,

met again with his Cabinet and announced that he was retiring from public life. I had not spoken to him during the weekend.

During the final months of his premiership, Bill Davis had taken one of the most controversial steps of his entire career. On June 12, 1984, he had reversed his long-time position and announced that the government would extend funding to all grades of the Catholic separate schools.

The more cynical pundits of the press ascribed this move to political motives. Nothing could be further from the truth. Politically it was a mistake, and Davis knew that he was taking a great risk by changing his position. The hard core of the Progressive Conservative Party is made up of Protestants, most of whom were strongly opposed to any further aid to the Catholic separate schools. The Liberals and the NDP were already on record as favouring the extension of the aid, and it was highly unlikely that the historically large and solid Liberal Catholic vote would significantly switch its allegiance to the Tories. Indeed, the best Catholic vote the Conservatives ever had was in 1971, when Davis campaigned on a policy of no extension of aid.

Davis's motivation was his strong belief that all the children of the province were entitled to equal educational opportunities. With a Catholic population that had risen from 30 per cent in 1971 to almost 50 per cent in 1986, there could be no doubt that the separate school boards were unable to afford the educational facilities and opportunities that the public school boards were providing.

The population change did not affect my opposing views, however, nor those of Ed Stewart and Bette Stephenson, then minister of education. In 1983 I had said to Davis, "It was a mistake to have set up two elementary school systems in the 1850s and protected them in the British North America Act. It was an even bigger mistake for Robarts to have extended separate school aid to Grades 9 and 10 in 1964 and I can see no reason for you to compound it." Former public school teacher Ed Stewart added, "Our major obligation is to strengthen and improve the public school system. This will weaken it."

Davis had two responses to our objections. The first was: "We cannot have a bifurcated system of financial aid any longer in Ontario. Whatever the theoretical arguments that you fellows raise, the fact is that almost half our students are in danger of receiving an inferior education and I don't accept that. Furthermore, if executed properly, separate school funding need not have a detrimental effect on the public school system." His second response was not to discuss this question with Stewart or me any more, but to choose a new set of advisers on the issue — a typical Davis ploy.

A few months later, Shirley Hodgins, my secretary, came wide-eyed into my office and said, "Cardinal Carter's secretary is on the line and would like to make an appointment for you to visit the Cardinal."

"No one can refuse a royal command from a prince of the church. Go ahead and make the appointment."

A few days later I was ushered into the office of His Eminence, G. Emmett Cardinal Carter, who was his usual charming, affable self. After the preliminaries, he got down to brass tacks. "You know what a serious problem the financing of education is to the Catholic community in Ontario."

"Your Eminence, I certainly do know that, especially with the ever-expanding school population. I also know the great problem the cost of education is generally in the province."

"The problem is, of course, much greater within the Catholic community," he rejoined.

"That was an early risk the Catholic community took when they set up their educational system. However, I am certainly not competent to argue this matter, nor do I intend to take any definitive position with you. I would be pleased to listen and learn whatever I can."

There followed a very pleasant half hour of discussion on Catholic educational problems and a lucid argument by the Cardinal for extension of aid. When it was over, I said, "I'm pleased that you took the time to discuss this with me. I assume you have no objection if I tell the premier of our meeting?"

When I told Davis of the Cardinal's summons, he chuckled and said that the meeting must have been set up by Joe Barnicke, a leading Tory and Catholic collector for the party.

I replied, "I remain opposed."

It was late afternoon on Saturday, January 26, 1985, when I and the other delegates to the Ontario Tory leadership convention crowded the Coliseum auditorium in Toronto's CNE grounds waiting on the results of the last ballot. The excitement was at its peak when the party president, David McFadden, walked onto the stage to announce the outcome: Frank Miller 869 and Larry Grossman 792. Frank Miller was the Premier of Ontario and heir to the forty-two-year Tory dynasty. I was at the convention with Bill Davis, who stood beside me gazing impassively ahead. On my other side stood Bill Kelly. Two tears trickled down Kelly's cheek. I said to myself, "For twenty-five years I have worked to prevent our party moving to the right. Now the real fight may be just beginning." It was not, I reflected, that Frank Miller lacked compassion. He was a decent man. Unfortunately, his belief in small entrepreneurship and his known opposition to certain of the government's programs had earned him the reputation, fostered by the press, of being a right-wing conservative. It would not be easy to shake that image.

Other than being a delegate, I had played no part in the campaign. I was the only one of the Big Blue Machine who did not choose a candidate and go all out for him. Had I done so, I would have chosen Roy McMurtry or Larry Grossman: McMurtry because of my admiraton for his humanity and compassion; Grossman because he was moderate in his views and an able administrator. My partner Herb Solway was very active in Dennis Timbrell's campaign and warned me constantly that only Timbrell could defeat Miller on the last ballot. He was right. Timbrell missed that ballot by only six votes.

After Miller's election his advisers were determined, to the point of paranoia, to get neither assistance nor advice from Davis's old gang. While Miller understandably wanted to distinguish his administration from Davis's, his people seemed to want vengeance — though for what, I never found out. The meetings of Miller's transition team, headed by Tom Campbell, a former deputy provincial treasurer and then chairman of Ontario Hydro, took place in the Four Seasons Hotel, which in party circles was nicknamed "the bunker." The motto adopted by the Miller clique was that they were "the little yellow train that crushed the Big Blue Machine." Their responsibility was to decide who would go into the new cabinet and which deputies and other public servants were to be shifted or appointed. Ed Stewart's advice was not sought. The team that Campbell headed included Tony Brebner, Michael Perik, David Melnik, Jim Anthony, and Bob Carman, who was secretary of the management board and brought some rational thought to the proceedings. A further unpleasant surprise to me was Miller's hesitancy about keeping John Tory on in the premier's office. When I heard that Miller wished to cut Tory adrift, I knew that he was getting bad advice. I made my only call to Miller during the transition period to urge him to keep John Tory.

On February 8, Miller announced his cabinet. While it was not a work of art, he had taken several steps along the road to reconciliation. He had also made several serious mistakes, which would never have happened if he had done more consultation with Davis and Stewart. I was delighted to see that David Rotenberg and Phil Gillies, both of whom I held in high regard, were included in the new cabinet. One casualty was Frank Drea, who was dropped in spite of intercession on his behalf by Davis. A popular politician, Drea was not going to run again and should not have been subjected to this embarrassment. Number one on Campbell's hit list was Bob Macaulay, the recently appointed chairman of the Ontario Energy Board, and a great friend of Davis's and mine. Macaulay, who had radically and brilliantly changed the board's function, had crossed Campbell by having a few unkind things to say about Hydro. Fortunately, Stewart got wind of the plan to fire Macaulay and convinced Miller to nix it.

In spite of these contretemps, I felt that if we could just get Miller settled into office, things might turn out all right. The party was so far ahead in the polls that everyone assumed an election would soon be called. In anticipation of Davis's remaining for one more election, Hugh Segal had a superb election organization well oiled and ready to go. Segal, however, was anathema to some members of Miller's team; nor was he a favourite of Miller's. After discussing the situation with Davis, Miller asked Norm Atkins to become the campaign chairman. Atkins, while not anxious for the appointment, agreed to take it, provided he had a free hand with organization. He then went to Antigua for a holiday.

Miller's advisers, unhappy about the choice of Atkins and overconfident of victory, convinced him to change his mind in favour of Pat Kinsella, who had been executive director of the 1981 campaign under Atkins. It was a huge mistake. While Kinsella was a competent organizer, he did not have enough clout or experience to keep Miller's coterie in line.

While all this was going on, I was busy practising law. Except for the occasional curiosity call to Stewart or Davis, I was getting my news from the newspapers. I was bitterly disappointed in the vengeful attitude of Tom Campbell, whom I had considered a friend, and wished that David Melnik, whom I had known for some time and liked, had had more experience. While I barely knew Michael Perik, and had no right to blame him, I did. Carman alone combined moderation, objectivity and experience in government, but he was there almost on sufferance. But Miller was premier and should have sought a wider and more tolerant spectrum of advice.

In the late winter, I received a surprise telephone call inviting me to a Thursday morning breakfast meeting in Frank Miller's suite at Sutton Place. The question of when an election should be called was on the agenda. We listened to a report from pollster Allan Gregg on the party's electoral prospects. The polls showed that the voters were supportive, but uncertain. There was a wide base of support, but it was not deep. Just how shallow it was, we were not told. I took the floor to say, "It would be a great mistake for us to call an election before the House assembles and we have the Speech from the Throne. In the electorate's eyes promises made during an election are like confetti at a wedding. We must have a full program of solid middle-of-the-road proposals backed up by bills presented to the House. Then you can judge what the public reaction is and decide whether to call an election." I could have saved my breath. Nobody was listening to this old fart. The same group was called together for another meeting, where we were told, not asked, about some new policy initiatives. I repeated my unwelcome views and met with the same non-response.

An election was called for May 2 before even a throne speech had been delivered by Miller's government. On election night the Conservatives won fifty-two seats, the Liberals forty-eight, and the New Democratic Party twenty-five.

How did we do so badly in an election, where we had started off with public support of about 50 per cent? Why did this sink to about 37 per cent? Every newspaper pundit, politician, taxicab driver, and, above all, every Tory worker, had his or her own answer: party disunity that led to the first badly managed Tory campaign in forty-two years; mishandling of the press, particularly on the leader's bus; Miller's refusal to debate Peterson publicly, and then not being accessible to the press, especially on the bus; his unsophisticated image (unwisely fostered by his handlers); the fresh appeal of David Peterson's Liberals; the bigotry stirred by the separate schools' issue.

My own view is that the premature election call denied the voters the necessary time to get to know and trust their new premier. The broad support for Miller shown in the early polls indicated that the electorate was prepared to give him the benefit of the doubt because of its favourable experience with previous Tory leaders. The public's doubts grew as Miller's handlers, contrary to his own nature, seemed to be sheltering him. People began to fear that Miller was not cast in the centrist, moderate mould of Frost, Robarts, and Davis.

In my view, the extension of aid to separate schools would not have been a factor in the election if Anglican Archbishop Lewis Garnsworthy had not inserted himself into the campaign with his intemperate criticism of Davis. In 1971, Archbishop Garnsworthy was a party to an ecumenical report advocating extension of aid to separate schools. When, in June 1984, Bill Davis announced his government's intention to extend the grants to Catholic separate schools, he also appointed a commission, headed by William Newnham, retiring president of Seneca

College, to tour the province and ascertain views on the terms and conditions and manner in which this should be achieved. Some time after the announcement, Garnsworthy requested and was given a private meeting with the Premier. To that meeting he brought Clarke MacDonald, a former moderator of the United Church. The Archbishop requested that a private meeting be arranged with the chairman of the commission, which would also be attended by Cardinal Carter. He said that meeting must be private, as he did not want to be accused of bigotry. The meeting was held with Newnham, Carter, MacDonald, Bette Stephenson, Ed Stewart, and Ed Nelligan, the commission vice-chairman.

At that meeting, Garnsworthy expressed his views with considerable force and truculence and in direct contradiction to his 1971 support for extension. He asked for and obtained yet another meeting with the chairman of the commission, the vice-chairman, and the secretary. When Garnsworthy later accused Bill Davis of having acted in a Hitlerian manner on the funding issue, I had to ask myself what manner of Christian churchman he was.

The day after the election, Miller resurrected Stewart and invited him and Bob Carman to a meeting in Bracebridge. It was decided to ask Davis and a few of his coterie for advice. The next day, Bill Davis, Hugh Segal, Ed Stewart, John Tory, and I flew to Miller's family lodge, to urge him not to resign, but to hang tough, while we gathered the party around him.

With the election almost a tie, the bidding was on for the support of the New Democratic Party. The NDP had started the campaign with some confidence that they would replace the Liberals as the official opposition and were stunned by the results, but they rallied quickly and decided to use their balance of power to their best advantage. There began a round of bargaining among representatives of the parties to see who would hustle the New Democratic Party into bed by conceding to some of their policy demands. Bob Elgie called me to discuss how far the Tory cabinet was willing to go. My response was: "We have forty-two years of governing that we can be proud of. Tell those guys to go screw themselves and let them defeat us in the House. Apart from the matter of pride and conscience, common sense should tell you that they are going to do it anyway."

I then called Frank Miller and repeated my views. Surprisingly, he seemed happy to hear them. "I am really glad you called me," he said. "I've been most uncomfortable with what I am being urged to do by my colleagues. You are giving me the advice my conscience wanted to hear." The next day, Miller withdrew from the bargaining.

When the Liberal-NDP pact was announced, I had serious reservations about its constitutionality. I believed then, and still do today, that to make an agreement not to have an election, even when defeated on major issues, is a breach of constitutional convention, if not the law. More important, here was an agreement under which the private members of the House had their voting rights taken away from them before specific issues were presented for their views. What kind of parliamentary democracy is that?

I was recently reminded of two lines from a poem by Walter Scott:

Behind four priests in sable stole
Sung requiem for the warrior's soul.

Let me write a requiem for the Big Blue Machine. Its heart and soul were the affection and respect in which its members held Bill Davis. I have participated actively in thirteen federal election campaigns and twelve provincial campaigns and I have never seen greater camaraderie than existed in the BBM, although we would at times disagree strongly and argue vociferously. Through a mixture of progressive, centrist policies, good management, and sophisticated electoral strategies, the machine became well-nigh invincible in its determination to provide Ontarians with solid Tory government.

CHAPTER SIXTEEN

NOT BY POLITICS ALONE

In the spring of 1951, I received a telephone call from Mabel Hees asking me to join the board of the National Ballet Company. Since the days of my sister's ballet lessons at The Boris Volkoff School, ballet had been my great love and the only art form of which I had even a rudimentary knowledge.

In the previous year, Eileen Woods, Sydney Mulqueen, and Pearl Whitehead, three women who were to become lifelong heroines to me, had satisfied themselves that Canada had the dancing talent to form a national professional ballet company. These three were a formidable group of "old Toronto" matrons; if anybody could achieve this objective, they could. They formed a committee and sent Stewart James, a young ballet lover, to Great Britain to get some advice from the leading figures of Britain's thriving ballet scene and to find someone of talent who would come to Canada to see whether their project was practical. James earned his place in Canadian cultural history by bringing back Celia Franca on the recommendation of Dame Ninette de Valois, then director of the Sadler's Wells Ballet.

In Franca Canada acquired one of its most valuable immigrants. She was then in the midst of an illustrious career as a dancer, choreographer, and artistic director. She had been a leading dancer with the Sadler's Wells Ballet, and de Valois described her as the "greatest dramatic dancer that the Wells has had." She was far more than that, however. She was a superb all-round classical dancer. At the Wells she had danced the Queen of the Wilis in *Giselle* to great acclaim, but because de Valois never chose her to dance the lead role of Giselle, which was reserved for Margot Fonteyn, balletomanes in the upper galleries took to wearing yellow rain slickers on which they wrote: "We want Franca." She had also served as an artistic director with the Metropolitan Ballet of London and as ballet mistress with Ballet Jooss.

On the committee's suggestion, Franca attended the Ballet Festival Association's performances in Toronto in November 1950 and came to the conclusion that it was possible to form a professional national ballet company in Canada. She returned to Toronto in February 1951 to start the job. The committee persuaded the T. Eaton Company to pay for the November trip and to give Franca part-time work while she started on the research necessary to put together a ballet company. From the beginning, Celia recognized that to succeed she would have to play the role of artistic director, prima ballerina, main adviser to the head of wardrobe, designer of scenery, adviser to the orchestra leader, public relations officer, and goader of the board of directors. Meanwhile the committee, now joined by Mabel Hees, went about the business of putting together a board of directors for the National Ballet Guild, which was being incorporated to operate the National Ballet Company.

The first board was headed by Z.R.B. (Bobs) Lash, a charming Toronto lawyer whose father had been one of the founding directors of the Royal Ontario Museum; in addition to Lash and the four ladies the board included Norman Seagram, George Craig, Brad Heintzman, Jack Allen, Martin Baldwin, the director of the Art Gallery of Ontario, Joe Whitmore, Arthur Gelber, and myself. Subsequently, we were joined by Vic Barnett, who toiled ceaselessly and fought with me constantly in fulfilment of his obligations as treasurer. For no reason other than that I had exhibited optimism and a willingness to work, I became chairman of the management committee. My role required me to work closely with the artistic staff and dancers as well as with the small administrative staff.

Two factions warred within the board: the careful, cautious men who wanted an accounting for the money spent and a balanced budget, and the enthusiastic, determined women who recognized that any great artistic project must lose a considerable amount of money at the outset. I was in the camp of the women and dunned everybody I knew for money during those formative years. Unfortunately, in my early thirties, I did not have as many wealthy friends to dun as I would have had in my fifties and sixties. After they got wind of my mission, what few friends I did have would cross the street when I approached.

One of my most successful financial strikes took place in the third year of the company's operations when we were scheduled to perform in New York, a prized opportunity to be seen by the continent's leading dance critics. Unfortunately, we had run out of money, and it looked as if the opportunity would be lost and the dancers deeply disappointed. One of my earliest clients, the then struggling Cadillac Development, had just succeeded in making its first important land sale. I pounced upon its president, Eph Diamond, and his partners, Joe Berman and Jack Kamin, and extracted $5,000 of their meagre profits, which got the company to New York and back.

The chief perk of my job was being able to rub shoulders with the many people of talent that Celia attracted in those early days. At the outset, Celia had set as a basic criterion that the dancers in the company, including the principals, would be Canadians or people who looked upon Canada as their permanent home. She was determined not to achieve a quick popular success by bringing in famous names from abroad who would draw at the box office, on the grounds that this would slow down the opportunities and reduce the drive of aspiring young Canadians, and also impede the growth of the company's *esprit de corps*. Celia used to say to me, "In time the world's great dancers will be flattered to dance with our company," and she was right.

Celia toured the country auditioning dancers and found that there was an amazing motherlode of Canadian talent, although very little of it had had any professional experience. David Adams, who had been with the Royal Winnipeg Ballet, had met Celia in England when he danced for a short time with Sadler's Wells, and then with the Metropolitan Ballet. He had returned to Canada and married Lois Smith, a talented ballerina from Vancouver who had never danced professionally. Under Celia's tutelage, the couple became the company's premier dancers.

The other two principals were also a married couple, Irene Apiné and Latvian-born Juri Gotshalks, who after the war had come to Halifax, where he taught dance. A great asset to the company, this pair were strong technical dancers, though their style was occasionally at variance with the more lyrical quality that Celia wanted to develop for the National Ballet.

Kay Ambrose, a leading illustrator and author of many books on ballet in Great Britain, was a great personal friend and admirer of Celia's. She came over from England to visit for two weeks in the early days and stayed for years. For the most part, she was unpaid, but we finally managed to find a pittance to employ her as a public relations officer, when in fact she was our leading costume designer and an extremely capable set designer. This artistic combination of Celia and Kay, with the teaching assistance of Betty Oliphant, the company's first ballet mistress, a position she held for more than twenty-five years, gave us a professionalism that might otherwise have taken many more years to achieve.

The opening night of the company's first short three-day run in Toronto was scheduled for November 12, 1951, at Eaton's Auditorium. In the weeks before the opening, I was spending little time at the office and a great deal at the rehearsal studios in the dirty, drafty, unrenovated St. Lawrence Hall. Until the National came on the scene, the hall had been used by indigent transients, and the city was most reluctant to rent it to us. My father was growing annoyed at my dedication to Terpsichore and suggested that I should trade my court gown for a tutu. My mother, on the other hand, was thrilled.

I had laid on a press conference for the announcement of the company's first season and to give the press an opportunity to meet some of the dancers. I decided that a beer and oyster lunch would suit and asked Coles, the caterers used by our family, to make arrangements. They explained that they couldn't take on the job because it would conflict with the oyster shuckers' union! I am a strong advocate of unions, but that was the limit. The management committee rolled up its sleeves and shucked scores of oysters until their hands bled.

Opening night arrived. The black-tie crowd settled back in their seats as the opening strains of Chopin heralded the beginning of a new Canadian institution. I closed my eyes and gave a quiet *shechianu* as the corps de ballet started to dance the Nocturne of *Les Sylphides*. It was not the best dancing the world has seen, but for me that night was the most memorable of the hundreds I have spent at the theatre.

It is not my intention to chronicle further the early history of the ballet, which has been done much better by others. What I wish to acknowledge are the dedication and discipline that fuelled all the artists and, together with Celia's genius and determination, inspired the formation of Canada's national company, a company that has become perhaps the country's finest contribution to the performing arts.

In the early years, Celia and I spent many days together planning the company's future. One late September we were at my family's cottage on Lake Couchiching near Orillia fishing for bass — although wormy perch were a more likely catch. Celia, a neophyte, had just hooked a fairly decent-sized perch when one of the great muskellunge that lurk in the weeds in Couchiching grabbed the perch and securely hooked itself on the small hook. She screamed, threw the rod at me and, to my undying shame, I took it. She continued to scream for twenty minutes as I played the line and gradually brought a large muskie right to the boat only to have it break the line in its final charge to the bottom. This story served to liven up many an evening at Celia's Tyndall Avenue flat, which she shared with Kay and dozens of itinerant artists as they passed through town.

On another occasion, Celia and I flew to New York to persuade Antony Tudor, then the ballet director for the Metropolitan Opera and a choreographer of great note, to teach the company his *Jardin aux Lilas*, a lovely romantic ballet that has remained a favourite of mine. He generously agreed to come for expenses and the munificent sum of $15 each time the company performed the ballet.

Some of the great names in the Canadian performing arts were associated with the ballet in the early days, including Walter Homburger, a gifted impresario and later general manager of the Toronto Symphony, who was the first company manager, when he wasn't building Glenn Gould's fine career. David Haber, also to become a prominent impresario, was our stage manager and had great talent and understanding of ballet and theatre. Celia Sutton, the wardrobe mistress, formed a fine team with Kay Ambrose. The company developed a corps of dedicated young dancers, among them Lillian Jarvis, Joyce Hill, Nadia Potts, Myrna Aaron, Colleen Kenney, Natalia Butko, Judie Colpman, Angela Leigh, Robert Ito, Hy Meadows, Andre Dufresne, and Katharine Stewart.

In 1958, I gave up the position of chairman of the management committee in favour of what I thought would be the relatively quiet role of president, following Tony Griffin. Celia and Betty must have been waiting for this to happen. In short order they descended upon me urging that it was essential to the future of the National Ballet that we have a full-time academic and dance school. Most of the promising young students were then receiving their training from Betty Oliphant's ballet school on Sherbourne Street. I was daunted by the prospect of starting and financing a full-time school and obtaining the physical plant as well as a residence to accommodate the out-of-town children. But there could be no gainsaying the logic of Celia's and Betty's argument, nor the force of their attack. I did not anticipate the opposition to these plans that I met within the board of directors, even from some on whom I normally counted for support. In the end the dauntless four women fell in behind me and again we carried the day.

I recognized quickly that it would be a great mistake to have the school as an adjunct of the National Ballet Company, no matter how close the relationship was between Betty, its principal, and Celia. I persuaded John Osler, later Mr. Justice Osler, to take over the presidency of the school and between us we managed to find an enthusiastic board. We located a building on Maitland Street, which is today still part of the greatly expanded school, and a residence on nearby Sherbourne Street. The crying need for a school in Canada and the talents of those involved brought the school almost instantaneous success. Today it is world famous.

During the school's second year, Betty and Celia showed up in my office saying that they had an exceptionally promising young pupil who required financial assistance to be able to come to the school. I told them that I would either give or arrange for a scholarship for the young student's school career. I called Pete Hardy at Labatt's and reported that I was doing him the great honour of cutting him in with me for half a scholarship for a young lady whose name was Veronica Tennant.

The funniest episode of my presidency occurred when the Ballets Russes came to Toronto to perform at Maple Leaf Gardens. Canadian relations with The Soviet Union were at a low ebb and city council decided that they would not entertain the ballet. To add to the insult, Mayor Nathan Phillips had passed a careless derogatory remark about the Russian ambassador to Canada, whose name was Aroutunian, whom he referred to as "Rootin' Tootin'." Balletomanes were outraged by the shabby treatment of the Ballets Russes, and I received many calls urging the National Ballet Company to entertain the visitors. The company was far too broke to provide lavish hospitality, and I had to figure out a way to do the job in style without digging too deeply into either the National's or my own pockets.

To add to my troubles, the Ballets Russes was coming on election day, when it was illegal to sell beer, wine, or spirits. Our party would have to be in a private residence spacious enough to accommodate the guest list. Even when restricted to the Russian company, the Canadian company, the board of directors, the staff, and sundry other notables, the numbers were sizeable. Someone remembered that the Cassels' large home in Rosedale was empty and the family kindly agreed to let us use it. After I convinced Shopsy's to contribute most of the food and a local distiller to contribute some of the liquor, I was able to afford the balance. The stage was now set for one of the great parties in Toronto's social history. The Russian ambassador would, of course, be present at the performance and the reception, so I called Mayor Phillips and offered him the opportunity to make up for his gaffe.

My wife and I went to the Cassels' house to make certain everything was ready and to greet the early guests. We had to miss the performance, but when I heard that prima ballerina Alicia Markova, a dancer of almost mythical grace and technique, had fallen flat on her prat, I was glad I hadn't been there to see it. After nearly all the guests had arrived, we were still waiting for the Russian ambassador. Finally, a large car drew up and disgorged its occupant, who was dressed in the *de rigueur* dinner jacket with a large red star hanging on his breast. I stepped forward and said, "Your Excellency, it's a great honour to have you here this evening."

He replied, "I'm not His Excellency. I lead the orchestra." My problems didn't end with the late arrival of the real Dr. Aroutunian. His Excellency's entrance was followed by that of Alicia Markova, who was, shall we say, in a less than sociable mood. Her attendant asked to be led to the private dining-room set aside for Madame Markova. I explained humbly that she was dining with everybody else and that a seat next to the ambassador had been reserved for her. Not to be mollified, the world's premiere ballerina flounced into the room without a hello. A few minutes later my wife, Suzie, clearly in a state of agitation came running over to me. An ill-mannered representative of Sol Hurok, the impresario who was managing the tour, had been telling her that usually Madame Markova and the company were entertained by heads of state at banquets of sumptuous quality and that our paltry efforts didn't measure up.

My problems, however, had just begun. The mayor arrived to pay his respects to the ambassador, accompanied by about twenty reporters. When I approached the ambassador to make the introduction, he sniffed that he had no intention of meeting anybody as ill-mannered as the mayor. It occurred to me at this stage that the evening wasn't going too well. I patiently explained to the ambassador that up until now the public had been on his side in the contretemps with the mayor. If he now refused to speak to the mayor, public opinion would quickly change, and he would lose the advantage. He reluctantly saw the logic of my argument and went out to greet the mayor. A rather tenuous reconciliation was effected to the snapping of many cameras.

When everything had settled down, and the guests were more or less contentedly dining, drinking, and dancing, I whispered to my wife, "Let's get the hell out of here before something else happens."

By 1960 I realized that I had had nearly ten years of working for the National Ballet and that the time had come to turn the job over to others, so I retired. It had been a fruitful decade for me. I had had the privilege of working both with the professional artists as well as with the dedicated amateurs on the board. The company was starting to receive international recognition. The standard of teaching for young Canadian dancers had improved tenfold right across the country. Seeing the best Canadian dancers competing with the best in the world gave me a satisfaction I could not have received from any other field of activity.

As soon as I learned to read, my mother started to ply me with books. When I was four and five, she would read to me from the various adventures of the Bobbsey Twins. On my own I later progressed to being enchanted by books and illustrated volumes on dinosaurs and other prehistoric life forms. Then one day my mother took me to the palaeontology galleries of the Royal Ontario Museum and the world of my fantasies came vividly to life. My fascination with dinosaurs was only the beginning. Roaming the vast galleries and corridors of the ROM, I became acquainted with its other treasures, with Egyptian mummies and ancient Chinese ceramics, with burnished medieval armour and fragile textiles, with rocks and minerals that lit up, and dazzling trays of brilliantly hued butterflies.

In 1983, Sydney Hermant, my former camp counsellor and religious school teacher at Holy Blossom Synagogue, who was chairman of the museum's board of trustees, finished his second term. He had taken the museum through a difficult period of physical expansion and renovation, which had necessitated a temporary closing. Hermant's second term in office ended in June 1983. Early that year, when Premier Bill Davis asked me to accept the appointment as Hermant's replacement, I did so with alacrity.

When my appointment was announced I expected some reaction from the press on account of my closeness to the government, but the only question they asked was what I was being paid. When they learned that it was a non-paying job, they immediately lost interest. Throughout my political experience, I have found the press interested in two things about appointments: the nature of the appointee's connection with the governing party and how much he or she is being paid. Whether the appointee is capable and suitable for the position never seems to be of concern to the media. But then how would the press understand those factors?

I was totally unprepared for the sad state of the ROM's finances. The museum was flat broke. It had a bank debt of just under $5 million; it was running an annual operating loss of about $0.5 million, and it was committed to a bicentennial project for which it had budgeted a further $0.5 million loss. And that was the *good* news.

The bad news was that while the recent enlargement and renovation of the museum had cost $55 million, a reasonable amount for the fine job that was done, that was only for the building shell and could not provide for the installation of the permanent galleries. Less than a fifth of these galleries had been opened, and these had been financed by bank borrowing up to the museum's maximum limit. The cost of the installation of the remainder of the galleries had been estimated to be a further $22 million, but a more accurate estimate would have been $35 million.

At a board meeting I attended before I took office, I was asked if I had any comment. I simply said, "I was under the misapprehension that I was being appointed chairman of the board. In fact I have been appointed as a trustee in bankruptcy for the Royal Ontario Museum. The institution is totally insolvent."

The ROM faces the same problems as any other museum or university in Canada. Most educational institutions in this country depend primarily on provincial governments for their funding and have failed to develop a tradition of obtaining large sums from the private sector. The ROM's early supporters had made generous amounts available to assist Charles Trick Currelly, the museum's founding spirit and first archeology curator, to purchase antiquities before the museum was built. A host of outstanding Canadians, such as Sir Edmund Walker, its founding chairman, George Croft, Major James Hahn, Bishop

White, Sigmund Samuel, Garfield Weston, Mrs. Robert Gouinlock, Mrs. H.D. Warren, Mrs. J. Edgar Stone, and John and Mary Yaremko had made significant donations to its collections. Colonel R.S. McLaughlin had donated the funds needed to build and maintain the McLaughlin Planetarium. There had never been an organized campaign for an endowment fund, however. Peter Swann, the director of the museum in the sixties, had recognized the need for money for collections and alone had raised about one hundred thousand dollars for future purchases. Swann then ran afoul of the board, which dismissed him in 1972. For the expansion in 1978 there had been a campaign chaired by Mona Campbell and John Devlin to raise capital funds from the private sector—the first since the museum came into being seventy years earlier—and the campaign raised about $10 million.

The restraint program instituted by the government of Ontario in the seventies had a strong impact on colleges and universities and on other educational and cultural institutions. For the museum, restraint coming in the midst of expansion was devastating. The expansion plan drawn up in 1977 had provided for the substantial budget increase necessary to an institution that was doubling in size. When the renovated museum reopened in 1982, the annual operating grant was only two-thirds of what had been originally planned in the seventies, a shortfall of about $7 million. While the original plan had been too extravagant, it was not possible to run a first-class institution on the diminished budget.

The first priority was to install the permanent galleries. It had been my view for some time that government policy should be directed at helping those volunteer social service, educational, and cultural institutions that were prepared to help themselves by matching campaigns. I made arrangements with the premier, Ed Stewart, and Bob Carman of the province's management board that if they would give us a grant of $10 million over five years for gallery installation the museum would raise at least as much. (In fact, the ROM board set an objective of $12 million to be raised from public and corporate donations.)

At my first board meeting in August 1983, I gave the trustees my view of the financial problems of the museum. "In the past, the boards of trustees and the chairmen of this institution have felt that it was not their responsibility to assist in funding, which they saw as a government responsibility. If that policy remains in force, this museum will not continue. We will not be able to install our galleries nor will we be able to balance our operating budget. This board of trustees is no different from a board of directors in the private sector. We are responsible for the financial health of this institution. While we obviously depend a great deal on the government, we must get money from many other sources. For the campaign to be successful, the board must set an example both in giving and in working." The board unanimously agreed to the public campaign and every member donated generously.

If I was to run a $12-million campaign, I needed some strong full-time help. The ROM had never had a full-time development officer. I took part in the search and interviewed several applicants for the position of executive director of the campaign. The one who appealed to me was Robert Howard, at that time the assistant development officer at the University of Toronto, an institution not well known for raising money. Howard, a chunky, laughing Varsity graduate, had for a short time played professional hockey with the New York Rangers and today he coaches young people's hockey. He is a person of high principles, who can mix with people at all levels. During the interview he asked, "What do you see as your role in this campaign?"

"Mr. Howard," I replied. "I want you to know that, for a cause I believe in, I can kissass with the best of them."

He laughed and said, "I want the job." We have been kissassing together for five years.

Eph Diamond and I had recently co-chaired the campaign for a new geriatric hospital at the Baycrest Centre for Geriatric Care and this experience now stood me in good stead. I had learned that the success of any fund-raising campaign is totally dependent on the quality and dedication of its leading canvassers and their knowledge of the need. For the ROM, which had just finished a building campaign, this factor was even more important; some donors were still paying their original pledges and weren't likely to be keen when the hat was passed again. I was fortunate to have the assistance of exceptionally able people. Dick Thomson, chairman of the Toronto-Dominion Bank, covered the banks; Arden Haynes, president of Imperial Oil, canvassed the oil companies; Jack Rhind, a long-time ROM supporter and chairman of Confederation Life, looked after the life insurance companies. Phil Holtby, president of Midland-Doherty, assisted by Jim Bullock of Cadillac Fairview and Bob Luba of Crownx, dunned the medium-sized corporations; Bob Stevens of Balek Cassels headed up the individual canvass together with Joan Thompson and Dibs Rhind, long-time ROM workers. With these people in place, I persuaded Wilfred Posluns, president of Dylex, to become chairman of the campaign, and Dick Ivey of London to become the honorary treasurer. With considerable help from Syd Loftus, a Dylex executive, Joe Chiappetta, an Italian lawyer, and Both von Bose, a German financial executive, we campaigned in some of the new and growing communities.

The fillip for both private and corporate donors was the establishment of two gift clubs, the Royal Corporate Circle and the Royal Terrace Club. These two organizations, now continuing institutions at the ROM, provide their members with special programs within the museum. They will be the basis of the ROM's future financial stability if we can persuade the members to renew after their initial gifts are paid up.

In the midst of the fund-raising arrangements, there was another major event to plan, the visit to the museum of Her Majesty Queen Elizabeth II and Prince Philip in September 1984. Their itinerary included a visit to the ROM for the dedication of the newly erected Terrace Gallery building, which was to house a great part of our collections.

Although I has not intended to launch the campaign till the fall of 1984, we decided to announce it in February and to commence in April. Howard and I figured that this would allow us to get started with the distribution of our cards and the lining up of our canvassers before the royal visit and its attendant publicity, which would give us the impetus and exposure we needed.

We came up with the splendid idea that the new Terrace

Gallery should be called The Queen Elizabeth II Terrace Gallery. An obliging provincial government obtained royal approval for that designation. The Queen was to spend an hour at the exhibition, dedicating the building, addressing the crowd, then touring the Ontario bicentennial exhibition, "Georgian Canada." This magnificent exhibition, put together by Don Webster and the Canadiana Department, included several pieces from the Queen's own private collection.

The museum was crowded to capacity with about 2,800 people the day the royal party arrived. I was pretty relaxed, but Suzie, who was accompanying Prince Philip, was anxious. Earlier she had asked Bill Davis's wife, Kathy, what she should talk to the Prince about. Kathy had replied, "Talk to him about fishing. He is a great trout fisherman." My wife had relayed this information to me and I volunteered to get Ed Crossman of the museum's ichthyology department to do her a memo on trout, which she struggled to commit to memory. On our walk through the museum to the Terrace Gallery, my wife gathered confidence, turned to Prince Philip, and said, "I understand that you are very interested in fishing."

"What gave you that idea?" came the devastating reply. Fortunately, Suzie rallied to talk of other things.

The royal visit went off without a serious hitch. For me one of the most gratifying moments occurred when I was able to present my daughter and son-in-law to Her Majesty—a perk that I regard as the only bit of patronage I received throughout my political career. I also made certain that many members of the staff and volunteers were presented.

The success of the gift clubs caused Bob Howard, Joan Thompson, the deputy chairman, who had become the campaign's spark-plug and main money raiser, and me to beef up our search for major gifts. We realized that no museum or gallery of world standing can maintain its position without the assistance of substantial benefactors. In the United States this is taken for granted, and museums and universities receive billions of dollars from private sources. If benefactors were to be found, a likely source was among families who had had a long tradition of interest in the ROM. We agreed that a gallery would be dedicated to anyone who contributed $1 million. In the midst of the campaign, three families who had been strong supporters of the institution came up with this munificent amount. The first were Liza and Ernie Samuel — Ernie being a grandson to Sigmund Samuel, to whom the museum was deeply indebted for his Canadiana contributions in its early stages. They dedicated our European gallery. The Weston family, whose patriarch, Garfield Weston, had been one of our most generous contributors in the twenties and thirties, dedicated the Exhibition Hall in his name. The Eaton family, who under the leadership of Signy, the matriarch of the family, has been a leading supporter of many cultural institutions in Canada, later agreed to dedicate the Eaton Court, which will enlarge the new building. All three of these families had hard-working members on our board, Nicky Eaton, Wendy Rebanks, and Ernie Samuel. Liz Samuel works on the members' volunteer committee. These examples encouraged others to help maintain our natural heritage. The McLaughlin Foundation, the museum's most generous supporter throughout its history, dedicated the mineralogy and geology gallery. The Canadian National Sportsmen's Shows, which shares the ROM's interest in the natural world, agreed to sponsor the bird gallery. These benefactors, along with the generous response to our newly instituted annual appeal for funds to our twenty thousand members, ensured the success of the campaign.

Though money was essential to the continued health of the ROM, money alone could not solve all the problems. The further priorities that Davis, Stewart, and I worked out were twofold. First, to build up public interest in and attendance at the ROM. Important as the work of the curatorial staff is, the museum was not built for the scholars but for the education and enjoyment of the public. We needed programs and activities that would pull in people of all ages and interests. We also had to upgrade our efforts at publicizing the museum's exhibitions. Call it huckster- ism if you will, but there is little point in offering the amenities of a world-class institution if no one comes to see it. The second priority was to strengthen the academic excellence that was slowly, but surely, deteriorating owing to lack of money and leadership.

Marketing and the popularization of the ROM's many educational programs was taken on with vigour. Several special exhibitions with both scholarly interest and public appeal have been brought in. Exhibitions like "Precious Legacy" containing Jewish artifacts from Czechoslovakia that showed the tragedy of the Holocaust, "Maya," which revealed the absorbing drama of that vanished Central American civilization (in this field Dr. Dave Pendergast and Dr. Elizabeth Graham of ROM had world renown), "Eye of the Beholder," which celebrated the beauty of personal adornment over the centuries, "*The Titanic*," with its underwater treasures, and a score of others have attracted thousands of visitors. Films, lectures, and other ongoing activities complement the galleries and exhibitions. More than a million people now visit the ROM every year, and another three-quarters of a million outside Toronto see its travelling exhibitions. It is the children, however, more than 200,000 of them a year, who make the ROM such a delightful place. Just as I came there as a wide-eyed youngster more than sixty years ago, now every day hundreds of children wander through its galleries with their eyes popping and their tongues wagging. Early this year Dr. Lou Levine saw two children gazing at the dinosaurs and one said to the other, "Wouldn't you love to crawl into that world?"

In 1984 entomologist Dr. David Barr was appointed associate director, curatorial, and we set out on the long road of restoring confidence between the board and management on one hand and the curatorial and other staff on the other. Later that year, Dr. James Cruise, the museum's director, informed me that he would not seek a third term. The board appointed a search committee of academics and members to find a new director. After a rigorous and lengthy search, in which fifteen outstanding candidates were interviewed, we found our new director, Dr. T. Cuyler Young, Jr., right at home in the museum. Dr. Young was the head of the West Asian department and had been a member of the museum staff for twenty-three years.

There is a flip side to the enjoyment of working with first-class academics. There is a vocal minority who exhibit a maddening narrowness of outlook and inflexibility. They see the work only through their own discipline and forget that they are part of a larger institution to which they owe a loyalty. My experience teaching at the University of Toronto and working at the ROM has taught me that there is no group of people more orthodox intellectually and less open to new ideas outside their fields than many of the very academics who are supposed to be seeking new insights. They believe that their academic customs are carved in stone. When any innovation is suggested by management it is pondered over until rigor mortis sets in.

My greatest frustration has been trying to expedite the installation of the ROM's permanent galleries. In the first three years, progress was barely discernible. As I said in my report to the lieutenant-governor-in-council, gallery installation was going "at a snail's pace and at the cost of a rake's progress."

In order to understand the complexity of the problem, you need to know that most galleries require a team consisting of curators, designers, preparators, theme designers, graphic designers, artists, and audio-visual technicians. These people all have to agree both on the story to be told and on the most creative way to tell it. Cuyler Young called for a survey of the staff of the museum to help determine the cause of the endless delays. It showed that the academics did not like working with the non-academics and that many believed they should have total control of the whole process. The non-academics disliked working with the academics, who they believed looked down on them. Cuyler, determined to rectify these delays and improve attitudes through a meaningful consultation with staff, arranged for Dr. Lou Levine to be appointed to the newly created post of associate director of exhibitions. The installation program now appears to be proceeding expeditiously. At the present time, 50 per cent of the galleries have been completed and there is as much permanent gallery space open today as there was when the museum closed for renovations. By the end of 1989 two-thirds of the galleries will be installed. While these mammoth changes are implemented, ROM is required to enlarge and expand its educational program for both young and old and to remain vibrant and exciting with exhibitions and public programs. No other museum institution in the world has attempted so formidable a creative task.

Early in my term there was disagreement between the board and management over special exhibitions. Experience in both North America and Europe has shown that to maintain attendance at museums and galleries, the institutions cannot rely on their permanent collections alone; they require a steady diet of special exhibitions to entice new visitors and keep the old. Previous management, unwilling to accept the policy on special exhibitions adopted by the board, provided us with a myriad of excuses. They alleged that staff time devoted to special exhibitions would slow down the installation of the permanent galleries. This was impossible; the process could not have been any slower. Another excuse was that the cost would be beyond the means of our budget. The board met this problem through a new policy of commercial sponsorships, a policy senior management endorsed but that met initial resistance among middle management.

Occasionally museum staff would go to great lengths to thwart the board. When I insisted on a banner indicating that the 1987 special exhibition on *The Titanic* was in the Sigmund Samuel Building and had been sponsored by the *Toronto Sun*, in a fit of pique some joker covered the whole wall of the building with the banner. I simply wrote a memo thanking the perpetrator. The result was that more than 5,600 people visited that building during spring break, compared with 360 the previous year.

My most open warfare has been with those I call the autonomous autocrats of the conservation department. The ROM has one of the best conservation departments in North America. It is also the most zealous in protecting its artifacts to the point of infinity.

The recent "Eye of the Beholder" exhibition was to be formally opened by the governor-general, the Honourable Jeanne Sauvé. When I visited a day or two before the opening, the lighting was so low that I could hardly see the objects. I was told that the conservation department had deemed it necessary to keep the light levels very low to protect the objects, many of which were hundreds of years old. I told Peta Daniels, the curator in charge of the exhibition, that I understood and would provide Her Excellency with a flashlight for the opening. The lighting was increased, but not by much.

On another occasion, I received a complaint about using an ancient steel sword for a birthday-cake-cutting ceremony, alleging that its life could be shortened by as much as 10 per cent. I inquired how long its life would then be. "About two million years," came the reply.

Happily these problems are largely in the past, and management and staff in all departments are working more harmoniously together in the interests of the institution we are all honoured to serve. The challenges facing the Royal Ontario Museum in the next decade are formidable, but they are more than equalled by the talent and energy of its staff and management.

In 1986 the government of Ontario changed, and David Peterson and the Liberals assumed power. The ROM has continued to receive the same high level of support and co-operation from Premier David Peterson, Minister of Culture and Communications Lily Oddie Munro, the treasurer, and the host of public servants it deals with as we had from the previous government. In June 1986, on the expiration of my first term, I proffered my resignation but it was not accepted by the premier, who extended many courtesies to me. When I finally do retire as chairman in 1989, it will be among my chief pleasures to watch the museum fulfil its destiny as a world-class institution.

In closing these reminiscences of my happy involvement in the arts, I feel I must bemoan the failure of a large segment of the community to understand that institutions of higher education, science, and culture need much greater support than they receive at present, not only from government, but from all levels of society. These institutions are essential to a richer quality of life for every segment of society, to Canada's ability to advance to the forefront of the international community, and to our country's economic well-being. The suggestion that culture is the "hobby of the rich" is misbegotten. The arts are enjoyed by every class and social group in the world. Music, dance, theatre, painting, sculpture, and literature spring from the native peoples of every continent and are the means by which they find self-expression and appreciate beauty. The arts are a major employer and an important part of our economy and tourist trade.

My experiences in many fund-raising ventures have taught me a sad lesson about the society we live in. The materialism that has engulfed North America in the past thirty years appals me. We have forgotten the obligations imposed by the Judaeo-Christian religions to devote one's time, efforts, and monies to better the lot of our less fortunate brethren. We are more concerned with fitting our houses and apartments with the latest audio equipment, three television sets, and the most sumptuous furnishings. In short, consumer goods are God, and selfishness reigns supreme. We expect all our duties and responsibilities to others to be taken on by the government, while at the same time it is lowering our taxes. If people are unwilling to help the unfortunate they are even less willing to help educational and cultural institutions. Too few citizens are willing to make the effort to help create an environment where the community may acquire higher values through the arts and promote world harmony through knowledge of other cultures.

Thus endeth the lesson.

NATIONALIST DREAMS

More than fifty-eight years have passed since my father told me that we were Conservatives because they were "more decent," and five decades have elapsed since the university days when I first held office in the Progressive Conservative Party. In that time I have seen leaders and policies come and go, and yet I have always found a core of Conservative principles in which I believe. Even today, when all three parties crowd each other to occupy the centre of the spectrum, the philosophical differences between them have been partially obliterated, and the average voter must look to such ephemera as the leader's "image" and the electoral views shown by the latest polls, I believe there still remain some ideological differences among the parties.

The philosophical threads that run through the Conservative Party's attitudes and policy since Confederation are embodied in the word "Tory," the name given to British Conservatives in the seventeenth century. Originally the Tory party stood for unswerving loyalty to the Crown, which today means loyalty primarily to parliamentary institutions and, on appropriate occasions, a willingness to sublimate private rights to the common interest; a belief in a strong defence policy with collective security under NATO; and a vision of Canada as a strong and unified nation, not a series of regions. Traditionally, the Progressive Conservative Party has favoured a nationalist economic policy as a means of realizing this "national dream."

In every election from the nineteenth century until 1945, Conservative Party policy emphasized protection of our industrial economy and, to the extent that it has been possible, our economic independence, through varying degrees of protectionist measures. From John A. Macdonald's introduction of tariffs to encourage Canadian manufacturing and industry, protectionism has been a traditional Conservative position. Sir Robert Borden in 1911 and R.B. Bennett in 1930 sought to limit Canadian dependence on trade with the United States; and in 1957 one of the arrows in John Diefenbaker's large quiver of policy issues was the transfer of 15 per cent of our trade from the United States to Great Britain, a policy that was tempered by a moderate protectionism to limit the growing control of foreign investors over Canadian resources.

By contrast, successive Liberal leaders and prime ministers traditionally talked in continental tones of increasing our relations and our trade with the United States. In 1970, in his book *Canada's First Century*, historian Donald Creighton wrote, "The decline and fall of the British Empire-Commonwealth and the growth of continentally organized North America were twin processes which had been going on now for over four decades and which successive Liberal governments in Canada had actively encouraged and assisted."

It was only in the mid-sixties that the strong nationalist views of Liberal Walter Gordon brought about an extraordinary change in the continentalist economic philosophy of the Liberal Party. Gordon's entire political life was dedicated to the principle of strengthening Canadians' control of their industrial and economic resources.

The combination of bad judgement, bureaucratic opposition and lack of support from Pearson for Gordon's first budget with its nationalistic goals hurt Gordon's authority and prestige. The failure of the Grits under his organizational direction to obtain a majority in 1965 was the *coup de grâce*, and he resigned as minister of finance. In June 1966, Mike Pearson, under pressure from Gordon's host of admirers, asked him to return to the cabinet, but Gordon required some assurances that steps would be taken to further economic nationalism. Gordon was then offered the position of minister without portfolio and given the responsibility of chairing a small committee to prepare a white paper on corporate structure and the Canadian economy, to be used as a basis for appropriate legislation. Gordon appointed Mel

Watkins, an able left-wing economist, as head of a task force to assist in the execution of this responsibility.

The Gordon report was presented to cabinet and, on February 15, 1968, Gordon tabled it in the House. Pearson already had announced his resignation and the Liberal Party was in the midst of a leadership race. Gordon resigned from the cabinet on March 11.

Gordon subsequently secured Pierre Elliott Trudeau's support for his report and endorsed Trudeau's leadership bid; but two years after the 1968 election, when no evidence of Trudeau's intention to follow through on these ideas was forthcoming, Gordon decided to jog Trudeau's memory. He created the Committee for an Independent Canada.

In the early part of 1970, I received a call from Walter Gordon. "I would very much appreciate it if you would come to a meeting of about eight or ten people," he said. "We are going to discuss the deep concern that some of us have about the extent of foreign ownership and control of our economy."

"Why me, Walter?"

"We wish this to be a non-partisan group, and we're anxious to have a high-profile Tory. In any event the roots of your party are embedded deep in nationalistic clay. Some of those fellows you have in Ottawa seem to be forgetting that."

As I was still Stanfield's national chairman of organization, I replied, "I will discuss it with Bob and get back to you."

Stanfield knew my nationalist sentiments and, with his blessing, I joined the loosely knit gang of self-styled, quixotic mule-riders known as the Committee for an Independent Canada. The CIC was a politically disparate group concerned about the effect on all aspects of national life of the ever-growing control of the Canadian economy by foreign, particularly American, corporations. The early members who come to mind where Abe Rotstein, a University of Toronto economist; Jack McClelland, the president of McClelland and Stewart; Peter C. Newman, well-known author and editor of *Maclean's* magazine; Pierre Berton, the chronicler of Canadian history; Senator Keith Davey (who did not last too long — working for a non-partisan organization was anathema to him); Dorothy Petrie (now Mrs.

Keith Davey), a prodigious worker for the committee and for the Liberal Party; Claude Ryan, publisher of *Le Devoir*; Jack Biddell, the chartered accountant with a thousand ingenious ideas; Mel Hurtig, the Edmonton publisher who has remained devoted to the cause; Flora MacDonald, who served as an early executive director; and Barbara Deprato, who succeeded Flora and was assisted by Jean McManus Zsolt. The original purpose of the committee was very simple. It was to collect a quarter of a million signatures on a petition requesting the government to take steps to limit foreign ownership of Canada's economy and resources.

The committee immediately took off, and people flocked to work for it. As branches were opened across the country, some form of central structure became essential. We decided that Gordon would be honorary chairman and McClelland would be chairman. We opened a small, decrepit, airless office for the staff, all of whom worked at starvation wages.

By early 1971 the CIC boasted several thousand members, and our petition had far exceeded its original objective. Aided by some vigorous news and editorial support from the *Toronto Star*, we had become a major source of interest across the country. The polls showed that we enjoyed the support of approximately 75 per cent of Canadians in every region of the country. The response from the public revealed to me how deeply many Canadians loved their country.

The time was propitious to act. An appointment was made for six or eight of us to meet with Prime Minister Trudeau in June, to be followed by meetings with Stanfield and David Lewis. About half an hour before our appointment with Trudeau, Walter Gordon took me aside and said that his previous cabinet association with Trudeau made it inappropriate for him to lead the delegation. Would I become the spokesman and leader? The first, last, and only time I had spoken to Trudeau he had called me a "sonofabitch" for forcing the 1968 television debate. With some misgivings I accepted.

Trudeau was warm and courteous. I briefly outlined the history and objectives of the committee. I pointed out the Liberal Party's public commitment to the committee's objectives. I emphasized the strong public support for our position. I dealt briefly with the dangers of the constantly increasing foreign investment and unfavourable balance of payments for the ten years prior to 1970. I ended by saying, "We understand, sir, that the cabinet has the preliminary draft of the Gray Report on foreign ownership, and the committee is looking forward to its release and to some specific commitments to act on its recommendations."

While Trudeau was quick to grasp many of the implications of the problems of foreign control of our industry, he was not prepared for our meeting. His response, which amounted to little more than the conventional platitudes, reinforced my view that his interest in crucial economic issues was never more than superficial. He expressed concern for the problems caused by the existing degree of foreign ownership. He said that the government's goals "are very close — though not identical — to those of the committee." He indicated that it would not be long before the government would present to the House certain measures like those we were suggesting and said that he looked forward to our support and assistance. At the end of the meeting Trudeau said to me, "This is a more pleasant occasion than the last time you and I met."

About a year later the government brought in a very weak bill setting up the Foreign Investment Review Agency. When the legislation was introduced, Gordon said to me, "This legislation is just a disgrace. It represents no steps of any consequence, and the committee must oppose it or the public will think the problem has been dealt with." I agreed and, in my recently appointed capacity as CIC chairman, I issued a public statement opposing the legislation on the grounds that it was a mere sop. The hearings on the legislation were undertaken by a parliamentary committee chaired by Bob Kaplan. I informed the committee secretary that the CIC wished to make representations on the bill. Kaplan called to inquire who would be appearing. I gave him three or four names, including Walter Gordon's and my own. He informed me that only I could speak for the CIC and that he would not allow Gordon to present his views in an independent capacity.

I was beside myself with anger and amazement. Gordon was the architect of the Liberal Party's return to power, the leading thinker and writer in the field, and Kaplan wanted to muzzle him at a public hearing. When the hearings were held, I made the preliminary remarks, then called on Gordon and others to express their opinions. Kaplan was furious. I whispered to him, "You interrupt and we will walk out and say that the Liberal Party wants to muzzle Walter Gordon." My threat worked.

The CIC-nurtured public opposition to the inadequacies of the projected Foreign Investment Review Agency caused the government to amend the bill to give it real teeth, and on the second go around the CIC supported it. There was great American resentment of the agency, whose mandate was to review any foreign investments of consequence. In many instances, I believe, FIRA did succeed in obtaining more beneficial terms as a condition for allowing foreign investment in the country.

In September 1974 the committee held a successful policy conference in Edmonton that produced many innovative ideas for the government of Canada, had they been interested — which they were not. I retired as chairman in 1975 to be ably succeeded by Mel Hurtig.

The rapid increase in the international flow of capital and the strengthening of Canadian pools of capital made the issue of economic nationalism more complex in the 1980s; public interest in the CIC message declined and the committee closed down in 1981.

Two years later Brian Mulroney was prime minister of Canada. It is not my intention to prepare a report card on this government (in which I have many close friends and former colleagues), although I am partisan and loyal enough to say that Mulroney has formed a cabinet of high calibre. I cannot, however, resist the temptation to express my views on those areas of his government's policy that have been my lifelong interests: economic nationalism and free trade; the law and national unity; defence and Middle East policy; and the performance of the leader.

My first experience with the new Tory power coincided with the visit by the Queen and Prince Philip to Canada. I received an invitation to attend the new prime minister's black-tie gala for the royal couple at Roy Thomson Hall. I said to Suzie, "Look, I am very busy until late that afternoon. We entertained the Queen and Prince at the ROM. Do you really want to go?" She replied, "It would be fun." I said "Okay, I'll go but I will not be able to put on my dinner jacket, as I'm working late. In any event, this is a late invitation and we will be up in the gods."

The morning of the gala, I forgot that we were going and put on a crumpled light-blue suit. We arrived at the concert hall barely on time, and to my surprise we were in the front and centre box with the premier of Alberta's box on one side and the premier of New Brunswick's box on the other side. There was also a row of people in front of us.

The royal couple arrived and were seated and Brian, to my surprise, waved to me. I waved back and said in my usual loud voice, "Why the hell would the Prime Minister wave at me? Probably because I'm the only person without a dinner jacket." Throughout the program, which left a lot to be desired, I grumbled audibly, even though Veronica Tennant was the mistress of ceremonies. The lights went on and I said, loudly, "Thank God that's over, it was awful, let's get going." The row in front of us stood up and turned around and there to my surprise was Sam Wakim, a lawyer, former member of Parliament, and a great friend of Brian Mulroney. He said to me, "Eddie, nice to see you." I introduced my wife. He said, "I'd like you to meet Brian's mother. And this is his sister. On the other side are Mila's mother and father, Dr. and Mrs. Dimitri Pivnicki." I expressed my delight at meeting them and then beat a hasty retreat. I now knew why Brian had waved.

Prime Minister Mulroney's support for the doctrine of freer trade with the United States, followed by the abandonment by the present Liberal Party of their century-old continentalist approach, has resulted in the most amazing reversals of policy in the history of both parties. These changes have required me to re-examine my beliefs, or at least to rearrange my prejudices. For me, any policy is merely a means to the ultimate end of achieving a healthy and independent country. Poor economic health weakens a nation. In reflecting upon the free trade issue I have considered the changed world economic circumstances of the late twentieth century and the ways in which nations must operate within the global economy to remain economically strong. Although I have not emerged from the free trade debate with the same views as I entered it with, I remain wedded to the moderate application of the principle of increasing Canadian control of our own industry. To me, the key question is whether free trade with the United States is inimical to greater Canadian control of our own economy, our own economic health and our own culture.

The Conservative Party's present free trade policy had an interesting genesis. During the 1983 leadership campaign, John Crosbie took the position that the country should enter into a free trade agreement with the United States. I received a telephone call from Senator Lowell Murray, who was managing Joe Clark's campaign, asking me as the former chairman of the Committee for an Independent Canada whether I would write a forceful letter to the newspaper attacking the Crosbie position. I flew down to Ottawa and discussed the matter with Clark and Murray. Murray and I then prepared a lengthy letter for publication. I sent it to Beland Honderich, publisher of the *Toronto Star*, who featured it prominently. The Crosbie supporters, particularly my friend Tom Kierans, were furious. My position appeared to have considerable support in the party and slowed down Crosbie's momentum.

When Brian Mulroney succeeded to the leadership, the issue appeared to be dead. Meanwhile the American trade deficit continued to grow, along with protectionist sentiment in the U.S. Congress. Canadian lumber, fish, hogs, and other commodities started to come under congressional attack in the United States as subsidized industries and the demand for countervailing duties on some Canadian items rose.

The publication in 1985 of the report of the Royal Commission on Economic Union and Development Prospects for Canada, a commission headed by Donald Macdonald, gave fresh impetus to the advocates of free trade with the United States. The Macdonald report received strong support from Ottawa bureaucrats, and Mulroney announced that he was starting discussions with the United States on a free trade agreement between the two countries. While I had real reservations about the effect of such an agreement, I felt a sneaking admiration for Mulroney's willingness to venture into such shark-infested waters.

Now the terms of the trade agreement are known, and the country is faced with one of the most important and difficult economic decisions in its history. In making this decision, it is fortunate that to a large extent we do not have to be concerned with the agreement's impact on our culture as, at Flora MacDonald's insistence, the government have for all practical purposes negotiated the cultural industries out of the agreement. A thoughtful consideration of the issue must examine the macroeconomics of world trade and the microeconomics of U.S.-Canadian trade. To date the debate has focused mainly on the microeconomic level. Most people recognize that problems of existing structure will make some Canadian industries less competitive. The decline of these industries will result in economic dislocation and loss of employment. At the same time, other Canadian industries will enlarge their markets and clearly benefit from free trade. Is the short-term pain worth the long-term gain? Those who are opposed to the treaty argue, "Who needs it? My ox is being gored. We must vigorously oppose it." Those who support it say, "The long-term advantage for some industries and the consumer is there. We must protect ourselves against American protectionism. Therefore we must support it." While important, neither argument convinces me. The problem must be examined in the context of world trade.

The ever-increasing flow of funds among countries has created a fluid global capital market very different from the static series of national capital markets that existed just a few decades ago. Tariff barriers are falling, and we hope that the coming round of GATT discussions will reduce them to an absolute minimum. Recent economic pacts, especially the formation of the European Economic Community, are having significant effects on trade relations. New technology and developments in communications are affecting almost every industry and every market. Finally, the booming Asian economies have transformed capital markets and manufacturing structures to an incredible degree. Obviously Canada cannot be a fortress against change. Our trade policy must adapt in order to take advantage of these radical shifts. Even if GATT negotiations are reasonably successful, they will not abolish internal protection policies. We need also the equivalent of a stronger domestic base to remain a significant international trader. Like the Japanese, we need a large enough home market to enable us to become important world traders.

In 1972 the *Canadian Forum* published a book called *An Industrial Strategy for Canada*, edited by Abe Rotstein. This book contains a thoughtful essay by Eric Kierans, Tom's father, who had a distinguished career as a minister in the governments of Quebec and Canada. Kierans makes the important point that the desire to maintain a vital measure of control of our own economy is not incompatible with free trade. However, it will require courageous tax and economic policies to achieve this compatibility. The nature of the Canadian economy and the large equity investment that American companies already have in this country undoubtedly make the venture more risky. The proposed agreement limits to some degree our right to restrict foreign investment. Can we afford to take the chance of competing with the Americans? The answer may well be that we cannot afford not to. In addition to the large degree of foreign ownership and the small domestic market, a basic weakness of Canada's economy is its poor productivity. This is aggravated by low U.S. environmental standards. The challenge of American competition and the larger quasi-domestic market may well eradicate this weakness. My own position is that I have more confidence in the Mulroney government's capacity to make it work that I have in Ed Broadbent's and John Turner's reasons for wanting to tear it up. By what hitherto unstated method do these two opponents of the deal propose to maintain our prosperity and high employment while propelling us into a disastrous trade war with our biggest customer?

While free trade is Brian Mulroney's most courageous initiative, it is not the one dearest to his heart. Most people who reach high office are ambitious to earn a place in history by making a lasting contribution to their country's welfare. In the case of Brian Mulroney, I have little doubt that "to bring about the full and active participation of Quebec in Canada's constitutional evolution" is his primary aim. He hopes that through this achievement he will make the Progressive Conservative Party an important and lasting force in Quebec's national political life and make himself the George Etienne-Cartier of the twentieth century. The signing of the Meech Lake Accord entered into by the first ministers of all the provinces and the federal government in 1987 agrees to amend the Constitution Act and is a significant step towards his objective.

This constitutional accord has been and continues to be the subject of debate in the House of Commons, in the Senate, and in several of the provincial legislatures. While both the federal Liberal Party and the federal New Democratic Party have announced clear support for the accord, an influential core within the Liberal Party, led by Pierre Trudeau, has voiced strong opposition to the proposed constitutional amendments.

The Meech Lake Accord was an achievement of considerable importance for the Prime Minister. It was a *tour de force* of negotiating skill. The major benefit of the accord is that it brings Quebec into the constitutional process by its acceptance of the Constitution Act of 1982 with its amendments. This very considerable achievement has been brought about because the signatories have agreed to amend the Constitution Act, section 2.1(b), by adding the words "the Constitution shall be interpreted in a manner consistent with the recognition that Quebec constitutes within Canada a distinct society." This is the recognition that Quebec demanded as its price for accepting the new constitution and charter of rights. But at what potential cost has Quebec's agreement been bought?

The concern that the "distinct society" acknowledgement could cause Quebec to request and obtain further provisions for special status in the future, thereby weakening the federal government's centralizing and unifying power, has some validity. I believe, however, that the risk is outweighed by the benefits of bringing Quebec into the constitutional process. It certainly does not lie in my mouth to criticize the Meech Lake Accord when I was prepared to recognize the *deux nations* amendment at the Montmorency Falls conference in 1967 — although there is a vast difference between a conference resolution and a constitutional amendment.

I feel justified, however, in criticizing Mulroney, the premiers, and the leaders of the opposition parties for their willingness to let the Supreme Court of Canada be balkanized under the accord. The formalizing of the right of Quebec, the only non-common-law province, to have three members on the nine-member court, is fit and proper; but the transfer of the power to appoint judges from the central government to the provinces weakens the court and thus endangers one of the great instruments of national unification. This amendment wrongly assumes that judges bring a regional bias and sit as westerners, Maritimers, or Ontarians instead of as Canadians. Obviously it is beneficial to have judges who come from various parts of the country and who together reflect the total Canadian experience; but what earthly excuse is there for transferring this jurisdiction to the provinces? In insisting on the right to appoint Supreme Court judges, the provinces are assuming that the jurists they appoint will represent their interests. This assumption should be unacceptable to the nation. I would be interested in the views of the Chief Justice of Canada on this aspect of the accord.

Many Canadians are attached to the view that, on the international scene, Canada's role epitomizes that decency my father found so important. Canada the "helpful fixer" is an image we are all familiar with. And yet, External Affairs' position on the Middle East is one in which I believe an unearned self-righteousness masquerading as decency conceals a long-standing insensitivity to Israel's legitimate concerns.

The Conservative Party since the war has always maintained a healthy suspicion of the bureaucrats of the Department of External Affairs. On assuming power, John Diefenbaker made himself Secretary of State for External Affairs. He said to me, "I do not trust those fellows, so they will report to me for a while." When Flora MacDonald became the minister under Joe Clark, she expressed similar reservations to me. In 1957 the wife of the under-secretary of the department, not knowing that Dorie Dunlop was George Hees' sister-in-law, said to her at a dinner, "I am appalled that these awful Conservatives have assumed power." The civil servants must be thrilled with their present minister, Joe Clark, who seems to have fallen to a considerable degree under their influence. Certainly the speech prepared for Clark by his bureaucrats for delivery to the Canada-Israel Committee on March 10 this year originated from a strong pro-Arab view that is of long standing in External Affairs. I came across it constantly in the fifties in my discussions with the department's officials for Mr. Diefenbaker.

Like tens of thousands of Canadian Jews, I was profoundly disappointed by Clark's speech to the committee. My reaction was not against the strong criticism he levelled at the Government of Israel's treatment of Palestinians in the West Bank and Gaza, a criticism with which most Canadians agreed. Three months earlier at a Negev dinner given in my honour, I had urged that Israel take steps to protect the civil rights of the Arabs within its borders. The difference between our speeches was that I acknowledged the extreme provocation and dire threats to Israel's existence that had brought about these excesses. There was no such balance in Clark's speech. It was a disastrous speech by a man whom I admire.

The speech clearly left the impression that if Israel would only cease mishandling the Palestinians, peace would descend on the Middle East. PLO terrorists financed by Libya and Syrian-protected assassins financed by Saudi Arabia would fold their tents and quietly steal away. Iran and Iraq would embrace, and Israel's neighbours would join her citizens in dancing the "hora." For forty years, the State of Israel has been endeavouring to reach a peaceful settlement with its neighbours. Except for Egypt, it cannot even gain recognition. These facts appear to have escaped the attention of the Department of External Affairs and its minister.

There are many Jews, both within and outside Israel, who are bitterly opposed to Yitzhak Shamir's policy of force. Israel is a democracy that allows strong anti-government views to be voiced and printed. In no other country in the Middle East is there a democratic form of government. In no other country in the Middle East is there the stability essential to prevent Communist domination of the area. What Clark has done is force Canadian Jews who were speaking out against the use of unnecessary force to silence their criticism so as not to be associated with his position.

I realize that the uninterested public and the unthinking press thought it was a great speech. Indeed, the most disturbing result of the Clark speech was what it revealed about the attitude of the non-Jewish community and their lack of knowledge of what has transpired over the past four decades in the Middle East. The day after Joe talked tough, the telephone lines of the Canadian Jewish Congress and other Jewish organizations were flooded with calls saying, "It's time somebody told you Jews where to get off," and other much more explicit statements.

Like many other Christians and Jews, immediately after the speech, I got in touch with the Prime Minister's Office to express my dismay. A few days later, Mulroney wrote to Sidney Spivak, the national chairman of the Canada-Israel Committee. While not cutting loose his secretary of state for external affairs or dissociating himself in any way, Mulroney endeavoured to restore some balance by writing: "History provides ample evidence of the antipathy of Israel's neighbours and the unacceptable use of terror against the Israeli people, challenging through violence their right to exist in the land which belongs to them. Throughout this too often tragic history, Canada has stood second to none in its support for Israel in its struggle to survive and prosper."

In the area of defence, which is very dear to my heart, I have nothing but praise for the current government. Last year saw the seventy-fifth anniversary of the Fort Garry Horse and I, along with hundreds of other old Garries, attended the celebrations in Winnipeg. The overwhelming consensus among my comrades-in-arms was that in the fields of national defence and of veterans' affairs the Mulroney government was the best Canadian administration since the war. You will hear this sentiment echoed throughout the legion halls and the armouries across the country and by the leaders of NATO. These Canadians express the strongest admiration for Minister of Defence Perrin Beatty, and for the efforts of Veterans Affairs Minister George Hees.

A short time ago I gave the Remembrance Day address at the Law Society of Upper Canada. As I said then and still believe:

> We must realize that a very real threat does exist from other nations and states; that these threats are to our freedom and to our liberty; that they are not fantasies manufactured by our chiefs of staff or in the Pentagon; that people have suffered and are suffering in Cambodia, Afghanistan, Ethiopia, Hungary, Czechoslovakia, Nicaragua and a host of other nations. . . .
>
> To me, the course of action is obvious and simple. We must first of all fulfil all of our NATO obligations and contribute at least as much as our wealth and resources can afford. Isolation is not a practical or moral solution either for Canada or for the North American continent as a whole. The second aspect of our policy must be close, intimate and supportive collaboration with the United States in both its international attempts to bring peace and its defence of this continent.

I have expressed in these memoirs my views of many Progressive Conservative Party leaders. Let me briefly assess therefore Brian Mulroney's personal performance as a leader. The Prime Minister had a shaky start, largely because his office adopted far too imperial a style and he personally thrust himself front and centre to justify every government policy or mistake. He was also beset by a series of cabinet ministers' misadventures, and his Irish sense of loyalty made him hesitate before acting. He is gaining experience, confidence and strength; his office is now more efficient and less imperial; he has achieved standing among Western world leaders; he is letting his ministers stand alone more frequently, although he is still in the limelight far too often. I believe if he bit his tongue a few times, desisted from bashing his opponents and left that to his cabinet colleagues it would be a big step towards his re-election. The present mood of the country is to be led by a statesman, not Sugar Ray Robinson. Mulroney's government has undertaken many needed reforms and I believe it is in the best interest of the country that he be given the opportunity to complete the courageous initiatives he has started. We might well know if my fellow countrymen agree with me by the time these memoirs are published.

There is no doubt that I am on the left side of the spectrum within my own party. Still, there are some things I believe we Tories all share, although they are not our exclusive property. An abiding patriotic love of this great northern land is foremost among them, closely followed by dedication to helping all Canadians enjoy a more fruitful life through a combination of private and governmental initiatives; recognition of the need to balance careful and constructive change with preservation of our national heritage and traditional values; and active commitment to the defence of the parliamentary process and of democracy everywhere.

I have always been an activist, a participant rather than an onlooker. As I look back at my life to date, enthusiastic involvement in the law, in politics, in the arts, and in health and education is the theme that pulls together the diverse images in my kaleidoscope of memories. This activism partly stems from the belief instilled in my sister Cecily and me by our parents that it is our patriotic duty to work for the principles we believe in. Yet I know my impulse to be in the thick of the action has had a deeper source: my love of Canada and my fellow Canadians.

Now that the book is completed I return first to helping Suzie get better and then with a clear conscience to the simple pleasures of the outdoors in the land I love. Canoeing in Quetico and the Territories beckons, and riding in Caledon or the Rockies. Canada is truly a great country, and how fortunate I was to be born here.

INDEX